# STUDY GUIDE

# MODERN MACROECONOMICS

## Fifth Edition

Robin Bade

Michael Parkin

Prentice Hall
Toronto

ISBN 0-13-031475-7

Acquisitions Editor: Dave Ward
Developmental Editor: Maurice Esses
Production Editor: Jennifer Therriault
Production Coordinator: Deborah Starks

1 2 3 4 5 05 04 03 02 01

Printed and bound in Canada

Acknowledgements

We thank our colleagues at the University of Western Ontario who have taught intermediate macro over the past 20 years. We also thank our many students who taught us just how difficult intermediate macro can be and just how useful a good Study Guide is to them. We also thank Jeannie Gillmore. Jeannie has worked every question in this Guide and checked the accuracy of every solution. We owe her a big "thank you."

Robin Bade

Michael Parkin

# Table of Contents

**Chapter 1**

# What is Macroeconomics?

## Perspective and Focus

This chapter tells you what macroeconomics is about. It introduces you to the *subject matter* of macroeconomics by describing the questions that macroeconomics is designed to answer. These questions are about macroeconomic performance—about what determines six key macroeconomic variables. These questions are:

- What determines the rate of growth of real GDP?
- What causes fluctuations in the rate of economic growth and of unemployment?
- What determines the average level of prices and the rate at which they rise—the inflation rate?
- What determines interest rates?
- What determines the Canadian balance of payments with the rest of the world?
- What determines the value of the dollar abroad?

The first three questions are the central and most important questions for macroeconomics, but all six define its subject matter.

The chapter goes on to *describe* the facts about macroeconomic performance. It also describes the problem of stabilizing the economy.

The questions that macroeconomists try to answer have turned out to be hard ones, and the answers that they have found are still controversial. Because of this fact the chapter makes you aware of the variety of opinion and the nature of the controversy in macroeconomics today.

## Learning Objectives

*After studying this chapter, you will be able to:*

- Explain what macroeconomics is about
- Describe the changing pace of economic expansion and inflation in the Canadian and world economies
- Describe the problem of stabilizing the economy
- Describe the main schools of thought on how the economy works and how it might be stabilized

## Increasing Your Productivity

How many times have you said to yourself "I worked hard for that exam and deserve a better grade"? The payoff from work depends partly on the number of hours we work. But it also depends on our *productivity*—on how effectively we use our work hours. You can increase your productivity in studying macroeconomics in a variety of ways. We give you our general advice on how to make your study effective in the preface of the textbook (on pages xvi and xvii). Here we focus on the two most important additional things to pay attention to as you begin your study of Chapter 1: *reading graphs* and *being skeptical and curious.*

### Reading Graphs

Graphs play an important part in macroeconomics. They convey a great deal of information to you and they enable you to convey a lot of information to your instructor. Don't just "look at" graphs—*read them.* When you read the text you know the order in which to proceed. You start at the top left-hand corner of the page and move rightward and downward. There is also a correct order in which to read a graph. Here it is:

1. Look at the $x$-axis and check that you understand the variable that is being measured along the axis and the units in which the variable is being measured.

2. Look at the $y$-axis and check that you understand the variable that is being measured along that axis and the units in which the variable is being measured.

3. Look at the curves in the graph *one at a time.* Be sure that you understand what each curve is telling you.

4. Look at any specially highlighted points and be sure that you understand why they are highlighted and what they are telling you.

5. Read the boxed notes.

6. Read the extended caption and as you do so look at the parts of the figure to which it draws your attention.

If you follow these rules each time you come to a diagram you will find that you make can read the text itself more quickly and with deeper and more lasting understanding.

### Being Skeptical and Curious

Don't take any facts about macroeconomic performance on trust. Check them out. Also be curious and ask questions, such as okay, these may be the facts in Canada but what about in the United States or Europe or Japan? Are the facts the same there?

Appendix A and Appendix B provide you with a good deal of data about Canadian macroeconomic performance between 1926 and 1998 and the macroeconomic performance of France, Germany, Italy, Japan, the United Kingdom, and the United States from 1968 to 1998. Use these appendixes whenever you get a chance and check how general or how special any particular feature of Canadian macroeconomic performance is.

## Self Test

### Fill in the Blanks

1. Macroeconomics is the study of ________ ________.
2. The unemployment rate is equal to the percentage of the ________ ________ that is either ________ ________ ________ and seeking ________ or on temporary ________.
3. Inflation is a ________ of ________ ________.
4. The recurring fluctuations in the pace of ________ ________ is called the business cycle.
5. Fiscal policy is changes in ________ ________ on ________ and ________ and ________ designed to influence the state of the economy.
6. Monetary policy is changes in ________ ________ and the quantity of ________ designed to influence the state of the economy.
7. ________ ________ are specific laws, rules, and regulations designed to modify the way people behave.
8. Macroeconomic policy targets include a ________ unemployment rate and a ________ inflation rate.
9. ________ macroeconomics is a body of theory based on the idea that the economy is a self-regulating mechanism that always tends towards ________.
10. ________ macroeconomics is a body of theory based on the idea that the economy has no self-regulating mechanism that can be relied upon to bring full employment.

### True or False

1. Real GDP is the goods and services that can be bought with the income of all the individuals in the economy.
2. The Canadian economy always grows, but the growth rate varies—sometimes it is rapid and sometimes it is slow, but it is always growing.
3. The unemployment rate is the percentage of the adult population that does not have jobs or are on temporary layoff from their regular jobs.
4. Inflation is a process in which money steadily loses its value in terms of the goods and services that it will buy.
5. An unexpected upturn in the inflation rate reduces the debts of borrowers and the wealth of lenders.
6. Macroeconomics studies what determines inflation, unemployment, real income growth, and interest rates. It does not study why the foreign exchange value of the dollar fluctuates.
7. Fluctuations in the pace of economic expansion is called the business cycle.
8. GDP fluctuates about trend GDP but because GDP exceeds trend GDP most of the time, trend GDP is positive.
9. Since World War II the Canadian business cycle has become less severe.
10. The Canadian economy has experienced only two periods of sustained growth since 1960—one beginning in 1960 and one beginning in 1982.

11. The Canadian price level fell during the Great Depression but increased every year since World War II. As a result the Canadian inflation has gradually increased.

12. When the rate of inflation decreased in Canada in the early 1980s, the Canadian price level continued to increase but at a slower rate.

13. Canadian inflation peaked during the mid-1970s at 25 percent a year. At the same time, inflation in the rest of the world was 13 percent a year.

14. Canada produces 4.6 percent of the world's total output and the United States produces 21 percent of it.

15. Since 1960, the growth rate of real income per person has been higher in Japan and the United States than in Canada. As a result, real income per person in the Canada is now less than that in Japan and the United States.

16. Since 1960, the gap between real income per person in Canada and in Central and South America has gradually become narrower.

17. Fiscal policy uses variations in interest rates to influence the state of the economy.

18. One of the targets of macroeconomic policy is mild fluctuations in the growth rate of real income and the unemployment rate.

19. To use wage and price controls in the hope of stabilizing the economy is to use a direct control.

20. Monetary policy is conducted by the government of Canada and the Bank of Canada, but when they can't agree the Bank of Canada takes control of monetary policy.

## Multiple Choice

1. Which of the following people would be counted as being unemployed?

(a) Mary quit her job last week so she could spend her time looking after her ailing grandmother.

(b) Tom starts a new job next week. He has spent the last two months searching full time for a job.

(c) Al teaches school in Newfoundland. He wants a teaching job in Alberta for next year and keeps watching the advertisements for teachers in Alberta.

(d) Jerry has a part-time job and wants a full-time one. He keeps reading the local newspaper for such a position.

(e) Martha is a novelist who has written five best sellers. Martha needs a break and has just decided to sail around the world for the next year.

2. The percentage of the labour force that is either out of work and seeking jobs or on temporary layoff is known as the

(a) discouraged worker effect.

(b) added worker effect.

(c) secondary worker effect.

(d) problem of ratio.

(e) unemployment rate.

3. Inflation

(a) is a relatively new phenomenon.

(b) was not experienced in Canada until the 1970s.

(c) became a problem when currencies ceased to be fixed in value to gold.

(d) is not a problem until it becomes a hyperinflation.

(e) none of the above.

4. Macroeconomics tries to explain

(a) why some unemployed workers become discouraged.

(b) why a country has a deficit on its international balance of payments.

(c) why real income growth in Canada has slowed in recent years.

(d) (b) and (c) .

(e) all of the above.

5. The business cycle in Canada

(a) expanded in the years immediately following the Korean War.

(b) was in a contraction phase for most of the 1960s.

(c) expanded in the years immediately following the Vietnam War.

(d) was in an expansion phase for most of the

1980s.

(e) none of the above.

6. Inflation in Canada

(a) was low at the time of the Korean War and the first OPEC oil shock.

(b) increased during the 1960s as the economy expanded.

(c) was low when the second OPEC oil shock occurred.

(d) increased during the 1980s as the economy expanded.

(e) (b) and (c) .

7. The growth rate of real income per person

(a) was higher in Japan than in Canada during the 1960s.

(b) slowed in Canada but not in Japan in the 1970s.

(c) was higher in the "Big 4" European economies and in the United States than in Japan in the 1960s.

(d) was higher in the United States than in Japan during the 1960s.

(e) (a) and (b) .

8. Inflation, on the average, was lower in Canada than in the rest of the world during

(a) the 1960s.

(b) the 1970s.

(c) the 1980s.

(d) the 1960s and the 1970s but not in the 1980s.

(e) (a), (b), and (c) .

9. Canada experienced a

(a) stronger expansion in the 1990s than the rest of the world.

(b) deeper recession in the 1970s than the rest of the world.

(c) less severe recession in the 1990s than the rest of the world.

(d) (b) and (c).

(e) (a) and (c) .

10. Changes in government expenditures on goods and services or taxes to influence the state of the economy is known as

(a) monetary policy.

(b) direct controls.

(c) fiscal policy.

(d) policy rules.

(e) policy targets.

11. Global policies influence the values of a small number of aggregate variables such as

(a) the government's budget deficit and the money supply.

(b) the money supply and the foreign exchange rate.

(c) the level of government expenditures on goods and services and the foreign exchange rate.

(d) the overall level of taxes and the government's budget deficit.

(e) all of the above.

12. Which of the following is an example of a policy rule?

(a) Cutting the money supply by 1 percent whenever the dollar depreciates by 0. 5 percent.

(b) A law enacted by parliament requiring the budget to be balanced.

(c) Increasing the growth rate of the money supply by 1 percent a year whenever the unemployment rate increases by 2 percent.

(d) (a) and (c) .

(e) (a), (b), and (c) .

13. Monetarists advocate that the government

(a) adopt fixed rules for the behaviour of the global macroeconomic variables.

(b) adopt fixed rules for the behaviour of the detailed macroeconomic variables.

(c) use discretionary policy for the behaviour of the global macroeconomic variables.

(d) use discretionary policy for the behaviour of the detailed macroeconomic variables.

(e) (a) and (d) .

14. Monetarists advocate that the government adopt fixed rules for the behaviour of which of the following variables?

(a) Government deficit.

(b) Government expenditures on goods and services.

(c) The price of oil.
(d) The average real wage rate.
(e) (a) and (b) .

15. Activists advocate that the government
(a) adopt fixed rules for the behaviour of the global variables.
(b) announce policy interventions as far ahead as possible.
(c) use discretionary policy for the behaviour of the global variables.
(d) do not announce policy changes before they are instituted.
(e) (c) and (d) .

16. Activists advocate that the government use discretionary policy to keep employment at its full employment level and inflation low and steady. Such actions are known as
(a) rationalizing the economy.
(b) fine tuning the economy.
(c) isolating the economy.
(d) dissecting the economy.
(e) automating the economy.

17. The body of theory based on the idea that the economy is a self-regulating mechanism that always tends towards full employment is known as
(a) Keynesian macroeconomics.
(b) classical macroeconomics.
(c) monetarist macroeconomics.
(d) new classical macroeconomics.
(e) real business cycle macroeconomics.

18. Which of the following is a body of theory based on the idea that if the economy is left to its own devices it can get stuck with a high and persistent level of unemployment and lost output?
(a) Monetarism.
(b) New classical macroeconomics.
(c) Classical macroeconomics.
(d) Keynesian macroeconomics.
(e) Real business cycle theory.

19. Explaining fluctuations in economic growth and unemployment as the consequence of price and wage stickiness and other failings of the market economy is the research agenda of
(a) new Keynesians.
(b) new classical macroeconomists.
(c) monetarists.
(d) global macroeconomists.
(e) macroeconomists who do not use micro foundations.

20. The microeconomic foundations of macroeconomics is the model of the behaviour of
(a) individual households and individual firms.
(b) individual firms but not individual households.
(c) government enterprises and organizations.
(d) foreign countries.
(e) (a) and (c) .

## Short Answer Questions

1. Briefly summarize the differences between Keynesian and classical macroeconomics.
2. Explain how monetary policy influences the state of the economy. Compare this influence with that of fiscal policy.
3. Do monetarists advocate rules or discretion in the conduct of macroeconomic policy?
4. Briefly describe the differences between the new classical and new Keynesian research programs on macroeconomics.
5. Explain direct controls and how they can be used to stabilize the economy.
6. (a) Explain what macroeconomics studies.

   (b) What does macroeconomics seek to understand?
7. (a) What is real GDP?

   (b) What is the growth in real GDP?
8. (a) What are macroeconomic policy targets?

   (b) What do these policy targets include?
9. Briefly compare the business cycle in Canada with that in the rest of the world from 1970 to 1997.

10. Explain the disagreement between monetarists and activists about how the economy works and the policy options that should be used. Do they agree on any aspects of these?

## Problem Solving

1. In Dream Land, there are 90 million people in the labour force. 10 million people are unemployed. Calculate the unemployment rate in Dream Land.
2. In 1982, actual real GDP was $3,166 billion and trend real GDP was $3,398 billion. Calculate the percentage deviation of real GDP from trend.
3. Classify the following statements according to whether it deals with a detailed or global policy, a policy rule or discretion, and/or is probably a recommendation by a monetarist or activist.

(a) The proposed cut in the capital gains tax rate is an important element of the long-term growth agenda.

(b) Fiscal policy typically provides a significant stimulus to the economy during recessions and early recovery.

(c) Effective job training programs to retrain workers are a key to increasing productivity and remaining internationally competitive.

(d) Investment in research and development and infrastructure, and the extension of research and development tax credits will help increase business productivity.

(e) The fundamental goal of Canada is the removal of all tariffs and the removal or reduction of nontariff trade barriers.

(f) Fundamental banking reform is critical to ensuring efficient operation of credit markets.

(g) The Bank of Canada has stated a policy goal of achieving, over time, price stability.

(h) Through most of the first half of 1991, the money supply stayed near the middle of its target.

# Answers

## Fill in the Blanks

1. aggregate economic activity
2. labour force, out of work, jobs, layoff
3. process, rising prices
4. economic expansion
5. government expenditures, goods, services, taxes
6. interest rates, money
7. Direct controls
8. low, low
9. Classical, full employment
10. Keynesian

## True or False

1T 5T 9T 13F 17F

2F 6F 10F 14F 18T

3F 7T 11F 15F 19T

4T 8F 12T 16F 20F

## Multiple Choice

1b 5d 9b 13a 17b

2e 6b 10c 14e 18d

3e 7a 11e 15e 19a

4d 8e 12e 16b 20e

## Short Answer Questions

1. Keynesian macroeconomics is a body of theory based on the idea that the economy has no self-regulating mechanism that can be relied upon to bring full employment. Left to its own devices, the economy can get stuck a long way from full employment.

   Classical macroeconomics is a body of theory based on the idea that the economy is a self-regulating mechanism that always tends towards full employment.
2. Monetary policy is the attempt by the Bank of Canada to influence the state of the economy by changing interest rates and the quantity of money. Fiscal policy is the attempt by the federal government to influence the state of the economy by changing government expenditures on goods and services and taxes.
3. Monetarists advocate that governments have

policies toward a limited number of global macroeconomic variables such as money supply growth, government expenditures on goods and services, taxes, and the government deficit. They advocate the adoption of fixed rules for the behaviour of these variables.

4. New classical macroeconomists believe that the classical view of the economy is a fruitful one and one that is likely to lead to better macroeconomic theory. Their goal is to explain such macroeconomic phenomenon as fluctuations in economic growth and unemployment as the "natural" consequences of a well functioning economy in which everyone is doing the best they can for themselves and in which markets work efficiently.

   New Keynesians believe that markets do not always work efficiently and that prices and wages are sticky, at least in the short run, so that the economy can get stuck a long way from full employment. Their research agenda is to explain fluctuations in economic growth and unemployment as the consequence of price and wage stickiness and other failings of the market economy.

5. Direct controls are specific laws, rules, and regulations designed to modify the way people behave.

   Examples of direct controls that influence the stability of the economy are wage and price controls that have sometimes been used in hope of keeping inflation in check.

6. (a) Macroeconomics is the study of aggregate economic activity.

   (b) Macroeconomics seeks to understand what determines unemployment, the real GDP growth rate, the price level and the inflation rate, the balance of international payments, and the exchange rate.

7. (a) Real GDP is a measure of the quantity of the goods and services that can be purchased with the income of all the individuals in the economy. It is a measure of living standards.

   (b) The growth in real GDP is a measure of the growth of people's real incomes. It is the pace of improvement in living standards.

8. (a) Macroeconomic policy targets are the goals of macroeconomic stabilization policy.

   (b) Macroeconomic policy targets include a high and sustained growth of real income, a low unemployment rate, mild fluctuations in the growth rate of real income and of the unemployment rate, and a low inflation rate.

9. From 1970 to 1997, the business cycle in the rest of the world lines up closely with that in Canada. But there are some differences in the degree of recession and recovery. Canada had deeper recessions in the mid 1970s, early 1980s, and early 1990s than did the rest of the world. The world had a greater recovery in the 1970s and 1990s.

10. Figure 1.9 summarizes the answer to this question. Monetarists are classical economists who believe that the market operates like a self-regulating mechanism, always tending towards full employment. Activists are Keynesian in their belief that the economy has a fundamental design problem that can keep it away from full employment for long periods at a time.

    On policy issues, monetarists believe that a fixed rule governing the money supply growth rate and possibly other rules governing the size of the federal budget deficit are best for achieving macroeconomic stability, whereas activists believe that discretionary changes in interest rates, taxes, and government expenditures are essential components of any stabilization policy.

    Some economists in each group favour stronger methods of achieving a balanced or more nearly balanced budget.

## Problem Solving

1. The unemployment rate is calculated by dividing the number of unemployed persons by the number of people in the labour force and multiplying the answer by 100. The unemployment rate is 11.1 percent.

2. In 1982, the percentage deviation of real GDP from trend was –6.8 percent. The deviation of real GDP from trend GDP is calculated as (actual GDP – trend GDP) ÷ trend GDP, expressed as a percentage.

3. (a) discretionary, activist

   (b) global, rule

   (c) detailed, activist

(d) detailed, activist
(e) detailed
(f) global
(g) global
(h) monetarist

Chapter 2

# Monitoring Macroeconomic Activity

## Perspective and Focus

A zillion things happen in the economy every day. This chapter tells you how economists organize their records of these events so they can keep track of the movements in the economy and develop theories that enable them to understand these events. The chapter makes three important distinctions. Those between:

- Stocks and flows
- Financial expenditure and intermediate transactions
- Income and expenditure

A stock is a value at a point in time while a flow is a rate per unit of time. The numbers of tapes or compact disks that you own are stocks—they are the numbers that you own at a given point in time. In contrast, the tapes or compact disks that you bought last week are flows—they are measured as the quantity bought per week.

Final expenditure is the purchase of a good or service by its final user. In contrast, an intermediate transaction is the purchase of a good or service to be used in the manufacture of some other good or service that eventually will be sold to its final user. For example, your purchases of tapes or compact disks are final expenditures. The purchases of plastic by EMI to use in the manufacture of tapes and compact disks are intermediate transactions.

But purchases of *new capital* equipment are final expenditures. If you buy a CD player or EMI buys a machine for pressing compact discs, the purchase is a final expenditure, not an intermediate transaction.

Income is the payment in return for the services of factors of production. In contrast, expenditure is the payment in exchange for final goods and services. For example, the wage you receive for working on the weekend is income. Your purchase of a textbook is expenditure.

This chapter also introduces you to two sets of key macroeconomic identities. They are:

- Aggregate expenditure equals aggregate income equals the value of aggregate output.
- Aggregate deficits across all sectors sum to zero.

## Learning Objectives

*After studying this chapter, you will be able to:*

- Explain the distinction between a flow and a stock
- Explain the distinction between expenditure on final goods and intermediate transactions
- Explain why aggregate income, expenditure, and product (or the value of output) are equal
- Explain the connection between the government budget deficit and the international trade deficit
- Define gross domestic product (GDP)
- Define nominal GDP and real GDP
- Explain what a balance sheet measures
- Define capital, wealth, and money
- Describe the main features of the debt explosion of the 1980s and 1990s
- Explain how economic growth and inflation are measured

## Increasing Your Productivity

Work hard to understand the important distinctions between:

(a) stocks and flows
(b) final expenditure and intermediate transactions
(c) income and expenditure

For at least the next week or two, ask yourself every time you encounter a transaction whether you are looking at a stock or a flow, an intermediate transaction or a final expenditure, or an income or an expenditure.

You probably won't have any trouble understanding the distinction between income and expenditure when using examples such as your wages from working in the college or university bookstore in comparison with your expenditure on textbooks. But when it comes to looking at the Canadian national income accounts, somehow things seem to get complicated. Problems 2 and 3 (on page 48 of your textbook) are designed to help you sort out and apply the distinctions between income and expenditure. When working the problems just apply the test: Is the transaction a payment for the services of a factor of production such as land, labour, or capital (or the residual profit)? If it is, then it is an income. Is the transaction a payment for a final good or service—a consumer good or a capital good? If it is, then it is an expenditure.

### Expenditure Equals Income Equals Value of Output

The key to understanding why aggregate expenditure equals aggregate income is an appreciation of the role played by inventories and profits. The change in value of the firms' inventories is considered part of aggregate expenditure. It is part of firms' investment. Thus if firms have produced something of value, even if it has not yet been sold to its final user, it is counted as expenditure on final goods and services.

Profit (or loss) is part of factor income. Aggregate income equals all the payments of wages and other factor incomes paid by firms to households plus the profit that firms have made but not yet paid out. A firm's profit equals its receipts from sales plus the change in the value of its unsold inventories minus the income it pays to factors of production. Thus profit plus income paid to factors of production equal receipts from sales of goods and services plus the change in the value of inventories. The sum of profit and the income paid to factors of production is factor incomes and the receipts from sales of goods and services plus the change in the value of inventories is expenditure on final goods and services. In aggregate, these are always equal.

Output can be valued either by what people are willing to pay for it or by what it costs to produce it. Since these two numbers are identical to each other, they are also equal to the value of output.

### Leakages Equal Injections

Work hard at Tables 2.2, 2.3, and 2.4 and the associated Figures 2.2, 2.3, and 2.4 and be sure that you understand (a) what we mean by leakages and injections and (b) why they are always equal to each other.

## Self Test

### Fill in the Blanks

1. A variable that measures a rate per unit of time is called a ___________. A variable that is measured at a point in time is called a ___________.
2. The stock of buildings, plant and equipment, houses, consumer durable goods, and inventories is called ___________. The purchase of new capital is called ___________ ___________, which is made up of ___________ ___________ and ___________ ___________.
3. The reduction in the value of capital that results from the use of the capital or from the passage of time is ___________. Total additions to the capital stock in a given period of time is ___________ ___________. The change in the capital stock is called ___________ which is equal to ___________ ___________ minus ___________.
4. The total sum of rent paid to the suppliers of land, wages paid to labour, interest paid to the suppliers of capital, and profit paid to the owners of firms is called ___________ ___________. The expenditure on all final goods and services produced during a specified time period is called ___________ ___________. The value of all final goods and services produced during a specified period is called ___________ ___________.
5. The goods and services bought by households, government, and foreigners minus the goods and services we buy from the rest of the world are ___________ ___________. Firm's purchases of new capital and their additions to inventory are ___________ goods, but their purchases of goods and services to be used by them in the production of goods and services are ___________ ___________. The increase in the value of a product when factors of production are used to transform it from one stage in the production or distribution process to the next is called ___________ ___________.
6. ___________ ___________ is the value of the goods and services bought by households. The income that households do not

spend on goods and services is called ________.

7. A flow out from the circular flow of income and expenditure is a ________ and a flow into the circular flow is an ________.
8. Expenditures by the government on final goods and services is called ________ ________ on goods and services. The benefits and subsidies paid by the government are called ________ ________. Total taxes paid minus transfer payments is called ________.
9. The flow of money from the rest of the world in exchange for Canadian-produced goods and services is ________; the flow to the rest of the world in exchange for foreign-produced goods and services is ________. ________ ________ is exports ________ imports.
10. The government's budget deficit and the Canadian deficit with the rest of the world are called the ________.
11. ________ ________ ________ is the total expenditure in a year on goods and services produced by Canadians wherever in the world that activity takes place. Gross ________ product is the total expenditure in a year on final goods and services produced in Canada. The total income, including profit, paid for the services of factors of production used to produce goods and services in Canada in a year is ________ ________.
12. The value of the goods and services produced in year measured in current year prices is called ________ ________. The value of the goods and services produced in year measured in base year prices is called is ________ ________.
13. Total income received by households is called ________ ________ and personal income minus personal income tax payments is called ________ ________.
14. The ________ ________ is that part of the economy engaged in illegal activities.
15. A ________ ________ is a statement about what someone owns and owes. Items that are owned are ________ and items that are owed are ________.
16. ________ assets are concrete, tangible objects and ________ assets are pieces of paper that represent promises to pay.
17. Total assets minus total liabilities is called ________ or ________ ________.
18. Anything generally acceptable in exchange for goods and services is called a ________. Any asset that serves as a medium of exchange is ________.
19. The rate of change of real GDP from one year to the next is called ________ ________.
20. The price level measured by the ratio of nominal GDP to real GDP all multiplied by 100 is called the ________ ________. The ________ ________ ________ is a measure of the price level that is based on the cost of a particular "basket" of goods and services consumed by urban Canadian families.

## True or False

1. The purchase of a new airplane by Air Canada is an expenditure on a final good but the purchase of the food that Air Canada serves on its flights is not.
2. Depreciation is the reduction in the value of capital that results from its use or from the passage of time.
3. The Canadian governments' payment of unemployment compensation benefits is part of its expenditures on goods and services.
4. Consumer expenditure is a flow, and net investment is a stock.
5. The flow of money from Japan to Canada in exchange for Canadian-produced goods and services is part of Canadian exports, and the flow of money from Canada to Japan in exchange for Japanese-produced goods and services is part of Canadian imports.
6. If households in Canada increase their expenditure on final goods and services, saving decreases and as a result investment decreases.

7. Leakages include taxes, saving and exports, and injections include government expenditures on goods and services, investment, and imports.
8. The government of Leisure Land has a budget deficit and households save less than firms invest. Leisure Land's stock of net financial assets is decreasing and the rest of the world's stock of net financial assets is increasing.
9. Canada has a deficit with the rest of the world. As a result, Canada lends to the rest of the world.
10. If consumer expenditure plus government expenditures on goods and services plus investment exceeds GDP, then investment must exceed saving if the government budget is balanced or the government has a budget deficit if saving exceeds investment.
11. GDP differs from GNP in that GNP values aggregate economic activity at market prices and GDP values aggregate economic activity at factor cost.
12. Domestic income is a net measure of aggregate economic activity in a year and it is measured at factor cost.
13. Real GDP is total expenditure on final goods and services, whereas nominal GDP is the inflation component of real GDP.
14. Personal disposable income is national income plus transfer payments from government minus business retained profits minus personal income tax payments.
15. When Earl withdraws $100 from his deposit at the Prairies Bank, the bank's balance sheet remains balanced because both its liabilities and assets decrease by $100.
16. The Azuma Bank makes a loan to Cathy to buy a boat and to Fred to buy some bonds. The Azuma Bank has increased its stock of financial assets, Cathy has increased her stock of real assets, and Fred has made no change to his stock of net financial assets.
17. Judy's wealth is equal to her stock of real assets. The loan she has taken to pay for this year at school has no effect on her wealth.
18. The underground economy is the part of the economy in which the medium of exchange used is not money.
19. Economic growth is the rate of change of either national income or nominal GDP.
20. The ratio of nominal GDP to real GDP multiplied by 100 is known as the GDP inflator.

## Multiple Choice

1. The total additions to the capital stock in a given period of time are
(a) inventory investment.
(b) fixed investment.
(c) net investment.
(d) gross investment.
(e) unintended investment.

2. Which of the following are stocks?
(a) expenditure on final goods and services but not intermediate transactions.
(b) the output of final goods and services but not those added to inventory.
(c) investment including the addition to inventories.
(d) the money that people have to spend.
(e) both (a) and (c).

3. Which of the following shows the equality of leakages and injections?
(a) $S + T + IM = I + G - EX$
(b) $S - T - IM = I - G + EX$
(c) $S + T + IM = I + G + EX$
(d) $S + I + IM = T + G + EX$
(e) $S + I + G = T + IM - EX$

4. In a country that has a government budget deficit
(a) leakages exceed injections.
(b) injections exceed leakages.
(c) exports exceed imports.
(d) imports exceed exports.
(e) none of the above.

5. When national income statisticians use the expenditure approach to measure GDP they do the following calculation:

(a) $C - I - G + EX + IM$
(b) $C + I + G + EX - IM$
(c) $C + I + G + T + EX + IM$
(d) $C + I + G - T + EX - IM$
(e) $C + I + G + T + EX - IM$

6. The two commonly used measures of the money supply in Canada today are
(a) M1 and M5.
(b) M2+ and M5.
(c) M1 and M2+.
(d) M2 and M4.
(e) M1 and M4.

7. The twin deficits are the
(a) private sector balance and the government sector balance.
(b) private sector balance and the rest of the world balance.
(c) net exports deficit and the private sector balance.
(d) government sector balance and the rest of the world balance.
(e) none of the above.

8. Which of the following is a stock?
(a) net exports.
(b) investment.
(c) government expenditures on goods and services.
(d) unemployment.
(e) interest rates.

9. During the 1980s and 1990s, Canadian federal government debt increased at an annual average rate of almost
(a) 30 percent.
(b) 20 percent.
(c) 14 percent.
(d) 40 percent.
(e) 4 percent.

10. Suppose you know that the government is running a budget deficit. Then
(a) saving must exceed investment.
(b) net exports must be positive.
(c) investment plus exports must exceed saving plus imports.
(d) the country's net exports can only be positive if saving exceeds investment.
(e) the budget deficit can be decreased only if net exports are increased.

11. Personal income is equal to
(a) national income + transfer payments from government – business retained profits.
(b) national income – transfer payments from government – business retained profits.
(c) national income + transfer payments from government + business retained profits.
(d) national income – transfer payments from government.
(e) national income – business retained profits.

12. Personal disposable income is equal to personal income minus
(a) dividend payments.
(b) personal saving.
(c) transfer payments.
(d) personal income tax payments.
(e) none of the above.

13. Mary's wealth is equal to her
(a) total assets.
(b) total assets and total liabilities.
(c) total assets minus her total liabilities.
(d) financial assets.
(e) financial assets minus her financial liabilities.

14. Which of the following would be included in GDP in the year 1999?
(a) The purchase in 1999 of a used 1998 car.
(b) The purchase in 1999 of a share of Bell Canada stock.
(c) The purchase in 1999 of a car produced in 1999.
(d) All of the above.
(e) Both (b) and (c) but not (a).

15. If net exports are zero and the government has a budget deficit, then
(a) the government's net financial assets decrease.
(b) the government's net financial assets increase.

(c) the private sector's net financial assets increase.

(d) both (a) and (c).

(e) real assets of the private sector decrease.

16. In 1998, Dream World's nominal GDP was \$100 billion and its real GDP was also \$100 billion. In 1999, its nominal GDP was \$110 billion and its real GDP was \$95 billion. In 1999, Dream World's economic growth rate was

(a) 10 percent.

(b) 5 percent.

(c) –5 percent.

(d) –10 percent.

(e) –11 percent.

17. Which of the following measures movements in the prices of goods and services typically consumed by urban Canadian families?

(a) The Consumer Producer Index.

(b) The Consumer Price Index.

(c) The GDP deflator.

(d) The GDP inflator.

(e) The CPI deflator.

18. The GDP deflator is equal to

(a) nominal GDP ÷ real GDP.

(b) nominal GDP x real GDP.

(c) (real GDP ÷ nominal GDP) x 100.

(d) (nominal GDP ÷ real GDP) x 100.

(e) nominal GDP – real GDP.

19. The price level as measured by the GDP deflator will be higher than that measured by the CPI if the

(a) prices of the goods typically consumed by households exceed other prices.

(b) basket of goods typically consumed by households doesn't change.

(c) prices of capital goods exceed the prices of other goods.

(d) economy experiences rapid growth in all sectors.

(e) none of the above.

20. On Sandy Isle, nominal GDP in 1999 was \$100 billion and real GDP was \$90 billion. In 1999, Sandy Isle's GDP deflator was

(a) 90.

(b) between 90 and 100.

(c) 100.

(d) between 100 and 110.

(e) more than 110.

## Short Answer Questions

1. Explain the difference between flow and stock variables. Give some examples of macroeconomic variables that highlight the difference between flows and stocks.

2. Explain the distinction between nominal GDP and real GDP.

3. Some economists have suggested that the official measure of GDP underestimates its true value. Why?

4. What are the twin deficits?

5. (a) What is gross national product (GNP)? What is gross domestic product (GDP)?

   (b) How are GNP and GDP valued?

   (c) What is the difference between GNP and GDP?

6. (a) What is domestic income?

   (b) What does domestic income measure?

7. (a) Using the expenditure approach to measure GDP, what equation is used by national income statisticians?

   (b) How does the expenditure approach value GDP?

8. Calculate business retained profits.

9. Some economists have suggested that the official estimates of GDP overestimate the true value of GDP. Why?

10. Canada experienced a debt explosion in the 1980s and 1990s. Among which agents of the economy did the level of indebtedness increase? Was this an explosion in nominal debt or real debt?

## Problem Solving

### Practice Problems

1. You are given the following information about the economy in Sunny Isle:

| Item | $ billion |
|---|---|
| GDP at market prices | 250 |
| Consumer expenditure | 100 |
| Investment | 75 |
| Government budget deficit | 20 |
| Net exports | –20 |

(a) Calculate saving.

(b) Calculate the taxes paid to the government.

(c) Calculate the change in the net financial assets of the government sector.

2. You are given the following data for an economy:

| Item | $ billion |
|---|---|
| Wages | 230 |
| Interest | 85 |
| Proprietors' income | 90 |
| Profit | 115 |
| Transfer payments | 35 |
| Consumer expenditure | 225 |
| Investment | 160 |
| Government expenditures | 175 |
| Imports | 124 |
| Exports | 118 |
| Total taxes paid | 150 |
| Depreciation | 34 |

(a) Calculate aggregate expenditure measured in market prices.

(b) Calculate domestic income.

(c) Calculate the government's budget *deficit*.

### Solutions to Practice Problems

1. (a) Calculate saving.

Saving is a leakage from the circular flow. Total leakages equal total injections. That is,

$S + T + IM = I + G + EX$

or,

$S = I + (G - T) + (EX - IM)$

$S = 75 + 20 + (-20)$

$S = \$75$ billion.

1. (b) Calculate the taxes paid to the government.

Households allocate their income between consumer expenditure, saving, and taxes. That is,

$Y = C + S + T$

or,

$250 = 100 + 75 + T$

$T = \$75$ billion.

1. (c) Calculate the change in the net financial assets of the government sector.

The change in the net financial assets of the government sector is equal to $T - G$, which is –$20 billion.

2. (a) Calculate aggregate expenditure measured in market prices.

Aggregate expenditure at market prices is equal to

$C + I + G + EX - IM$,

which is

225 + 160 + 175 + 118 – 124

or $554 billion.

2. (b) Calculate domestic income.

Domestic income is the total income paid for the services of factors of production used to produce goods and services. It is the sum of wages, interest, proprietors' income, and profit. That is,

230 + 85 + 90 + 115

or $520 billion.

2. (c) Calculate the government's budget *deficit*.

The government's budget deficit is equal to $G - T$, where $T$ is taxes. Taxes equal total taxes paid minus transfer payments. That is, 150 – 35, or $115 billion. The budget deficit is equal to 175 – 115, which is $60 billion.

## Problems to Solve

1. On June 1, 1999, Terry owned a 1993 boat with a current market value of $4,000. In the year from June 1, 1999 to June 1, 2000, the market value of the boat dropped to $3,200. On June 1, 2000, Terry sold the 1993 boat and replaced it with a 1996 boat valued at $6,000. Her capital stock on June 1, 2000 was the same $6,000.

   (a) What was the change in Terry's capital stock from June 1, 1999 to June 1, 2000?

   (b) What was Terry's gross investment?

2. Suppose that you purchase a strawberry flavoured ice-cream bar from your local grocery store for $1.50. The store bought the ice-cream bar from a wholesaler for $1.20; the wholesaler bought it from the manufacturer for $0.98; the manufacturer bought the milk for $0.06, the strawberries for $0.12, the sugar for $0.04, and electricity for $0.20, paid wages to its workers of $0.36, and made a $0.20 profit. The profit was paid to the stockholders as a dividend.

   (a) What is the total flow of money in this story of the strawberry flavoured ice-cream bar?

   (b) What is the expenditure on final goods and services?

3. In problem 2, what is the value added by the manufacturer? The value added by the wholesaler? The value added by the grocery store?

4. In problem 2, what are the factor incomes paid.

5. Firms produce $1,000 worth of goods and services and pay incomes of $1,000 to households. If households purchase $900 worth of goods and services and save $100 and firms do not purchase any new capital equipment, then the only investment is inventory investment. By what amount do the firms' inventories change?

6. This year in Leisure Land, consumer expenditure is $3,657.3 billion, investment is $741 billion, government expenditures on goods and services are $1,098.1 billion, exports are $672.8 billion, imports are $704 billion, and indirect taxes less subsidies are $469.4 billion.

   (a) What is gross domestic product at market prices?

   (b) What is gross domestic product at factor cost?

7. On December 31, 1999, George had $25 of currency, $150 in his savings account, $200 in savings bonds, a $1,000 bank loan, $1,200 on his Visa account, and a car worth $1,500, and a CD player and CDs worth $1,000. Calculate George's

   (a) total financial assets.

   (b) total financial liabilities.

   (c) total real assets.

   (d) total assets.

   (e) total liabilities.

   (f) net worth.

8. You are given the following information about an economy:

| Item | $ billion |
|---|---|
| Wages | 4,000 |
| Interest | 200 |
| Proprietors' income | 1,000 |
| Profits | 500 |
| Income taxes | 300 |
| Indirect taxes less subsidies | 50 |
| Capital consumption | 30 |

Calculate:

(a) domestic income.

(b) gross domestic product at factor cost.

(c) net domestic product at market prices.

(d) gross domestic product at market prices.

9. You are given the following information about Dream Land:

| Item | $ billion |
|---|---|
| GDP | 5,000 |
| Net exports | 250 |
| Government expenditures | 1,700 |
| Consumer expenditure | 2,000 |

(a) If the budget is balanced, what is saving?

(b) Calculate investment.

(c) Calculate the change in net financial assets of households and firms.

(d) Is Dream Land borrowing or lending to the rest of the world?

(e) Calculate the change in the net financial assets of the rest of the world.

10. You are given the following data for Desert Kingdom, which is a closed economy:

| Item | $ billion |
|---|---|
| Wages | 130 |
| Interest | 35 |
| Proprietors' income | 40 |
| Profit (all distributed) | 75 |
| Transfer payments | 45 |
| Consumer expenditure | 145 |
| Investment | 80 |
| Government expenditures | 75 |
| Imports | 6 |
| Exports | 18 |
| Total taxes paid | 50 |
| Depreciation | 10 |

Calculate:

(a) gross aggregate expenditure using the expenditure approach.

(b) gross domestic income using the factor incomes approach.

(c) the government's budget *deficit*.

(d) personal income.

(e) indirect taxes less subsidies.

## Answers

### Fill in the Blanks

1. flow, stock
2. capital, investment, fixed investment, inventory investment
3. depreciation, gross investment, net investment, gross investment, depreciation
4. aggregate income, aggregate expenditure, aggregate product
5. final goods and services, final, intermediate transactions, value added
6. Consumer expenditure, saving
7. leakage, injection
8. government expenditures, transfer payments, taxes
9. exports, imports, net exports, minus
10. twin deficits
11. gross national product, domestic, domestic income
12. nominal GDP, real GDP
13. personal income, personal disposable income
14. underground economy
15. balance sheet, assets, liabilities
16. real, financial
17. wealth, net worth
18. medium of exchange, money
19. economic growth
20. GDP deflator, Consumer Price Index

### True or False

1T 5T 9F 13F 17F
2T 6F 10T 14T 18F
3F 7F 11F 15T 19F
4F 8T 12T 16T 20F

### Multiple Choice

1d 5b 9c 13d 17b
2d 6c 10d 14c 18d
3c 7d 11a 15d 19d
4e 8d 12d 16c 20e

### Short Answer Questions

1. A flow is a variable that measures a rate per unit of time. Examples of macroeconomic flows are income and expenditure that are expressed as dollars per unit of time. A stock is a variable measured at a point in time. An example of a macroeconomic stock is the total quantity of money in the economy at a given point in time.
2. Nominal GDP is the value of goods and services produced in a year measured in current year prices. Real GDP is the value of the goods and services produced in a year when output is valued at the prices prevailing in a base year.
3. The measured GDP omits the underground economy. The underground economy is the part of the economy that is engaged in illegal activities and includes criminal activity, such as drug dealing, and activities that are not themselves illegal but are concealed to avoid government regulations or the payment of taxes, such as underreporting tips.
4. The government's budget deficit and the Canadian deficit with the rest of the world are called the twin deficits.
5. (a) Gross national product is the total expenditure in a year on final goods and services produced by Canadians wherever in the world that activity takes place. Gross domestic product is the total expenditure on final goods and services in a year in Canada.

   (b) Both GNP and GDP are valued at market prices, which are the prices paid by the final user.

   (c) The difference between GDP and GDP is known as net investment income from non-residents. It is not large for most countries and is small for Canada.
6. (a) Domestic income is the total income, including profit, paid for the services of factors of production used to produce goods and services in Canada in a year.

   (b) Domestic income measures net aggregate economic activity because firms deduct the depreciation of their capital stock in calculating profit.
7. (a) National income statisticians use the following equation to obtain a measure of

GDP:

$Y = C + I + G + EX - IM$.

(b) The expenditure approach values GDP at market prices.

8. Business retained profits are those profits not distributed to households in the form of dividends.
9. Some economists suggest that the official estimates of GDP overestimate the true value of GDP because they omit the cost of pollution and the destruction of natural resources such as lakes and forests. These costs could be very large if the worst-case scenarios about global warming and ozone layer depletion are correct.
10. The debt explosion of the 1980s and 1990s occurred because of an enormous increase in the overall level of indebtedness among individuals, firms, and government. In nominal terms, federal government debt increased at an average rate of 13.5 percent a year. Federal government debt also increased in real terms—at an average rate of 10 percent a year. Federal government debt also increased as a percentage of GDP.

Problem Solving

1. (a) $2,000
   (b) $2,800
2. (a) $4.66
   (b) $1.50
3. $0.56, $0.22, $0.30
4. $1.50
5. $100
6. (a) $5,465.2 billion
   (b) $4,995.8 billion
7. (a) $375
   (b) $2,200
   (c) $2,500
   (d) $2,875
   (e) $2,200
   (f) $675
8. (a) $5,700 billion
   (b) $5,730 billion
   (c) $5,750 billion
   (d) $5,780 billion
9. (a) $1,300 billion
   (b) $1,050 billion
   (c) $250 billion
   (d) lending
   (e) –$250 billion
10. (a) $312 billion
   (b) $290 billion
   (c) $70 billion
   (d) $325 billion
   (e) $22 billion

## Chapter 3

# The Economy at Full Employment: The Classical Model

## Perspective and Focus

This chapter studies a macroeconomic model. A macroeconomic model describes how households, firms, governments, and foreigners make decisions and how these decisions are coordinated in markets. A macroeconomic model explains some variables—endogenous variables—and other variables—exogenous variables—are determined outside the model.

The macroeconomic model studied in chapter 3 is the classical model. The classical model enables us to understand the economy at full employment. Real endogenous variables determined in the classical model are: real GDP; saving, investment, and the real interest rate; employment and the real wage rate. Nominal endogenous variables are the price level and the money wage rate. In the classical model the capital stock and the state of technology, government expenditures, taxes, and the quantity of money are exogenous. They are determined outside the model.

We study the classical model to understand the situation towards which the economy is persistently pulled. The classical model serves as a foundation on which to build other macroeconomic models.

## Learning Objectives

*After studying this chapter, you will be able to:*

- Describe the classical macroeconomic model
- Explain the relationship between employment and real GDP
- Explain how labour market equilibrium determines potential GDP at full employment
- Explain how capital market equilibrium determines investment, saving, and the real interest rate at full employment
- Explain how the quantity of money determines the price level at full employment
- Compare the economy at different full-employment positions and different price levels

## Increasing Your Productivity

Work hard to understand the important relationships between:

(a) the slope of the short-run production function and the labour demand curve
(b) equilibrium in the labour market and potential GDP
(c) the price level and the quantity of money

### The Slope of the Short-run Production Function and the Labour Demand Curve

The slope of the short-run production function measures the marginal product of labour. The demand for labour is the relationship between the quantity of labour employed and the real wage rate.

The goal of all firms is to maximize profit by hiring the quantity of labour at which the cost of the last hour of labour employed brings in an equal amount of revenue. Firms realize this goal by hiring the quantity of labour at the point where the wage rate equals the marginal product of labour multiplied by the price of output. Equivalently, they hire the quantity of labour such that the real wage rate equals the marginal product of labour.

The labour demand curve shows the relationship between the quantity of labour employed and the real wage rate. The real wage is equivalent to the marginal product of labour which is the slope of the short-run production function.

### Equilibrium in the Labour Market and Potential GDP

The short-run production function shows the relationship between real GDP and the quantity of labour employed. At labour market equilibrium, employment is at its full-employment level and the quantity of real GDP produced by the full-employment quantity of labour is potential GDP.

### The Price Level and the Quantity of Money

The inflation rate equals the growth rate of the quantity of money.

The price level is proportionate to the quantity of money. The factor of proportionality depends on the propensity to hold money and potential GDP.

## Self Test

### Fill in the Blanks

1. A ________ ________ is a description of how households, firms, governments, and foreigners make economic decisions and how these decisions are coordinated in markets.
2. An ________ variable is a variable whose value is determined by a model.
3. Variables whose values are determined outside a model are ________ variables.
4. ________ ________ is a body of laws and generalizations about how the economy works based on macroeconomic models.
5. The classical model explain how real GDP and other variables are determined at ________ ________.
6. The unemployment rate at full employment is the ________ ________ ________.
7. ________ ________ is the level of real GDP at full employment.
8. The short-run production function is the relationship between the ________ ________ ________ ________ and the ________ ________ ________ when all other influences on production remain the same.
9. The slope of the short-run production function measures the ________ ________ ________ ________.
10. The demand for labour is the relationship between the ________ ________ ________ ________ and the ________ ________ ________ other things remaining the same.
11. The short-run production function and the demand for labour curve shift as a result of ________ ________ and ________ ________.
12. ________ is working and searching for a job.
13. ________ and ________ is nonmarket activity.
14. The amount of time allocated to working is the ________ ________ ________ ________.
15. Changes in ________ and ________ ________ shift the labour supply curve.
16. When the real wage rate is ________ the equilibrium, an excess demand for labour forces the real wage rate ________ to its equilibrium level.
17. The main factors that influence saving decisions are ________ ________, ________, ________, and ________.
18. The greater the expected profit rate from new capital, the ________ is the amount of investment. The ________ the real interest rate, the lower is the amount of investment.
19. The ________ interest rate equals the ________ rate of interest plus the inflation rate.
20. The opportunity cost of holding money is the ________ ________ ________.

### True or False

1. In Canada, real GDP, employment, the real wage rate, and the inflation rate increase over time.
2. A movement along the short-run production function occurs when the quantity of physical capital increases.
3. As the amount of labour hours increases along the short-run production function, the marginal product of labour decreases.

4. Firms maximize profit by employing the quantity of labour such that the marginal product of labour multiplied by the price of the output equals the real wage rate.

5. An increase in capital stock shifts the short-run production function upward and creates a movement along the demand for labour curve.

6. When the short-run production function shifts downward, the marginal product of labour falls, and the demand for labour curve shifts leftward.

7. As the real wage rate rises, the substitution effect and the income effect work together to increase the quantity of labour supplied.

8. The labour supply curve does not become backward bending because of the intertemporal substitution of work.

9. An increase in population, the real interest rate, or the real wage rate shifts the labour supply curve rightward.

10. At full-employment equilibrium, the quantity of labour demanded equals the quantity of labour supplied, there is no tendency for the real wage rate to change, and the quantity of real GDP produced is potential GDP.

11. Along the saving supply curve, the higher the interest rate, the greater is the quantity of saving.

12. A firm expects a profit rate of 10 percent a year from some new capital. If the real interest rate is 8 percent, the firm will buy the new capital.

13. Kate has an annual income of $40,000 and a demand for money of $1,000. Kate's propensity to hold money is 0.25.

14. The lower the nominal interest rate, the smaller is the propensity to hold money.

15. The real interest rate is determined in the capital market by investment demand and saving supply.

16. When the inflation rate rises, the quantity of money demanded increases because the opportunity cost of holding money decreases.

17. The inflation rate equals the growth rate of the quantity of money.

18. The return on money holding is equal to the inflation rate.

19. The price level is inversely related to the quantity of money.

20. The quantity of money has a larger effect on the price level at a high inflation rate than it does at a low inflation rate.

## Multiple Choice

1. A macroeconomic model
(a) is a detailed description of the economy.
(b) is a selective description of the economy that emphasizes some things and ignores others.
(c) explains exogenous variables only.
(d) explains exogenous variables and endogenous variables.
(e) is a body of laws and generalizations about how the economy works.

2. The classical model is applicable
(a) when there is a surplus or a shortage of labour.
(b) whenever the quantity of money demanded equals the quantity of money supplied.
(c) only when the inflation rate is zero and unemployment is at its natural rate.
(d) only at full employment.
(e) at all levels of employment.

3. Employment in the country of Sparta is increasing with no change in capital or technology. Which of the following is true?
(a) Real GDP is decreasing.
(b) Real GDP and marginal product of labour are increasing.
(c) Real GDP and marginal product of labour are decreasing.
(d) Marginal product of labour is decreasing.
(e) Marginal product of labour is increasing.

4. The demand for labour curve is downward sloping because
(a) the supply of labour curve is upward sloping.
(b) the demand curve shifts when the short-run production function shifts.
(c) as the price level falls output decreases and the demand for labour increases.
(d) as the price level falls output increases and the demand for labour increases.
(e) the marginal product of labour diminishes as employment increases.

5. A firm that produces candles pays a wage rate of $20 per hour. The marginal product of the last hour of labour is 5 candles per hour and each candle sells for $5. To maximize profit, the firm
(a) decreases the number of employees.
(b) increases the wage rate it pays to its employees.
(c) hires more employees.
(d) increases its physical capital but does not change the number of employees.
(e) increases its physical capital and decreases the number of employees.

6. When capital accumulation and technological change shift the short-run production function upward, real GDP
(a) increases at every level of employment and the marginal product of labour decreases.
(b) increases at every level of employment and the marginal product of labour does not change.
(c) does not change because the supply of labour does not change.
(d) and the marginal product of labour increase at every level of employment and the demand for labour curve shifts rightward.
(e) and the supply of labour increase.

7. The marginal cost of an extra hour spent on nonwork activities is the
(a) marginal product of labour minus the inflation rate.
(b) marginal product of labour plus the inflation rate.
(c) real wage rate.
(d) wage rate.
(e) real interest rate.

8. The opportunity cost of work today versus work later increases if
(a) today's real wage rate increases permanently.
(b) tomorrow's real wage rate increases.
(c) the real interest rate rises.
(d) the real interest rate falls.
(e) (a) and (d).

9. If the only effects working on the quantity of labour supplied are the income effect and the substitution, then when the substitution effect is greater than the income effect, the labour supply curve
(a) is vertical.
(b) is horizontal.
(c) bends backwards.
(d) is upward sloping.
(e) has an increasing slope.

10. When the real interest rate rises, the labour
(a) supply does not change today but it increases in the future.
(b) supply decreases today and returns to its original level in the future.
(c) demand curve shifts rightward.
(d) supply curve shifts rightward.
(e) (c) and (d)

11. At potential GDP
(a) the labour market is in equilibrium with the quantity of labour demanded equal to the quantity supplied.
(b) there is no necessary relationship between the quantity of labour demanded and the quantity supplied.
(c) the real wage adjusts so that it equals the money wage.
(d) the real wage rate must be rising because the marginal product of labour is rising.
(e) the demand for labour curve is vertical.

12. The opportunity cost of consumption is
(a) saving.
(b) is greater for lenders than for borrowers.
(c) is greater for borrowers than for lenders.
(d) the real interest rate.
(e) investment.

13. Saving supply is the relationship between the quantity of saving and
(a) the quantity of investment.
(b) the real interest rate.
(c) disposable income.
(d) wealth
(e) the quantity of capital.

14. The higher the real interest rate
(a) the greater is the amount of investment and the less is the saving supply.
(b) the less is the amount of investment and the greater is the saving supply.
(c) the greater is the expected profit rate.
(d) the steeper is the slope of the saving supply curve.
(e) the greater is a household's wealth.

15. The propensity to hold money is the ratio of
(a) money income to the quantity of money demanded.
(b) real GDP to money income.
(c) the quantity of money demanded to money income.
(d) the quantity of money demanded to real GDP.
(e) the quantity of money demanded to the price level.

16. The real interest rate
(a) is less than the nominal interest rate.
(b) is greater than the nominal interest rate.
(c) is greater than the inflation rate.
(d) equals the nominal interest rate plus the inflation rate.
(e) equals the nominal interest rate minus the inflation rate.

17. The opportunity cost of holding money is
(a) the inflation rate.
(b) minus the inflation rate
(c) the goods and services that you do not purchase with the money.
(d) the nominal interest rate.
(e) the real interest rate.

18. The inflation rate equals
(a) 1 – the propensity to hold money.
(b) 1 – the growth rate of money.
(c) 1 + the growth rate of money.
(d) the growth rate of money.
(e) 1 + the propensity to hold money.

19. If the Bank of Canada decreases the quantity of money supplied, all other things remaining the same
(a) the price level falls.
(b) the price level rises.
(c) the inflation rate rises.
(d) equilibrium in the money market no longer exists.
(e) the real interest rate rises.

20. The Canadian economy was close to full employment in
(a) 1982.
(b) 1933.
(c) 1991.
(d) 1973.
(e) 1999.

## Short Answer Questions

1. (a) What is a macroeconomic model?

(b) What are exogenous and endogenous variables?

2. Describe the shape of the short-run production function.

3. (a) What is the marginal product of labour?

(b) How is the marginal product of labour measured?

4. How do the substitution effect and the income effect change the quantity of labour supplied?
5. What happens to the supply of labour when the real interest rate rises?
6. Describe the relationship between labour market equilibrium and potential GDP.
7. How does a firm decide whether to invest in new capital?
8. (a) What is the propensity to hold money?

   (b) What determines the propensity to hold money?
9. (a) What is the relationship between the inflation rate and the growth rate of the quantity of money?

   (b) What is the relationship between the price level and the quantity of money?
10. Contrast the effect of the quantity of money on the price level at different inflation rates.

## Problem Solving

### Practice Problems

1. Figure 3.1 shows the economy of Whitesand, an island country in the South Pacific whose unit of currency is the seashell.

   (a) What is the quantity of labour employed at full employment?

   (b) What is the real wage rate at full employment?

   (c) What is the marginal product of labour at full employment?

   (d) What is potential GDP?
2. You are given the following information about an economy:

   The short-run production function is

   $y = 50L - 2.5L^2$,

   where $y$ is real GDP and $L$ is the quantity of labour employed.

   The supply of labour is determined by

   $LS = 0.2w$,

   where $w$ is the real wage rate.

   (a) Calculate the quantity of labour employed and the real wage rate at equilibrium.

   (b) Calculate potential GDP.

**Figure 3.1**

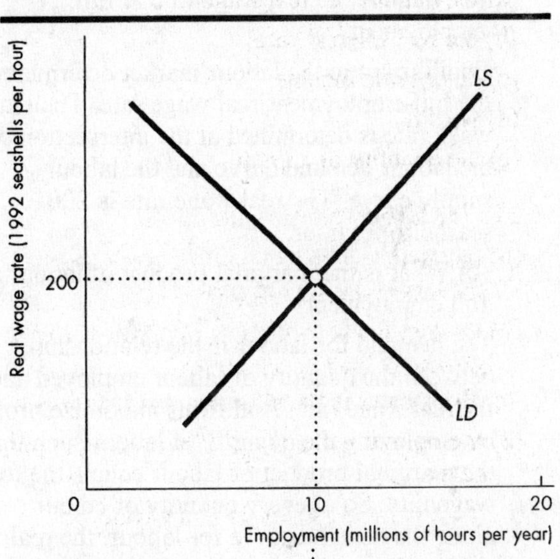


**(a) Labour market**

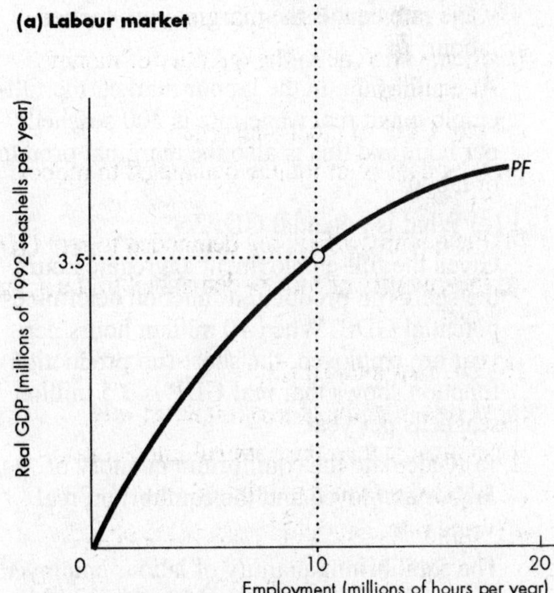


**(b) Production function**

**Solutions to Practice Problems**

1. (a) What is the quantity of labour employed at full employment?

Equilibrium in the labour market determines the full-employment aggregate hours. Equilibrium in the labour market occurs at the intersection of the labour demand curve and the labour supply curve. The quantity of labour employed at full employment is 10 million hours per year.

1. (b) What is the real wage rate at full employment?

Equilibrium in the labour market determines the full-employment real wage rate. The real wage rate is determined at the intersection of the labour demand curve and the labour supply curve. The real wage rate is 200 seashells per hour.

1. (c) What is the marginal product of labour at full employment?

The demand for labour is the relationship between the quantity of labour employed and the real wage rate. And firms maximize profit by employing the quantity of labour such that the marginal product of labour equals the real wage rate. So at every quantity of labour along the demand curve for labour, the real wage rate equals the marginal product of labour.

At equilibrium in the labour market, the full-employment real wage rate is 200 seashells per hour and this is also the marginal product of labour.

1 (d) What is potential GDP?

Given the full-employment aggregate hours, the short-run production function determines potential GDP. When 10 million hours per year are employed, the short-run production function shows that real GDP is 3.5 million seashells per year.

2. (a) Calculate the equilibrium quantity of labour employed and the equilibrium real wage rate.

The equilibrium quantity of labour employed occurs at the point where the quantity of labour demanded equals the quantity of labour supplied.

The slope of the short-run production function measures the marginal product of labour.

Firms hire labour such that the marginal product of labour equals the real wage rate, so the slope of the short-run production function gives us the equation for the labour demand curve.

The short-run production function is

$y = 50L - 2.5L^2$.

So,

$w = 50 - 5L$

or

$LD = 10 - .2w$.

At equilibrium, $LS = LD$.

$LD = 10 - 0.2w$ and $LS = 0.2w$.

Equating these two equations and solving for $w$ gives

$10 - 0.2w = 0.2w$.

$w = 25$.

The real wage rate is 25. The equilibrium quantity of labour is

$LD = LS = 5$.

2. (b) Calculate potential GDP.

Substitute $L = 5$, the quantity of employment at full employment into the formula for the short-run production function to calculate potential GDP.

$y = 50(5) - 2.5(5)^2 = 187.5$

Potential GDP is 187.5.

## Problems to Solve

1. Figure 3.2 shows the economy of Bluesand, an isolated island country off the South American coast whose unit of currency is the seashell.

   (a) What is the quantity of labour employed at full employment?

   (b) What is the real wage rate at full employment?

   (c) What is the marginal product of labour at full employment?

   (d) What is potential GDP?

2. You are given the following information about an economy:

   The short-run production function is

   $y = 40L - 2L^2$,

   where $y$ is real GDP and $L$ is the quantity of labour employed.

   The supply of labour is determined by $LS = 0.25w$,

   where $w$ is the real wage rate.

   (a) Calculate the equilibrium quantity of labour employed.

   (b) Calculate the equilibrium real wage rate.

   (c) Calculate potential GDP.

3. In the economy described in problem 2, a technological advance makes labour more productive, so that at each level of employment real GDP is 50 percent higher than that described by the equation

   $y = 40L - 2L^2$.

   (a) Calculate the equilibrium quantity of labour employed.

   (b) (b) Calculate the equilibrium real wage rate.

   (c) Calculate potential GDP.

**Figure 3.2**

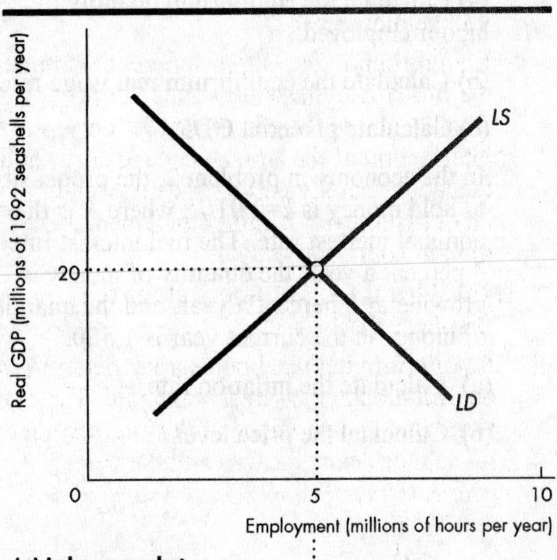


**(a) Labour market**

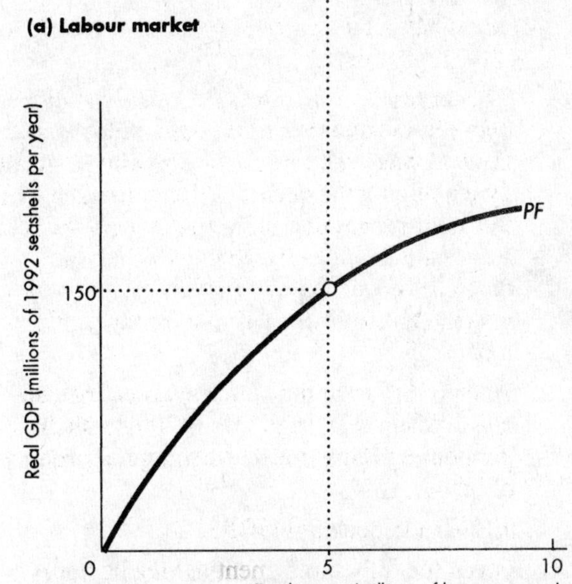


**(b) Production function**

4. In the economy described in problem 2, a technological advance makes labour more productive, so that at each level of employment real GDP is 50 percent higher than that described by the equation

   $y = 40L - 2L^2$.

   At the same time, immigration increases and the new supply of labour is determined by

   $LS = 0.5w$,

where $w$ is the real wage rate.

(a) Calculate the equilibrium quantity of labour employed.

(b) Calculate the equilibrium real wage rate.

(c) Calculate potential GDP.

5. In the economy in problem 2, the propensity to hold money is $k=0.01/R$, where $R$ is the nominal interest rate. The real interest rate is 3 percent a year, the quantity of money is growing at 8 percent a year, and the quantity of money in the current year is 1,500.

(a) Calculate the inflation rate.

(b) Calculate the price level.

## Answers

### Fill in the Blanks

1. macroeconomic model
2. endogenous
3. exogenous
4. Macroeconomic theory
5. full employment
6. natural unemployment rate
7. Potential GDP
8. maximum attainable real GDP, quantity of labour supplied
9. marginal product of labour
10. quantity of labour employed, real wage rate
11. capital accumulation, technological change
12. Market activity
13. Leisure, home production
14. quantity of labour supplied
15. population, real interest rate
16. below, upward
17. real interest rate, disposable income, wealth
18. greater, higher
19. nominal, real
20. nominal interest rate

### True or False

1F 5F 9F 13F 17T
2F 6T 10T 14F 18F
3T 7F 11T 15T 19F
4F 8T 12T 16F 20T

### Multiple Choice

1b 5c 9c 13b 17d
2d 6d 10d 14b 18d
3d 7c 11a 15c 19a
4e 8c 12d 16e 20e

## Short Answer Questions

1. (a) A macroeconomic model is a description of how households, firms, government, and foreigners make economic decisions and how these decisions are coordinated in markets. A macroeconomic model is selective—it is not a detailed description. It emphasizes some things and ignores others.

   (b) Exogenous variables are variables whose values are determined outside a model. Endogenous variables are variables whose values are determined by a model.
2. The short-run production function slopes upward—an increase in employment brings an increase in real GDP. The slope is not constant. It starts out steep and becomes flatter and flatter as employment increases.
3. (a) The marginal product of labour is the increase in output produced as a result of employing an additional hour of labour.

   (b) To calculate the marginal product of labour, measure the slope of the short-run production function at a given point.
4. The substitution effect encourages more work. The higher the real wage rate, the greater is the quantity of labour supplied. The income effect is ambiguous. At low wage rates, an increase in income will likely induce an increase in the quantity of labour supplied, but at a high enough income level, an increase in income will likely induce a decrease in the quantity of labour supplied.
5. As the real interest rate rises, the greater is the tendency to work today and take more leisure in the future. The reason is that an extra dollar earned today earns interest at a higher rate and is worth more than a dollar earned in the future. When the real interest rate rises, other things remaining the same, there is a substitution away from working in the future towards working today, and the labour supply curve shifts rightward.
6. Labour market equilibrium determines the real wage rate and the level of employment. At the labour market equilibrium, employment is at its full-employment level. And the quantity of real GDP produced by the full-employment quantity of labour is potential GDP.
7. To decide whether to invest in new capital, a firm compares the expected profit rate with the real interest rate. When the expected profit rate exceeds the real interest rate, the firm invests in the new capital. When the real interest rate exceeds the expected profit rate, the firm does not invest in the new capital.
8. (a) The propensity to hold money is the ratio of the quantity of money demanded to money income.

   (b) The higher the rate of interest the more it pays to convert unspent income into earning assets and the smaller is the average quantity of money held. So, the propensity to hold money is determined by the interest rate and the higher the interest rate, the smaller is the propensity to hold money.
9. (a) The inflation rate is equal to the growth rate of the quantity of money.

   (b) The price level is proportional to the quantity of money.
10. When the price level is high relative to the quantity of money, the influence of a change in the quantity of money on the price level is large. When the price level is low relative to the quantity of money, the influence of a change in the quantity of money on the price level is small.

## Problem Solving

1. (a) 5 million hours per year

   (b) 20 seashells per hour

   (c) 20 seashells per hour

   (d) 150 million seashells per year
2. (a) 5

   (b) 20

   (c) 150
3. (a) 6

   (b) 24

   (c) 252
4. (a) 7.5

   (b) 15

   (c) 281.25
5. (a) 7 percent per year

   (b) 100

**Chapter 4**

# Departures from Full Employment: The Aggregate Demand-Aggregate Supply Model

## Perspective and Focus

You now know (from Chapter 1) what macroeconomics is about and (from Chapter 2) how we go about observing and measuring the main flows and stocks that keep track of our macroeconomic performance. In Chapter 3 we discussed the economy at full employment. Your job in this chapter is to move forward and learn what makes our economy fluctuate around full employment, how real GDP and the price level are determined—the tendency for real GDP to grow all the time, what determines the cycles in economic activity, and the tendency for prices to rise—for there to be inflation.

## Learning Objectives

*After studying this chapter, you will be able to:*

- Set out and explain the aggregate demand-aggregate supply model
- Explain what determines aggregate demand
- Explain what determines aggregate supply
- Explain how aggregate demand and aggregate supply interact to determine real GDP and the price level
- Use the aggregate demand-aggregate supply model to explain the performance of the Canadian economy during the 1980s and 1990s
- Explain the difference between the classical and Keynesian models of aggregate demand and aggregate supply
- Explain how the classical and Keynesian models interpret fluctuations in real GDP and the price level
- Describe the objectives of the research programs of new classical and new Keynesian macroeconomists

## Increasing Your Productivity

There are just two things to watch in this chapter that cause real problems for students time and time again. Get them right and you are way ahead of the game.

1. The direction of shift of the *SAS* curve.
2. What happens when long-run aggregate supply changes.

### Directions of Shift of the *SAS* Curve

An increase in short-run aggregate supply shifts the *SAS* curve to the right. A decrease in short-run aggregate supply shifts the *SAS* curve to the left. Don't be confused by the positions of the *SAS* curves in the vertical direction. When short-run aggregate supply has fallen, the new *SAS* curve intersects the *LAS* curve at a higher price level than the original *SAS* curve. But short-run aggregate supply has fallen. The quantity of real GDP supplied at a given price level is lower on the new *SAS* curve than on the original *SAS* curve. Take a look at Figure 4.6(a) and convince yourself of this fact.

### Effects of a Change in Long-Run Aggregate Supply

When long-run aggregate supply increases both the long-run aggregate supply curve and the short-run aggregate supply curve shift to the right. The new *SAS* curve intersects the *AD* curve at a level of real GDP below the new long-run aggregate supply level. That is, with an increase in long-run aggregate supply, long-run real GDP increases by more than actual real GDP. Figure 4.7(c) illustrates this case.

Work through the opposite case—that of a decrease in long-run aggregate supply. Draw a diagram as you follow the story that we are about to tell. A decrease in long-run aggregate supply (for example resulting from a major drought) shifts the long-run aggregate supply curve to the left. The short-run aggregate supply curve shifts leftward with it. The new short-run aggregate supply curve intersects the aggregate demand curve at a level of real GDP above the long-run level. That is, the fall in actual real GDP is smaller than the fall in long-run real GDP.

Does your diagram agree with this account? If it doesn't draw it again. Make your short-run aggregate supply curve shift leftward to intersect the new *LAS* curve at the same price level as the original *SAS* curve intersects the original *LAS* curve. In other words, make a diagram that looks like Figure 4.7(c) except make the *LAS* and *SAS* curves move in the opposite direction from the shifts shown in that figure.

## Self Test

### Fill in the Blanks

1. The aggregate quantity of goods and services demanded is the total value (measured in constant dollars) of __________ __________, __________, __________ __________, and __________ __________.
2. The aggregate demand schedule lists the __________ __________ __________ at each __________ level, holding constant all other influences on the buying plans of households, firms, governments, and foreigners.
3. The aggregate demand curve is a graph of the __________ __________.
4. Aggregate demand is the relationship between the quantity of __________ __________ demanded and the __________ __________.
5. The aggregate quantity of goods and services supplied is the total value (measured in __________ dollars) of all the goods and services __________ in the economy.
6. The aggregate __________ __________ lists the quantity of real GDP supplied at each price level, holding constant all other influences on firms' production plans.
7. The aggregate supply curve is a graph of the __________ __________ __________.
8. Long-run aggregate __________ is the quantity of real GDP __________ when all __________ __________ and __________ have adjusted so that each firm is producing its profit-maximizing output and there is __________ __________.
9. The short-run aggregate supply schedule is a list of the quantities of real GDP supplied at each price level, holding constant the __________ of the factors of production and, in particular, the __________ __________.
10. The short-run aggregate supply curve is a __________ of the short-run aggregate supply schedule.
11. __________ __________ is the relationship between the quantity of real GDP supplied and the price level.
12. The situation in which the quantity of real GDP demanded equals the quantity of real GDP supplied is called a __________ __________.
13. When macroeconomic equilibrium occurs on the long-run aggregate supply curve, the economy is at a __________ __________.
14. When macroeconomic equilibrium occurs at a level of real GDP below long-run aggregate supply, the economy is at an __________ __________.
15. When macroeconomic equilibrium occurs at a level of real GDP above long-run aggregate supply, the economy is at an __________ __________.
16. When real GDP is less than long-run aggregate supply, a __________ __________ exists.
17. Households' income minus total taxes paid is __________ __________.
18. __________ __________ is money expressed in terms of the quantity of goods and services that it can buy.
19. A measure of the price of domestic goods and services relative to the price of foreign goods and services is the __________ __________.
20. The __________ __________ __________ is the money wage rate divided by the price level.

### True or False

1. Between 1970 and 1998, inflation in Canada was most rapid in the late 1970s and early 1980s.
2. Both Canada and the rest of the world experienced a recession in 1982 and an expansion with increasing inflation through the 1980s.

3. From 1970 to 1998, real GDP in Canada increased by a smaller percentage than did real GDP in the rest of the world.

4. The aggregate demand schedule lists the quantity of real GDP demanded at each price level, taking account of variations in all other influences on the purchasing plans of households, firms, governments, and foreigners.

5. Aggregate demand decreases when government expenditures on goods and services decrease, consumption expenditure decreases, and investment increases.

6. Long-run aggregate supply is the quantity of real GDP supplied when all wage rates and prices have adjusted so that each firm is producing its profit-maximizing output and there is full employment.

7. Macroeconomic equilibrium is a situation in which the quantity of real GDP demanded is equal to the quantity of real GDP supplied in the long run.

8. When the economy is at an unemployment equilibrium or at an above full-employment equilibrium, a GDP gap exists.

9. The real exchange rate rises when the price of foreign goods and services increase or the price of domestic goods and services decrease.

10. A shift of the aggregate demand curve to the left is a decrease in aggregate demand.

11. Long-run aggregate supply increases when a technological change increases productivity or the labour force increases. Long-run aggregate supply decreases when wage rates increase.

12. When short-run aggregate supply increases, the short-run aggregate supply curve shifts leftward.

13. The price level rises and unemployment increases when either short-run aggregate supply or aggregate demand increases.

14. The classical model has just one aggregate supply curve and that curve is vertical. The Keynesian model has a short-run aggregate supply curve that is horizontal.

15. New classical and new Keynesian macroeconomists agree that macroeconomic models should use the basic ideas of microeconomics but they cannot agree on the most promising route to progress and increased knowledge.

## Multiple Choice

1. The aggregate quantity of goods and services demanded is
(a) the total quantity demanded of all goods and services produced domestically plus the quantity of goods and services imported.
(b) the total value (measured in current dollars) of consumer expenditure, investment, and government expenditures on goods and services.
(c) the quantity of real GDP demanded.
(d) the total quantity demanded of all goods and services produced domestically minus those that remain unsold and are put into inventory.
(e) none of the above.

2. Long-run aggregate supply is the level of real GDP that
(a) varies with the price level so that the long-run aggregate supply curve is upward sloping.
(b) varies so that the long-run aggregate supply is negatively sloped.
(c) varies at a given price level so that the long-run aggregate supply curve is horizontal.
(d) never varies so that the long-run aggregate supply curve is vertical.
(e) none of the above.

3. The economy in at an unemployment equilibrium if the macroeconomic equilibrium occurs at a
(a) level of real GDP below long-run aggregate supply.
(b) level of real GDP on the long-run aggregate supply curve.
(c) level of real GDP above long-run aggregate supply.
(d) level of real GDP either above or below long-run aggregate supply.
(e) (a), (c), and (d).

4. Aggregate demand curve shifts to the left if
(a) disposable income increases.
(b) investment increases.
(c) business confidence improves.
(d) all of the above.
(e) none of the above.

5. The aggregate demand curve slopes downward because as the price level increases, other things being equal,
(a) the quantity of real money decreases and consumer expenditure decreases. As a result the quantity of real GDP demanded decreases.
(b) the real exchange rate increases and the demand for domestically-produced goods and services decreases. As a result the quantity of real GDP demanded decreases.
(c) the quantity of real money decreases and consumer expenditure increases. As a result, the quantity of real GDP demanded decreases.
(d) both (a) and (b).
(e) all of the above.

6. The short-run aggregate supply curve slopes upward because when
(a) the price level changes, wage rates also change.
(b) the price level changes, wage rates do not change.
(c) wage rates change, the price level does not change.
(d) wage rates change, the price level changes.
(e) none of the above.

7. Long-run aggregate supply increases if
(a) the labour force increases.
(b) the natural rate of unemployment decreases.
(c) the wage rate increases.
(d) both (a) and (b).
(e) all the above.

8. Short-run aggregate supply increases if
(a) the labour force increases or the capital stock increases.
(b) the natural rate of unemployment decreases.
(c) technological change increases productivity.
(d) both (a) and (b).
(e) all of the above.

9. Aggregate demand increases if
(a) government expenditures on goods and services increase.
(b) a tax cut increases disposable income and increases consumer expenditure.
(c) business confidence improves and investment increases.
(d) the dollar weakens on the foreign exchange market and net exports increase.
(e) all of the above.

10. Short-run aggregate supply increases, but long-run aggregate supply does not change if
(a) wage rates increase.
(b) the minimum wage rate is increased.
(c) labour unions push for higher wage rates.
(d) all the above.
(e) none of the above.

11. Both the long-run and the short-run aggregate supply increase if
(a) the labour force decreases.
(b) the natural rate of unemployment increases.
(c) the capital stock decreases.
(d) technological change increases productivity.
(e) all of the above.

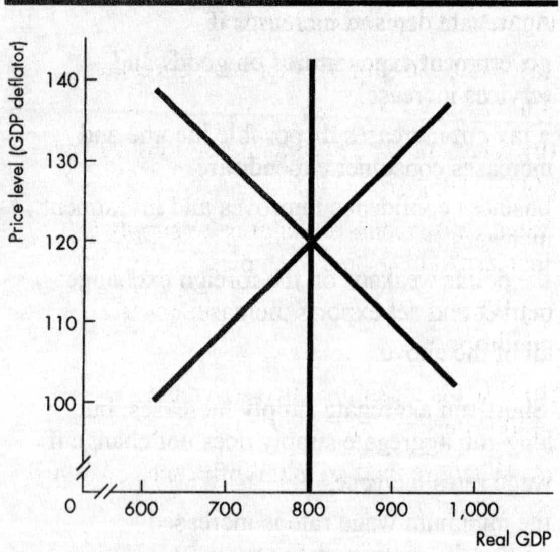


**Figure 4.1** Fantasy Land has the aggregate demand and aggregate supply curves shown above.

12. Use Figure 4.1. At the macroeconomic equilibrium
(a) real GDP is at its long-run level.
(b) the price level is 120.
(c) unemployment is zero.
(d) both (a) and (b).
(e) all of the above.

13. Use Figure 4.1. An increase in aggregate demand of 100 units
(a) increases real GDP by 100 units.
(b) increases the price level by 10 units.
(c) decreases the natural rate of unemployment.
(d) increases real GDP by 50 units.
(e) none of the above.

14. Use Figure 4.1. An increase in long-run aggregate supply of 200 units
(a) increases real GDP to 900 units.
(b) increases the price level to 130.
(c) decreases the price level to 110.
(d) increases the natural rate of unemployment.
(e) both (a) and (c).

15. Use Figure 4.1. An increase in wage rates that shifts the short-run aggregate supply to the left by 200 units
(a) moves the economy to an unemployment equilibrium, so wage rates will quickly fall to restore full employment.
(b) increases the price level to 130.
(c) moves the economy to an unemployment equilibrium, so aggregate demand will automatically increase to restore full employment.
(d) increases the natural rate of unemployment.
(e) both (b) and (d).

16. In classical macroeconomics, an increase in aggregate demand is induced by
(a) an increase in the money supply.
(b) a cut in taxes.
(c) an increase in government expenditures.
(d) an increase in investment.
(e) all of the above.

**Figure 4.2** Magic Empire has the following aggregate demand and aggregate supply curves.

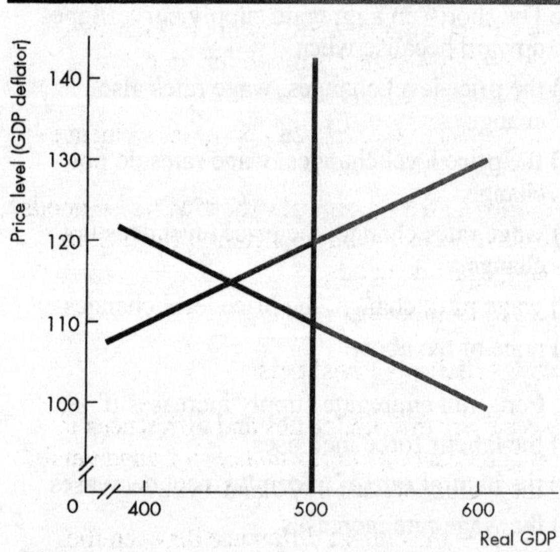


17. Use Figure 4.2. At the macroeconomic equilibrium
(a) real GDP is 500 and the price level is 110.
(b) real GDP is 500 and the price level is 120.
(c) real GDP is 450 and the price level is 115.
(d) unemployment is above the natural rate.
(e) both (c) and (d).

18. Use Figure 4.2. An increase in aggregate demand of 100 units
(a) increases real GDP by 100 units.
(b )increases the GDP deflator by 5.
(c) decreases the natural rate of unemployment.
(d) increases real GDP by 50 units.
(e) both (b) and (d).

19. Use Figure 4.2. A severe drought decreases long-run aggregate supply by 100 units and
(a) moves the economy to a full-employment equilibrium.
(b) moves the economy to an above full-employment equilibrium.
(c) decreases the natural rate of unemployment.
(d) does not change the macroeconomic equilibrium.
(e) both (a) and (c).

20. In Keynesian macroeconomics,
(a) important influences on aggregate demand are fiscal policy and those coming from the rest of the world.
(b) a change in the money supply influences aggregate demand through its effects on investment.
(c) changes in taxes are an important influence on aggregate demand.
(d) changes in government expenditures on goods and services are an important influence on aggregate demand.
(e) all of the above.

## Short Answer Questions

1. What are the similarities and differences in macroeconomic performance in Canada and the world between 1970 and 1998?

2. What is the crucial difference between the aggregate demand-aggregate supply model and the micro demand-supply model?

3. Briefly summarize the Keynesian explanation of the 1980s.

4. What is meant by the quantity of real GDP demanded?

5. (a) What determines the position of the aggregate demand curve?

(b) What factors cause aggregate demand to increase? Give some examples.

6. (a) What is meant by long-run aggregate supply?

(b) What are the determinants of long-run aggregate supply?

7. What causes long-run aggregate supply to increase? Give some examples.

8. (a) What is meant by full-employment equilibrium?

(b) What is meant by unemployment equilibrium?

9. (a) What are the two main influences on firms' investment?

(b) Briefly explain each influence.

10. What are the predictions of the classical model?

## Problem Solving

### Practice Problems

1. Leisure Land has the following aggregate demand and aggregate supply curves:

| | | |
|---|---|---|
| *AD* curve | $y^d = 2{,}000 - 10P$ | (4.1) |
| *SAS* curve | $y^s = -500 + 10P$ | (4.2) |
| *LAS* curve | $y^s = 600$ | (4.3) |

(a) What is the macroeconomic equilibrium?

(b) A severe drought decreases aggregate supply by 150 units. What is the new macroeconomic equilibrium?

(c) In part (a), Leisure Land is at an above full-employment equilibrium. What is Leisure Land's long-run equilibrium?

**Solutions to Practice Problems**

1. (a) What is the macroeconomic equilibrium?

Macroeconomic equilibrium occurs at the intersection of the aggregate demand and short-run aggregate supply curves. Figure 4.3 shows the macroeconomic equilibrium.

To find the equilibrium real GDP ($y^*$) and price level ($P^*$) solve the equations to the *AD* and *SAS* curves. At the equilibrium,

*AD* curve $y^* = 2{,}000 - 10P^*$ (4.1)

*SAS* curve $y^* = -500 + 10P^*$ (4.2)

Add Equations (4.1) and (4.2) to give

$2y^* = 1{,}500.$

That is, $y^* = 750.$

Substitute 750 for $y^*$ in Equation 4.2 to give

$750 = -500 + 10P^*$

$P^* = 125.$

Equilibrium real GDP is 750 and the equilibrium price level is 125.

**Figure 4.3**

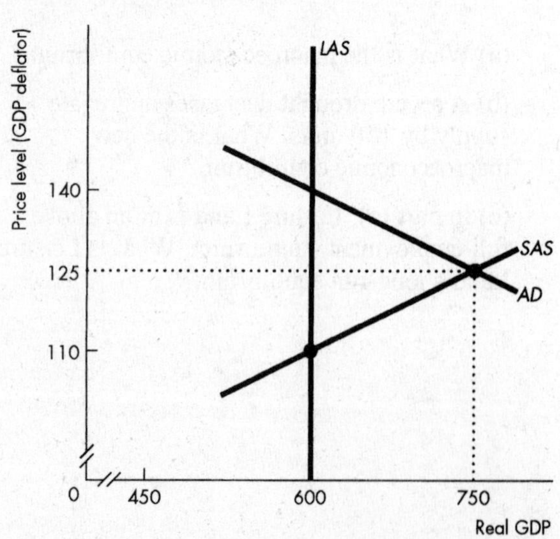


(b) A severe drought decreases aggregate supply by 150 units. What is the new macroeconomic equilibrium?

A decrease in aggregate supply shifts both the long-run and short-run aggregate supply curves to the left. Figure 4.4 shows the *LAS* and the *SAS* curves shifting to the left by 150 units. The *LAS* curve shifts from $LAS_0$ to $LAS_1$, and the *SAS* curve shifts from $SAS_0$ to $SAS_1$.

Figure 4.4 shows that the new equilibrium real GDP is between 600 and 750 and that the new equilibrium price level is above 125. The new macroeconomic equilibrium lies to the right of the $LAS_1$ curve, so the economy is at an above full-employment equilibrium.

Before we can find the actual values of the new equilibrium we must find the equation to the $SAS_1$ curve. The $SAS_1$ curve is such that real GDP supplied at each price level is 150 units less than on $SAS_0$. That is, the $SAS_1$ curve is

$y^s = -500 + 10P - 150.$ (4.4)

To find the new equilibrium, solve Equations (4.1) and (4.4) for $y^*$ and $P^*$. That is,

*AD* curve $y^* = 2{,}000 - 10P^*$ (4.1)

$SAS_1$ curve $y^* = -650 + 10P^*$ (4.4)

Add Equations (4.4) and (4.1) to give

$2y^* = 1{,}350.$

That is, $y^* = 675.$

Substitute 675 for $y^*$ in Equation 4.4 to give

$675 = -650 + 10P^*$

$P^* = 132.5.$

Equilibrium real GDP is 675, and the equilibrium price level is 132.5. Notice that this macroeconomic equilibrium matches that shown in Figure 4.4.

**Figure 4.4**

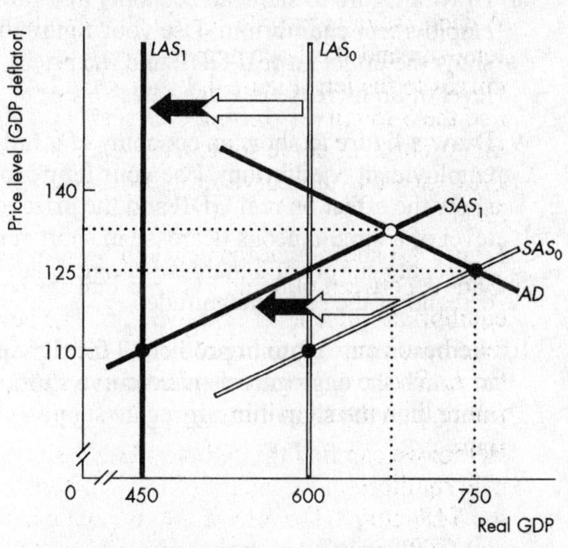


(c) In part (a), Leisure Land is at an above full-employment equilibrium. What is Leisure Land's long-run equilibrium?

At an above full-employment equilibrium there is a shortage of labour and wage rates will automatically begin to rise. The rise in wage rates shifts the short-run aggregate supply curve to the left. Wage rates will continue to rise until the macroeconomic equilibrium lies on the long-run aggregate supply curve. Figure 4.5 shows the *SAS* curve shifting to the left, and the macroeconomic equilibrium moving up the aggregate demand curve, as shown by the arrows. The short-run aggregate supply curve comes to a halt when it reaches $SAS_2$.

Figure 4.5 shows that the new equilibrium real GDP is 600 and the new equilibrium price level exceeds 132.5. The new macroeconomic equilibrium lies on the *LAS* curve, so the economy is at full-employment equilibrium.

To find the new equilibrium, solve Equation (4.1) and (4.3) for $y^*$ and $P^*$. That is,

| | | |
|---|---|---|
| *AD* curve | $y^* = 2{,}000 - 10P^*$ | (4.1) |
| *LAS* curve | $y^* = 600$ | (4.3) |

Set Equation (4.3) equal to (4.1) to give

$$600 = 2{,}000 - 10P^*.$$

That is, $P^* = 140$.

Equilibrium real GDP is 600, and the equilibrium price level is 140. Notice that this macroeconomic equilibrium matches that shown on Figure 4.5.

**Figure 4.5**

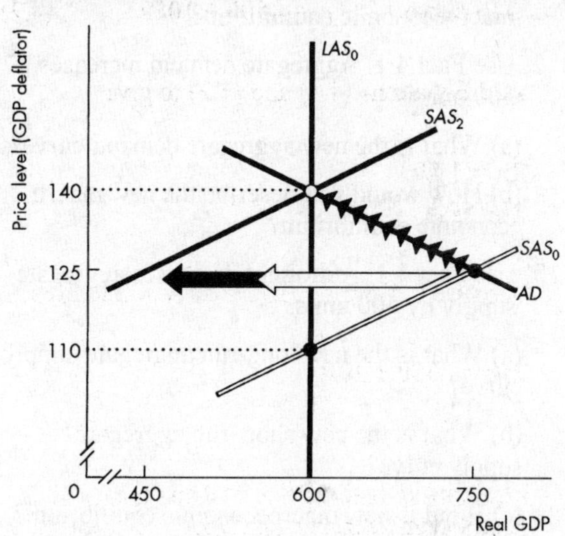

## Problems to Solve

**Fact 4.1** Sunny Isle has the following aggregate demand and aggregate supply curves:

| | |
|---|---|
| *AD* curve | $y^d = 4{,}000 - 20P$ |
| *SAS* curve | $y^s = 20P$ |
| *LAS* curve | $y^s = 2{,}000$ |

1. Use Fact 4.1. What is macroeconomic equilibrium? How would you describe the macroeconomic equilibrium?

2. Use Fact 4.1. Aggregate demand increases by 500 units.

   (a) What is the new aggregate demand curve?

   (b) How would you describe the new macroeconomic equilibrium?

3. Use Fact 4.1. A drought decreases aggregate supply by 500 units.

   (a) What is the new long-run aggregate supply curve?

   (b) What is the new short-run aggregate supply curve?

   (c) What is new macroeconomic equilibrium?

   (d) How would describe the macroeconomic equilibrium?

4. Long-run aggregate supply increases to $4.7 trillion, and at the same time equilibrium real GDP increases to only $4.6 trillion. How big is the GDP gap?

5. Mark lives in a country that has a price level of 100. Mark has $5,000 in the bank. What happens to the quantity of real money Mark has when the price level

   (a) increases by 10 percent?

   (b) decreases by 5 percent?

6. Draw a figure to show an economy at full-employment equilibrium. Use your figure to show the effect on real GDP and the price level of a decrease in firms' confidence about future profits.

7. Draw a figure to show an economy at a full-employment equilibrium. Use your figure to show the effect on real GDP and the price level of a technological advance.

8. Draw a figure to show an economy at a full-employment equilibrium. Use your figure to show the effect on real GDP and the price level of an increase in wage rates.

9. Draw a figure to show an economy at a full-employment equilibrium. Use your figure to show the effect on real GDP and the price level of a simultaneous decrease in short-run aggregate supply and increase in aggregate demand of the same magnitude.

10. Redraw your figure in problem 9 for the case in which the aggregate demand curve shifts by more than the short-run aggregate supply curve.

## Answers

### Fill in the Blanks

1. consumer expenditure, investment, government expenditures, net exports
2. quantity of real GDP demanded, price
3. aggregate demand schedule
4. real GDP, price level
5. constant, produced
6. supply schedule
7. aggregate supply schedule
8. supply, supplied, wage rates, prices, full employment
9. prices, wage rate
10. graph
11. Aggregate supply
12. macroeconomic equilibrium
13. full-employment equilibrium
14. unemployment equilibrium
15. above full-employment equilibrium
16. GDP gap
17. disposable income
18. real money
19. real exchange rate
20. real wage rate

### True or False

1T 4F 7F 10T 13F
2F 5F 8F 11F 14T
3T 6T 9F 12F 15T

### Multiple Choice

1c 5a 9e 13d 17e
2e 6b 10e 14e 18a
3a 7d 11d 15b 19a
4e 8e 12d 16e 20e

### Short Answer Questions

1. The similarities are the tendency for real GDP to grow and prices to rise. The differences are the overall scale of expansion and rising prices, the changing pace of expansion and inflation, and the occurrence of recessions.
2. The most important difference is that the aggregate demand-aggregate supply model explains how aggregate variables, such as the price level and real GDP are determined, while the micro demand-supply model explains how the prices and quantities of individual goods and services, such as pizza and banking services are determined.
3. The Keynesian explanation of the recession of the early 1980s is that it resulted from a sharp increase in world oil prices combined with slow growth of aggregate demand. The recovery of the 1980s resulted from strong aggregate demand growth. The most important influence on aggregate demand during the recovery was the expansionary fiscal policy—the persistent government budget deficit.
4. The quantity of real GDP demanded is the total value (measured in constant dollars) of consumer expenditure, investment, government expenditures on goods and services, and net exports.
5. (a) The position of the aggregate demand curve is determined by all influences on the quantity of real GDP demanded other than the price level.
   (b) Aggregate demand increases if taxes decrease, interest rates fall, business confidence increases, government expenditures increase, the money supply increases, rest-of-world income increases, foreign prices increase, or the dollar weakens on the foreign exchange market.
6. (a) Long-run aggregate supply is the quantity of real GDP supplied when all wage rates and prices have adjusted so that each firm is producing its profit-maximizing output and there is full employment.
   (b) Long-run aggregate supply is determined by the size of the labour force, the size of the capital stock, the state of technology, and the natural rate of unemployment.
7. Long-run aggregate supply increases when the labour force increases, the natural rate of unemployment decreases, the capital stock increases, or technological change increases productivity.
8. (a) Full-employment equilibrium is a situation in which macroeconomic equilibrium occurs at a point on the long-run aggregate supply curve. Unemployment is at its natural rate.

(b) An unemployment equilibrium is a situation in which macroeconomic equilibrium occurs at a level of real GDP below long-run aggregate supply.

9. (a) The two main influences in firms' investment are interest rates and the state of confidence.

   (b) The higher the interest rate, the more expensive it is for firms to borrow, the greater is the inducement for firms to economize on purchases of new plant and equipment, and the lower is investment.

   The major influence on firms' investment is their state of confidence about future business prospects. When firms anticipate an expanding and booming economy, investment is high; and when firms anticipate a slack, depressed economy, investment is low.

10. According to the classical model, a change in the money supply leads to a change in the price level but no change in real GDP. Money growth causes inflation but not real GDP growth.

    Advances in technology, accumulation of capital, and growth in the labour force lead to growth in real GDP. Other things remaining the same, these factors lead to falling prices, but prices don't actually fall because a steadily rising money supply more than offsets this tendency.

    Changes in taxes and government expenditures have no influence on real GDP and the price level. But they do influence interest rates and the composition of aggregate demand.

## Problem Solving

1. Equilibrium real GDP is 2,000, and the price level is 100. The macroeconomic equilibrium lies on the long-run aggregate supply curve, so the equilibrium is a full-employment equilibrium.
2. (a) $y^d = 4{,}500 - 20P$.

   (b) Equilibrium real GDP is 2,250, and the price level is 112.5. The macroeconomic equilibrium lies to the right of the long-run aggregate supply curve, so the equilibrium is an above full-employment equilibrium.
3. (a) $y^s = 1{,}500$.

   (b) $y^s = 20P - 500$.

   (c) Equilibrium real GDP is 1,750, and the price level is 112.5. The macroeconomic equilibrium lies to the right of the long-run aggregate supply curve, so the equilibrium is an above full-employment equilibrium.
4. A real GDP gap arises if equilibrium real GDP is less than long-run real GDP. The GDP gap is equal to $0.1 trillion.
5. (a) Mark's real money decreases by $454.55.

   (b) Mark's real money increases by $263.16.
6. Figure 4.6 shows that a decrease in firms' confidence about future profits decreases real GDP and lowers the price level.

**Figure 4.6**

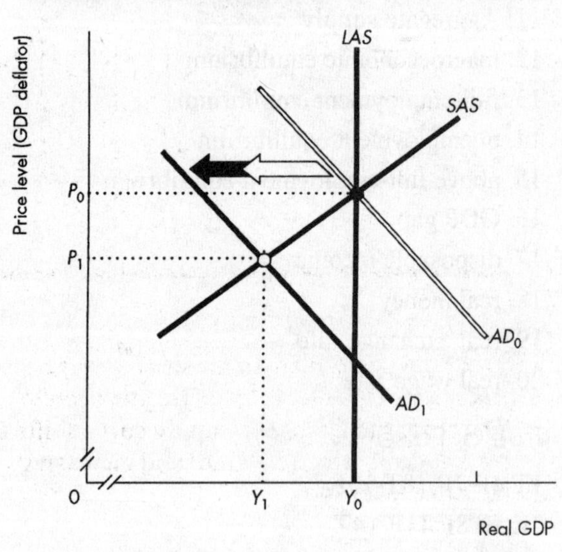

7. Figure 4.7 shows that technological advance increases long-run aggregate supply and short-run aggregate supply increasing real GDP and lowering the price level.

**Figure 4.7**

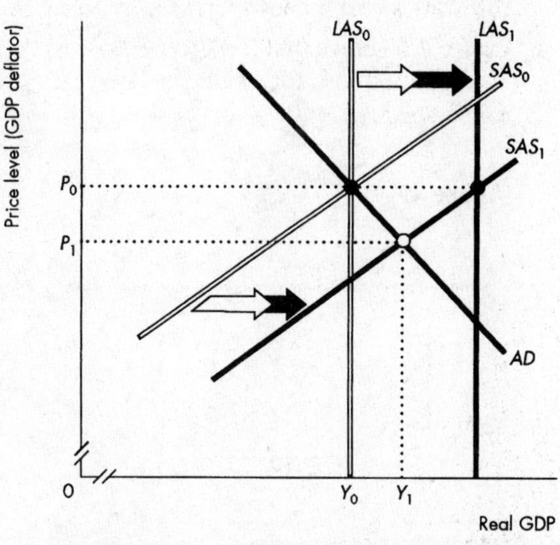


8. Figure 4.8 shows that an increase in wage rates decreases short-run aggregate supply. The short-run aggregate supply curve shifts to the left decreasing real GDP and increasing the price level.

**Figure 4.8**

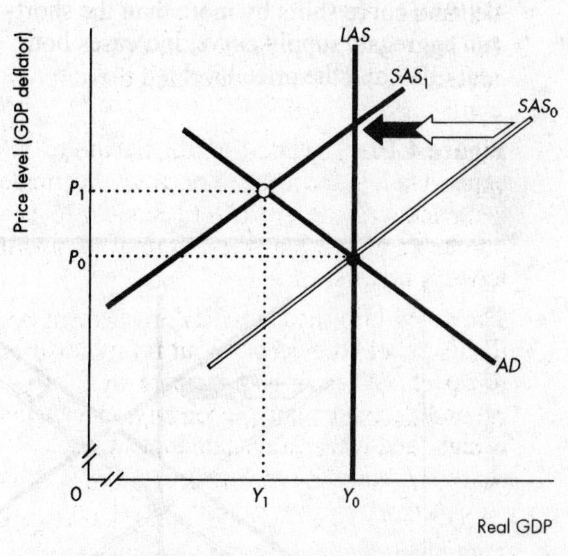


9. Figure 4.9 shows that a simultaneous increase in aggregate demand and decrease in aggregate supply of the same magnitude increase the price level and have no effect on real GDP.

**Figure 4.9**

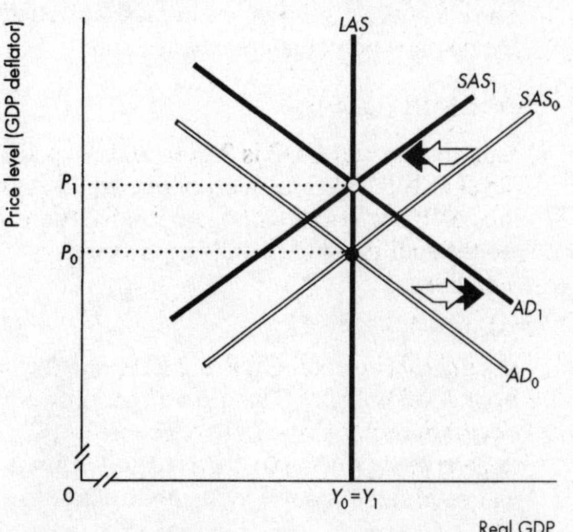

10. Figure 4.10 shows that a simultaneous increase in aggregate demand and decrease in aggregate supply, where the aggregate demand curve shifts by more than the short-run aggregate supply curve, increases both real GDP and the price level.

**Figure 4.10**

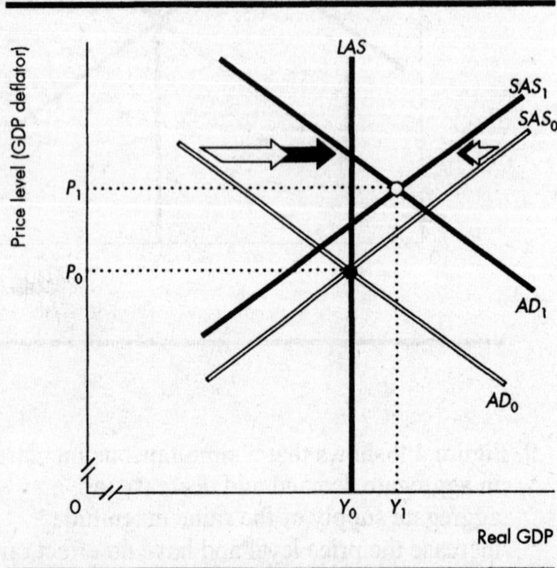

**Chapter 5**

# Aggregate Expenditure and Income

## Perspective and Focus

You have now studied aggregate demand and aggregate supply and know, in general terms, how real GDP and the price level are determined. This chapter is the first of four that take you behind the scenes of the aggregate demand curve. You are going to take the aggregate demand curve to pieces and study it in great detail.

To do this you are going to temporarily freeze the price level. Don't be confused about what this means. The price level is not actually fixed. You are going to study simply what happens in the economy at a particular price level. You are going to learn about the forces that influence the position of the aggregate demand curve and that make the aggregate demand curve shift to the right (for an increase in demand) and to the left (for a decrease in demand). It is easier to study the influences on the aggregate demand curve by working out what happens at a particular price level. That is why we freeze the price level in this and following three chapters.

Chapter 5 examines the immediate determinants of the components of aggregate expenditure—consumer expenditure, investment, government expenditures on goods and services and net exports. The chapter begins by describing these components of aggregate expenditure and showing how they have fluctuated in recent years. It then explains what determines the various components of expenditure and finally shows you how to calculate equilibrium expenditure and the multiplier effect of a change in the components of aggregate expenditure.

## Learning Objectives

*After studying this chapter, you will be able to:*

- Describe the components of aggregate expenditure, the relative importance of each, and the extent to which each fluctuates
- Set out a simple model of consumption and saving
- Describe the relationship between consumption and income in the Canadian economy
- Explain how equilibrium expenditure is determined
- Explain how the economy converges to equilibrium expenditure
- Define and derive the multiplier
- Define and derive the fiscal policy multipliers
- Explain the effects of changes in investment, government expenditures, taxes, and exports on equilibrium expenditure

## Increasing Your Productivity

The key to understanding what is going on in this chapter is to make a sharp distinction between actual and planned expenditure. Actual consumer expenditure plus investment plus government expenditures plus net exports is always equal to real GDP *by definition. Planned* consumer expenditure plus investment plus government expenditures plus net exports equals real GDP only *in equilibrium*.

Consumption plans, government expenditures plans and net export plans are always fulfilled. Investment plans *are not* always fulfilled. Firms have a desired level of investment but actual investment equals desired investment plus the unintended change in inventories. If sales are less than planned, inventories accumulate and because inventories are part of investment, *actual* investment exceeds *planned* investment. If sales exceed expectations, inventories decline and *actual* investment is below *planned* investment.

The fact that investment is not always equal to its planned level has two implications:

1. The economy is not always in a state of equilibrium expenditure.
2. When the economy is not at equilibrium expenditure forces work moving it toward such an equilibrium.

Since actual GDP equals the sum of consumer expenditure, investment, government expenditures on goods and services, and net exports, when there is an unintended accumulation of inventories, actual investment exceeds planned investment and planned expenditure is less than real GDP. In such a situation, firms cut back production to lower inventories and real GDP decreases. It keeps on decreasing until planned expenditure and actual expenditure are equal. Conversely, if inventories fall below the desired level, then planned expenditure exceeds actual expenditure and firms take steps to increase production. In this case, real GDP increases and continues to do so until actual expenditure equals planned expenditure.

These ideas are the essence of this chapter. The rest of the chapter follows mechanically and is easy to understand once you have understood these fundamental ideas. The diagrammatic and algebraic presentation of the determination of equilibrium expenditure, the convergence to it, and the multiplier effect that operates when there is a change in investment or exports or government expenditures can all be understood using these essential concepts.

An appendix to the chapter presents the algebra of equilibrium expenditure and the multipliers. Study the appendix carefully and do attempt to understand how they are derived and what they mean. Translate into plain English after you have learnt how to derive them. But do not attempt to memorize all these formulas.

## Self Test

### Fill in the Blanks

1. The consumption function is the relationship between ________ ________ and ________ ________.
2. The amount of consumer expenditure that is independent of the level of income is ________. The amount of consumer expenditure that varies with disposable income is ________ ________.
3. The saving function is the relationship between ________ and ________. Negative saving is called ________.
4. The average propensity to consume is the ratio of ________ ________ to ________ ________. The marginal propensity to consume is the ratio of the ________ in consumer expenditure to the ________ in disposable income.
5. The ________ propensity to save is the ratio of saving to disposable income. The ________ propensity to save is the ratio of a change in saving to a change in disposable income.
6. The average relationship between consumer expenditure and personal disposable income over several decades is called the ________-________ ________ and the relationship between consumer expenditure and personal disposable income in a particular year is called the ________-________ ________.
7. The sum of planned consumer expenditure, investment, government expenditures on goods and services, and net exports is ________ ________. Equilibrium expenditure exists when real GDP equals ________ ________ ________.
8. Taxes that do not vary with income are called ________ ________ and taxes that vary as income varies are called ________.
9. The aggregate expenditure curve is a curve showing aggregate planned expenditure at each level of ________ ________.
10. Expenditure that does not depend on real GDP is called ________.
11. The ________ is the ratio of the change in real GDP to the change in investment that caused it.
12. The government expenditures multiplier is the ratio of the change in ________ to the change in ________ that caused it.
13. The ratio of the change in ________ to the change in ________ that caused it is called the autonomous tax multiplier.
14. The ratio of the change in real GDP to the change in government expenditures when taxes change by the same amount as government expenditures is called the ________ ________.
15. The marginal propensity to consume out of real GDP is the fraction of each additional dollar of ________ ________ that

_________ spend on goods and services.

16. The ________ ________ ________ is the fraction of an additional dollar of income paid out in taxes.

17. The __________ ________ ________ _________ is the ratio of the change in real GDP to the change in the marginal tax rate that caused it.

18. The relationship between taxes paid and income is called the ________ ________.

19. The import function is the relationship between the quantity of _________ and _________ _________.

20. The change in imports resulting from a one-dollar increase in real GDP is called the _________ _________ _________ _________.

True or False

1. Government expenditure is the largest component of aggregate expenditure, investment is the second largest component, and consumer expenditure is the third largest.

2. Exports, imports, and investment are the most volatile components of aggregate expenditure.

3. If consumer expenditure is $10,000 when disposable income is zero, then saving is equal to –$10,000.

4. A household with zero disposable income spends $5,000 a year on basic food, clothing, and shelter. Its autonomous consumer expenditure is $5,000 a year.

5. The ratio of consumer expenditure to disposable income is the average propensity to consume.

6. The ratio of a change in saving to a change in disposable income is the marginal propensity to save.

7. When real GDP increases, consumer expenditure increases as the economy moves up its consumption function. At the same time, saving decreases as the economy moves down its saving function.

8. Along a linear consumption function the marginal propensity to consume is a constant, but as disposable income increases the average propensity to consume decreases.

9. As real GDP decreases, induced expenditure and aggregate expenditure decrease, but autonomous expenditure does not change.

10. Autonomous expenditure is the fraction of aggregate expenditure that depends on real GDP.

11. As disposable income increases both the marginal propensity to consume and the marginal propensity to save increase.

12. If all taxes are autonomous, the investment multiplier in a closed economy is $1/(1 - b)$.

13. The autonomous tax multiplier in a closed economy is $-by/(1 - b)$.

14. In a closed economy, the balanced budget multiplier is 2 and it tells us that if government expenditures on goods and services are increased by $1 trillion and autonomous taxes are increased by $1 trillion to pay for such expenditure, then real GDP will increase by $2 trillion.

15. Aggregate expenditure is the quantity of nominal GDP demanded at a given price level.

16. At real GDP below equilibrium expenditure, planned expenditure is greater than actual expenditure, so inventory investment is lower than intended.

17. The multiplier process occurs because as real GDP increases consumer expenditure increases, which leads to an increase in investment.

18. The magnitude of the government expenditures multiplier is the same as the autonomous tax multiplier.

19. The government budget deficit fluctuates over the business cycle and in such a way that allows it to work as an automatic stabilizer.

20. The multiplier in an open economy is smaller than in a closed economy.

## Multiple Choice

1. Planned consumer expenditure is given by 0.050 + 0.7$y$ trillion. If income is zero, then planned consumer expenditure is

(a) $0.025 trillion.
(b) $0.050 trillion.
(c) $0.075 trillion.
(d) $0.010 trillion.
(e) $0.070 trillion.

2. If the marginal propensity to save is 0.25, then an increase in disposable income of $40,000 increases saving by

(a) $1,000.
(b) $ 5,000.
(c) $15,000.
(d) $30,000.
(e) $10,000.

3. When disposable income is $40,000 a year, consumer expenditure is $35,000. The average propensity to consume is

(a) 40,000/35,000.
(b) 75,000/35,000.
(c) 40,000 × 35,000.
(d) 35,000/40,000.
(e) 40,000 – 35,000.

4. The slope of the saving function

(a) is the reciprocal of the slope of the consumption function.
(b) is the same as the slope of the consumption function.
(c) plus the slope of the consumption function equals one.
(d) is at least as large as the slope of the consumption function.
(e) is larger than the slope of the consumption function.

**Fact 5.1.** Magic Empire's consumption function is

$$c = 10 + 0.75(y - t).$$

Magic Empire is a closed economy, government expenditures are $10 billion, and autonomous taxes are $8 billion. There are no income taxes in Magic Empire. Investment is $15 billion.

5. Use Fact 5.1. Equilibrium expenditure occurs at a real GDP of

(a) $116 billion.
(b) $164 billion.
(c) $148 trillion.
(d) $38.67 trillion.
(e) $65.33 trillion.

6. Use Fact 5.1.The government expenditures multiplier is

(a) 0.75.
(b) 0.25.
(c) 4.
(d) 1.33.
(e) 3.

7. Use Fact 5.1. A $1 billion increase in government expenditures, which is paid for by an increase in autonomous taxes increases real GDP by

(a) $0 billion.
(b) $1 billion.
(c) $2 billion.
(d) $3 billion.
(e) $4 billion.

8. Use Fact 5.1. A $2 billion increase in autonomous taxes increases real GDP by

(a) $4 billion.
(b) $3 billion.
(c) $2 billion.
(d) –$3 billion.
(e) –$6 billion.

9. In Dream World the investment multiplier is 4. A $1 trillion decrease in investment changes real GDP by

(a) –$2 trillion.
(b) $0.25 trillion.
(c) $40 trillion.
(d) –$4 trillion.
(e) $0.4 trillion.

10. Sandy Island is a closed economy, and its marginal propensity to save is 0.4. Its autonomous tax multiplier is equal to

(a) –1.5.

(b) –2.976.

(c) –0.855.

(d) –5.970.

(e) –9.888.

11. In a closed economy which has induced taxes, investment changes. Real GDP changes by an amount equal to the change in investment multiplied by

(a) $\frac{1}{1-b(1-t_1)}$.

(b) $\frac{1-b}{1+t_1}$.

(c) $\frac{1-b}{1-t_1}$.

(d) $\frac{1}{1-b(1-t_1)}$.

(e) $\frac{1}{b-y}$.

**Fact 5.2.** Desert Empire is a closed economy. Its consumer expenditure is $200 billion when disposable income is zero and its marginal propensity to consume is 0.8. Investment is $500 billion. Government expenditures are $100 billion and taxes are 10 percent of income.

12. Use Fact 5.2. At equilibrium expenditure, real GDP is approximately equal to

(a) $800 billion.

(b) $880 billion.

(c) $1,000 billion.

(d) $2,000 billion.

(e) $2,857 billion.

13. Use Fact 5.2. At equilibrium expenditure, the government budget deficit is

(a) $185.7 billion.

(b) $85.7 billion.

(c) –$185.7 billion.

(d) –$85.7 billion.

(e) none of the above.

14. Use Fact 5.2. If investment increases by $10 billion, real GDP increases by

(a) $10 billion.

(b) more than $10 billion but less than $20 billion.

(c) more than $20 billion but less than $30 billion.

(d) more than $30 billion but less than $40 billion.

(e) $50 billion.

15. Use Fact 5.2. The government can balance its budget by

(a) increasing private investment.

(b) increasing government expenditures.

(c) raising the marginal tax rate.

(d) introducing autonomous taxes.

(e) increasing consumer expenditure.

16. The multiplier process takes place because the initial change in real GDP

(a) produces an additional change in consumer expenditure.

(b) produces an additional change in government expenditures as taxes change.

(c) produces an additional change in investment as saving changes.

(d) (a) and (c).

(e) all the above.

17. Treasure Island is an open economy. Its autonomous imports are $0.05 trillion and its marginal propensity to import is 0.1. Treasure Island's import function is

(a) 0.10 + 0.5*y* trillion dollars.

(b) 0.05 + 0.1*y* trillion dollars.

(c) 0.05 + 0.5*y* trillion dollars.

(d) 0.15 + 0.1*y* trillion dollars.

(e) 0.01 + 1.5*y* trillion dollars.

18. The import function can be written as

(a) $im = iy - m_0m$.

(b) $im = im_0 + my$.

(c) $im = im_0 - m$.

(d) $im = a + by$.

(e) $im = im_0 - im(y - t)$.

19. An economy has a given level of government expenditures and a fixed marginal tax rate. As real GDP fluctuates, and its fluctuations are lessened because

(a) investment automatically moves in the opposite direction to real GDP.

(b) taxes automatically move in the opposite direction to real GDP.

(c) the government budget deficit automatically moves in the opposite direction to real GDP.

(d) all of the above.

(e) none of the above.

20. On Coral Island the marginal propensity to consume is 0.75, the marginal tax rate is 0.2, and the marginal propensity to import is 0.1. If Coral Island is a closed economy, the investment multiplier is

(a) 2.5 and if it is an open economy the investment multiplier is 4.

(b) 3.4 and if it is an open economy the investment multiplier is 1.5.

(c) 2.5 and if it is an open economy the investment multiplier is 2.

(d) 0.5 and if it is an open economy the investment multiplier is 0.9.

(e) 4.2 and if it is an open economy the investment multiplier is 2.6.

## Short Answer Questions

1. What are the components of aggregate expenditure and what is the relative importance of each of them?

2. Explain what autonomous consumer expenditure is and what induced consumer expenditure is.

3. Derive the balanced budget multiplier.

4. Distinguish between average propensity to save and marginal propensity to save.

5. (a) Define the long-run consumption function.

(b) Define the short-run consumption function.

6. What is the investment multiplier?

7. (a) Define the marginal tax rate.

(b) Define the marginal tax rate multiplier.

(c) What effect does a higher marginal tax rate have on the investment multiplier?

8. Explain the term marginal propensity to consume.

9. Explain why consumer expenditure plus saving always equals income minus taxes.

10. What is the difference between the government expenditures multiplier in the closed economy and the government expenditures multiplier in the open economy.

## Problem Solving

### Practice Problems

1. Rose Land is a closed economy. Its consumption function is

$c = 100 + 0.75(y - t_0)$ billion dollars.

Investment is $350 billion, government expenditures are $200 billion, and autonomous taxes are $150 billion. There are no induced taxes.

(a) What is real GDP at equilibrium expenditure?

(b) What is consumer expenditure?

(c) If government expenditures decrease by $50 billion, what is the change in real GDP?

(d) What is the government expenditures multiplier?

### Solutions to Practice Problems

1. (a) What is real GDP at equilibrium expenditure?

Equilibrium expenditure occurs when aggregate planned expenditure equals real GDP. Aggregate planned expenditure is equal to

$$e_p = c_p + i_p + g_p.$$

Substitute $100 + 0.75(y - t_0)$ for $c_p$, $350 billion for $i_p$ and $200 billion for $g_p$ to give

$$e_p = 100 + 0.75(y - t) + 350 + 200.$$

Substitute \$150 billion for $t$ to give

$e_p = 100 + 0.75(y - 150) + 350 + 200$
$e_p = 537.5 + 0.75y$.

At equilibrium expenditure, real GDP equals aggregate planned expenditure. That is,
$y = e_p$
$y = 537.5 + 0.75y$
$y$ = \$2,150 billion

1\. (b) What is consumer expenditure?
Consumer expenditure is determined from the consumption function $c = 100 + 0.75(y - t_0)$. Substitute \$2,150 billion for $y$ and \$150 billion for $t_0$ to give
$c = 100 + 0.75(2{,}150 - 150)$
c = \$1,600 billion.

1\. (c) If government expenditures decrease by \$50 billion, what is the change in real GDP?
The change in real GDP equals

$$\Delta y = \frac{1}{1-b}\Delta g.$$

Substitute –50 for the change in government expenditures and 0.75 for $b$ to give

$$\Delta y = \frac{1}{1-0.75} \times (-50)$$

$$\Delta y = -\$200.$$

Real GDP decreases by \$200 billion.
1\. (d) What is the government expenditures multiplier?
The government expenditures multiplier is

$$\frac{1}{1-b}.$$

Substitute 0.75 for $b$. The government expenditures multiplier is 4.

## Problems to Solve

1. In Star Kingdom, the consumption function in billions of dollars is

   $c = 50 + 0.6(y - t_0)$.

   Autonomous taxes are \$8 billion, planned investment is \$7.5 billion, and planned government expenditures are \$10 billion. Star Kingdom is a closed economy and there are no induced taxes.

   (a) What is planned consumer expenditure when real GDP is zero?

   (b) What is planned consumer expenditure?

   (c) What is aggregate planned expenditure?

   (d) What is real GDP at equilibrium expenditure?

**Fact 5.3.** On Green Island, the consumption function is

$c = 100 + 0.75(y - t_0)$ billion dollars.

Planned investment is \$500 billion, planned government expenditures are \$400 billion, and autonomous taxes are \$400 billion. Green Island is a closed economy, and there are no induced taxes.

2. Use Fact 5.3. At equilibrium expenditure, calculate:

   (a) real GDP.

   (b) consumer expenditure.

   (c) the government's budget deficit.

3. Use Fact 5.3. The government of Green Island cuts its purchases of goods and services by \$100 billion. Calculate:

   (a) the change in real income.

   (b) the change in consumer expenditure.

   (c) the change in the government budget deficit.

   (d) the government expenditures multiplier.

4. Use Fact 5.3. The government of Green Island makes a balanced budget cut of \$100 billion.

Calculate:

(a) the change in real income.

(b) the change in consumer expenditure.

(c) the balanced budget multiplier.

5. In Faraway Land, when disposable income is zero, consumer expenditure is $5,000 and when disposable income increases by $1,000, consumer expenditure increases by $600.

(a) What is the marginal propensity to save?

(b) When disposable income is $24,000, what is saving?

(c) When disposable income is $24,000, what is the average propensity to save?

6. In Fantasy Land all taxes are autonomous. Real GDP is $2 billion and the government expenditures multiplier is 4. If the government expenditures multiplier increases to 5, what is real GDP at the new equilibrium expenditure?

7. Carla's disposable income is $40,000 per year and she saves $5,000 a year. Calculate:

(a) Carla's average propensity to save.

(b) Carla's average propensity to consume.

8. If an increase in aggregate income of $200 million increases consumer expenditure by $150 million, what is the marginal propensity to consume?

**Fact 5.4.** Green Country is an open economy. Its consumption function is

$c = 100 + 0.75(y - t)$ million dollars.

Investment is $400 million, government expenditures are $300 million, autonomous taxes are $400 million, exports are $100 million, and its import function is

$im = 50 + 0.3y$ million dollars.

9. Use Fact 5.4. Calculate:

(a) equilibrium real GDP.

(b) equilibrium consumer expenditure.

(c) the government's budget deficit.

The government cuts its expenditures on goods and services to $200 million. Calculate:

(d) the change in real GDP.

(e) the change in consumer expenditure.

(f) the change in the government's budget deficit.

(g) the government expenditures multiplier.

10. Use Fact 5.4. If taxes are not autonomous but induced and given by the tax function

$t = 0.15y$,

what now are the answers to problem 9?

## Answers

### Fill in the Blanks

1. consumer expenditure, disposable income
2. autonomous consumer expenditure, induced consumer expenditure
3. saving, disposable income, dissaving
4. consumer expenditure, disposable income, change, change
5. average, marginal
6. long-run consumption function, short-run consumption function
7. aggregate planned expenditure, aggregate planned expenditure
8. autonomous taxes, induced taxes
9. real GDP
10. autonomous expenditure
11. investment multiplier
12. real GDP, government expenditures
13. real GDP, autonomous taxes
14. balanced budget multiplier
15. real GDP, households
16. marginal tax rate
17. marginal tax rate multiplier
18. tax function
19. imports, real GDP
20. marginal propensity to import

### True or False

1F 5T 9T 13F 17F
2F 6T 10F 14F 18F
3T 7F 11F 15F 19T
4T 8T 12T 16T 20T

### Multiple Choice

1b 5a 9d 13c 17b
2e 6c 10a 14d 18b
3d 7b 11d 15b 19c
4c 8e 12e 16a 20c

### Short Answer Questions

1. The components of aggregate expenditure are consumer expenditure, investment, government expenditures on goods and services, and net exports.

   Consumer expenditure, the largest component, comprises just less than 60 percent of the total. Government expenditures on goods and services accounts for between 20 and 25 percent, investment accounts for between 14 and 21 percent, and net exports fluctuate around zero percent of aggregate expenditure.
2. Autonomous consumer expenditure is consumer expenditure that is independent of the level of income.

   Induced consumer expenditure is consumer expenditure that varies with disposable income.
3. The balanced budget multiplier is the ratio of the change in real GDP to the change in government expenditures that produced it, when that increase in expenditures is financed by an equal change in autonomous taxes.

   We can calculate the balanced budget multiplier by adding the government expenditures multiplier, associated with the increase in government expenditures, and the autonomous tax multiplier, associated with the increase in autonomous taxes.

   The balanced budget multiplier is derived as:

$$\frac{1}{1-b}+\frac{-b}{1-b}$$

$$=\frac{1-b}{1-b}=1.$$

4. The average propensity to save is the ratio of saving to disposable income. The marginal propensity to save is the ratio of a *change* in saving to a *change* in disposable income.
5. (a) The long-run consumption function is the average relationship between consumer expenditure and personal disposable income over several decades.

   (b) The short-run consumption function is the relationship between consumer expenditure and personal disposable income in a particular year.
6. The investment multiplier is the ratio of the change in real GDP to the change in investment that caused it.
7. (a) The marginal tax rate is the fraction of an additional dollar of income paid out in taxes.

(b) The marginal tax rate multiplier is the ratio of the change in real GDP to the change in the marginal tax rate that caused it.

(c) An increase in the marginal tax rate ($t_1$) decreases disposable income and decreases consumer expenditure. The marginal propensity to consume out of real GDP, which is equal to $b(1 - t_1)$, declines.

The investment multiplier is equal to

$$\frac{1}{1-b(1-t_1)}.$$

So an increase in $t_1$ decreases $b(1 - t_1)$, which increases $1 - b(1 - t_1)$ and decreases the multiplier.

8. The marginal propensity to consume is the ratio of a change in consumer expenditure to a change in disposable income.
9. Households receive income in payment for the services of the factors of production that they own. Part of their income is paid out in taxes and what is left is disposable income (income minus taxes). Households allocate their disposable income between consumer expenditure and saving. So income minus taxes always equals consumer expenditure plus saving.
10. The government expenditures multiplier in the closed economy is

$$\frac{1}{1-b(1-t_1)}.$$

The government expenditures multiplier in the open economy is

$$\frac{1}{1-b(1-t_1)+m}.$$

The multiplier in the open economy is smaller. It is smaller because imports are an additional leakage from the circular flow of income and expenditure.

## Problem Solving

1. (a) $45.2 billion
   (b) $c_p = 45.2 + 0.6y$
   (c) $e_p = 62.7 + 0.6y$
   (d) $156.75 billion
2. (a) $2,800 billion
   (b) $1,900 billion
   (c) $0
3. (a) –$400 billion
   (b) –$300 billion
   (c) –$100 billion
   (d) 4
4. (a) –$100 billion
   (b) $0
   (c) 1
5. (a) 0.4
   (b) $4,600
   (c) 0.19
6. $2.5 billion
7. (a) 0.125
   (b) 0.875
8. 0.75
9. (a) $1,000 million
   (b) $550 million
   (c) –$100 million
   (d) –$181.82 million
   (e) –$136.36 million
   (f) –$100 million
   (g) 1.82
10. (a) $1,283.02 million
   (b) $917.92 million
   (c) $107.55 million
   (d) –$150.94 million
   (e) –$96.23 million
   (f) –$77.36 million
   (g) 1.51

**Chapter 6**

# The *IS-LM* Model of Aggregate Demand

## Perspective and Focus

In Chapter 5, you learnt how to determine equilibrium expenditure, for a *given level of investment*. But investment is influenced by many economic factors, and one of the key influences on investment is the cost of capital, as measured by the interest rate. Fluctuations in interest rates, among other things, bring fluctuations in investment. In this chapter, you study the influences on investment. Because investment is influenced by the interest rate and investment influences equilibrium expenditure, there is a relationship between aggregate expenditure and the interest rate. This relationship is called the *IS* curve.

Since equilibrium expenditure depends on the interest rate, we cannot determine the actual level of aggregate expenditure until we know the interest rate. This chapter takes that next step and shows you how interest rates are determined in the markets for financial assets and money. In studying the determination of the interest rate in the market for money, you will discover that the demand for money depends on income. Because the demand for money depends on income the equilibrium interest rate also depends on income. This fact gives rise to another relationship between the interest rate and real GDP, a relationship called the *LM* curve. You will learn about the *LM* curve in this chapter.

Bringing the *IS* and *LM* curves together enables us to determine equilibrium aggregate expenditure and the interest rate simultaneously. The chapter also teaches you how to do this.

## Learning Objectives

*After studying this chapter, you will be able to:*

- Describe the fluctuations in Canadian investment and interest rates during the 1980s and 1990s
- Explain what determines investment
- Explain the distinction between the nominal interest rate and the real interest rate
- Define and derive the investment function
- Describe the shifts in the Canadian investment function between 1970 and 1998
- Define and derive the *IS* curve
- Describe the fluctuations in Canada money supply and interest rates during the 1980s and 1990s
- Explain what determines the demand for money
- Describe the shifts in the Canadian demand for money function between 1970 and 1998
- Define and derive the *LM* curve
- Determine the equilibrium interest rate and real GDP
- Derive the aggregate demand curve

## Increasing Your Productivity

The *IS-LM* analysis lies at the heart of the theory of aggregate demand and it is important that you master this material at this stage of your study. Do not attempt to go beyond this point without being thoroughly on top of this material.

A key thing to remember when studying *IS* and *LM* curves is that they are a different type of curve from any other that you have thus far encountered in your study of economics. You have been accustomed to curves that describe plans of consumers and producers and how those plans are influenced by prices—demand and supply curves. The *IS* and *LM* curves are *not* like demand and supply curves. The *IS* and *LM* curves are curves that trace out an *equilibrium relationship*.

Along the *IS* curve, the market for goods and services is in equilibrium in the sense that aggregate planned expenditure equals real GDP. At points to the left of the *IS* curve, aggregate planned expenditure exceeds real GDP. At points the right of the *IS* curve, aggregate planned expenditure is less than real GDP. Only when the economy is on the *IS* curve is aggregate planned expenditure is equal to real GDP.

Work at understanding the intuition behind the slope of the *IS* curve. The curve slopes downward because: The lower the interest rate, the greater the level of planned investment; and the greater the level of planned investment, the higher the level of equilibrium expenditure and equilibrium real GDP.

Like the *IS* curve, the *LM* curve is also an equilibrium relationship. Along the *LM* curve the quantity of money demanded equals the quantity of money supplied. If the economy was to the left of the *LM* curve, the quantity of money demanded would be less than the quantity of money supplied. If the economy was the right of the *LM* curve, the quantity of money demanded would exceed the quantity of money supplied. Only on the *LM* curve is the money market in equilibrium.

Where the *IS* and *LM* curves intersect, there is *simultaneous equilibrium* in the markets for goods and money.

You have already learnt, in Chapter 5, that when aggregate planned expenditure is less than actual expenditure, actual expenditure falls until actual expenditure and planned expenditure are equal. Thus whenever the economy is to the right of the *IS* curve, forces operate to bring the economy back onto the *IS* curve. These forces are changes in production—real GDP. Inventories are piling up above their planned level, so firms cutback their production and real GDP decreases. Conversely, when the economy is to the left of the *IS* curve forces operate in the opposite direction. Inventories are below their planned level, so firms increase production and real GDP increases.

Similarly, if the economy is off the *LM* curve, forces operate to bring it back onto that curve. These forces are changes in interest rates. If the economy is to the right of the *LM* curve, interest rates rise and if the economy is to the left of the *LM* curve, interest rates fall.

The combined effect of all these forces keep the economy moving toward the intersection point of the *IS* and *LM* curves.

With the tools of the *IS-LM* model, you are able to derive the aggregate demand curve explicitly. To do this, you vary the price level and enquire how the level of aggregate demand changes as the price level changes, *everything else held constant*. A change in the price level changes the real money supply and shifts the *LM* curve. The lower the price level, the larger is the quantity of real money supplied and the farther to the right is the *LM* curve, and at the intersection point with the *IS* curve the higher is equilibrium real GDP and the lower is the interest rate. The points traced by the falling price level and the rising equilibrium real GDP form the aggregate demand curve. As the economy moves along an aggregate demand curve the interest rate changes. Specifically, as the price level decreases and real GDP increases along the aggregate demand curve, the interest rate falls.

Although the algebra of the *IS-LM* model is presented as an appendix in this chapter, it will definitely require careful study. Do not attempt to memorize the formulas for equilibrium income, interest rate, and the aggregate demand curve. But do attempt to understand how they are derived and what they mean. Translate each of them into plain English after you have learnt how to derive it.

Work harder at this chapter than any other you have ever worked on and do all the exercises as many times as is necessary to feel completely on top of this material. A thorough knowledge of this chapter will pay handsome dividends in subsequent parts of the course.

## Self Test

### Fill in the Blanks

1. The ________ interest rate is equal to the ________ interest rate minus the inflation rate.
2. The ________ interest rate is the interest rate actually paid in dollar terms.
3. ________ ________ is the planned rate of purchase of new capital.
4. The rate of return on a piece of capital equipment is equal to the ________ ________ received from using the equipment expressed as a percentage of the equipment's ________.
5. The investment function is the relationship between ________ and the ________ ________, holding all other influences constant.
6. The *IS* curve is the relationship between ________ ________ and the interest rate such that aggregate planned expenditure equals ________ ________.
7. When government expenditures increase, the

*IS* curve shifts _________ by an amount _________ _________ the increase in government expenditures.

8. The quantity of _________ _________ is the amount of money that people plan to hold on a given day in given circumstances.

9. The quantity of money divided by the price level is _______ _______.

10. The _______ the level of real income and the _______ the rate of interest, the larger is the quantity of money demanded.

11. The demand for money function is the relationship between the quantity of real money demanded and the factors on which it depends: ___________________ and the _______ _______.

12. A curve that shows the quantity of real money demanded at a given _______ _______ as the interest rate varies is the demand curve for _______ _______.

13. The ratio of the quantity of real money demanded to real income is called the _______ _______ _______ _______.

14. The relationship between the interest rate and real GDP such that the quantity of _______ demanded equals the quantity supplied is the *LM* curve.

15. When the real money supply decreases, the *LM* curve shifts _________.

## True or False

1. At points below the *LM* curve, the demand for money is less than the supply of money.

2. The relationship between aggregate planned expenditure in a given period of time and the price level is known as the aggregate demand curve.

3. The *IS* curve shifts if government expenditures, taxes, or any other component of autonomous expenditure changes.

4. The quantity of money demanded is the amount of money that people plan to hold on a given day in given circumstances.

5. The demand curve for real money shows the quantity of real money demanded at a given real income assuming that the interest rate remains constant.

6. If a bond pays $10 a year in perpetuity and its current market price is $100, then the interest rate is 10 percent—$10 divided by $100 expressed as a percent.

7. A change in the real money supply does not shift the *LM* curve.

8. A change in the demand for money arising from any source other than a change in real GDP or a change in the interest rate shifts the *LM* curve.

9. Along the *IS* curve, planned leakages equal planned injections.

10. The real interest rate is equal to the nominal interest rate plus the inflation rate.

11. The real interest rate is the interest rate really paid and received after taking inflation into account.

12. If the economy is at a point above the *LM* curve, the real GDP adjusts to restore money market equilibrium.

13. If the economy is off the *IS* curve then investment adjusts to restore equilibrium.

14. As an economy moves up its *LM* curve the demand for money is constant.

15. As an economy moves down its *IS* curve, the interest rate decreases and so investment increases. As investment increases, aggregate expenditure increases and the *IS* curve shifts to the left.

16. An increase in the money supply shifts the *LM* curve to the right, decreasing the interest rate and increasing the quantity of money demanded.

17. As real income increases, the demand for money increases and consumer expenditure increases. The *LM* curve shifts to the left and the *IS* curve shifts to the right. The interest rate increases.

18. An increase in interest rates decreases investment but does not shift the *IS* curve.

19. As an economy moves up its *IS* curve, leakages and injections both decrease by the same amount.

20. As an economy moves up along its *LM* curve the demand for money decreases because the interest rate increases.

## Multiple Choice

1. Investment projects are undertaken when the

(a) opportunity cost of holding money is greater than the real interest rate.

(b) interest rate is greater than the rate of return.

(c) rate of return is greater than the inflation rate.

(d) rate of return is greater than the opportunity cost of holding money.

(e) rate of return is greater than the interest rate.

2. The relationship between investment and the interest rate, holding all other influences on investment constant, is known as the

(a) interest rate function.

(b) capital function.

(c) investment function.

(d) *IS* function.

(e) aggregate expenditure function.

3. Which of the following equations describes the investment function?

(a) $i = i_0 - hr \quad i_0, h > 0$.

(b) $i = i_0 + hr \quad i_0, h > 0$.

(c) $i = hr - i_0 \quad i_0, h > 0$.

(d) $i = i_0 \div hr \quad i_0, h > 0$.

(e) $i = hr \div i_0 \quad i_0, h > 0$.

4. The relationship between real GDP and the interest rate such that aggregate planned expenditure—planned consumer expenditure plus investment plus government expenditures—is equal to real GDP is known as the

(a) investment function.

(b) *IS* curve.

(c) *LM* curve.

(d) short-run aggregate supply curve.

(e) demand for money function.

5. Along an *IS* curve,

(a) aggregate planned expenditure is less than real GDP.

(b) aggregate planned expenditure is greater than real GDP.

(c) aggregate planned expenditure equals real GDP.

(d) aggregate planned expenditure may be greater or less than real GDP.

(e) the rate of return on capital always equals the inflation rate.

6. Because the *IS* curve slopes downward,

(a) an increase in the interest rate brings about an increase in real GDP in order to keep the economy at an expenditure equilibrium.

(b) a constant interest rate brings about an increase in real GDP in order to keep the economy at an expenditure equilibrium.

(c) a decrease in the interest rate brings about a decrease in real GDP in order to keep the economy at an expenditure equilibrium.

(d) a decrease in the interest rate brings about an increase in real GDP in order to keep the economy at an expenditure equilibrium.

(e) an increase in the interest rate causes real GDP to remain constant in order to keep the economy at an expenditure equilibrium.

7. Since $b$ is a fraction, $1 - b$ is also a fraction, and $1/(1 - b)$ is a number

(a) larger than one.

(b) equal to one.

(c) less than one.

(d) which is negative.

(e) equal to zero.

8. An increase in government expenditures shifts the *IS* curve by $1/(1 - b)$

(a) times the change in government expenditures.

(b) divided by the change in government expenditures.

(c) plus the change in government expenditures.

(d) minus the change in government expenditures.

(e) none of the above.

9. The measure of money that includes currency in circulation, demand deposits, personal savings deposits, and nonpersonal notice deposits and deposits at other financial

institutions is

(a) M1.

(b) M2+.

(c) M3.

(d) M2.

(e) L.

10. The quantity of money demanded depends on

(a) price level.

(b) real income.

(c) interest rate.

(d) both (a) and (b).

(e) all the above.

11. The interest rate is the opportunity cost of holding money, therefore

(a) the higher the rate of interest, the smaller is the quantity of money people are planning to hold.

(b) the lower the rate of interest, the smaller is the quantity of money people are planning to hold.

(c) the higher the rate of interest, the greater is the quantity of money people are planning to hold.

(d) the lower the rate of interest, the greater is the quantity of bonds people are planning to hold.

(e) none of the above.

12. The combinations of real GDP and the interest rate at which the quantity of money demanded equals the quantity supplied traces out the

(a) *IS* curve.

(b) *LM* curve.

(c) long-run aggregate supply curve.

(d) short-run aggregate supply curve.

(e) none of the above.

13. If the economy is at a point to the right of the *IS* curve, investment

(a) plus government expenditures exceeds saving plus taxes.

(b) plus government expenditures equals saving plus taxes.

(c) minus government expenditures exceeds saving plus taxes.

(d) plus government expenditures is less than saving plus taxes.

(e) minus government expenditures is less than saving plus taxes.

14. A movement downward along *IS* curve results when

(a) the interest rate increases.

(b) business taxes decrease.

(c) real income increases.

(d) expected future profits increase.

(e) government expenditures increase.

15. In the closed economy *IS-LM* model, equilibrium occurs when

(a) the quantity of money supplied equals injections and the quantity of money demanded equals leakages.

(b) the quantity of money supplied equals the quantity of money demanded and investment equals saving.

(c) the quantity of money supplied equals the quantity of money demanded and investment plus government expenditures equals taxes plus saving.

(d) investment equals saving and government expenditures equal taxes.

(e) none the above.

16. Which of the following statements about the *IS* curve in a closed economy is *false*?

(a) The *IS* curve is steeper than the investment function.

(b) The *IS* curve describes an equilibrium of flows.

(c) Along the *IS* curve, the increase in investment resulting from a decline in the interest rate equals the increase in saving resulting from the increase in income.

(d) The more sensitive investment is to changes in interest rate, the flatter is the *IS* curve.

(e) Both (a) and (c).

17. If the quantity of money demanded exceeds the quantity of money supplied,

(a) a decrease in the interest rate can restore equilibrium in the money market.

(b) the economy is to the right of the *LM* curve.

(c) an increase in the price level can not restore equilibrium in the money market.

(d) an increase in government expenditures will restore equilibrium in the money market.

(e) both (a) and (b).

18. Coral Island is a closed economy and its marginal propensity to consume is 0.75. An increase in taxes of $100

(a) moves the economy up its *LM* curve.

(b) moves the economy down its *IS* curve.

(c) shifts the *IS* curve to the right by 100.

(d) shifts the *IS* curve to the left by 300.

(e) none of the above.

19. In a closed economy, a decrease in government expenditures

(a) shifts the *LM* curve to the right.

(b) shifts the *IS* curve to the left.

(c) shifts the *IS* curve to the right.

(d) leaves the *IS* curve unchanged.

(e) both (a) and (c).

20. An increase in government expenditures matched by an increase in taxes

(a) shifts the *LM* curve to the right.

(b) shifts the *IS* curve to the left.

(c) shifts the *IS* curve to the right.

(d) leaves the *IS* curve unchanged.

(e) both (a) and (c).

## Short Answer Questions

1. How does the nominal interest rate differ from the real interest rate?.

2.What does the quantity of money demanded depend on?

3. What happens to the *IS* curve when

(a) taxes decline?

(b) government expenditures increase?

(c) interest rates increase?

4. (a) What are the two main determinants of investment?

(b)What is meant by investment demand?

5. (a) What is the rate of return on a piece of capital equipment equal to.

(b) What determines whether a particular investment is worthwhile.

6. What happens to the *LM* curve when

(a)both the price level and the money supply increase by the same percentage?

(b)the price level decreases?

7. What are the effects of a change in interest rate or a change of the rate of return on capital on the investment function?

8. Explain the change in aggregate expenditure as an economy moves down its *IS* curve.

9. Explain why an increase in government expenditures shifts the *IS* curve to the right.

10. Use the *IS-LM* model to explain why the aggregate demand curve slopes downward.

## Problem Solving

### Practice Problems

1. Rose Land is a closed economy. Its consumption function is

$c = 100 + 0.75(y - t_0)$ billion dollars.

Its investment function is

$i = 1{,}000 - 25r$ billion dollars.

Government expenditures are $200 billion and autonomous taxes are $150 billion. There are no induced taxes.

(a) What is the equation to Rose Land's *IS* curve?

(b) Calculate the slope of the *IS* curve.

(c) Rose Land's demand for money is

$M^d = (100 + 0.2y - 5r)P$.

If Rose Land's supply of money is 1,000 and its price level is 1, what is the equation to Rose Land's *LM* curve?

(d) What is the slope of Rose Land's *LM* curve?

(e) Calculate Rose Land's equilibrium interest rate and equilibrium real GDP.

(f) Find the equation to Rose Land's aggregate demand curve.

## Solutions to Practice Problems

1. (a) What is the equation to Rose Land's *IS* curve?

Along the *IS* curve, aggregate planned expenditure equals real GDP. The equation to the *IS* curve is calculated as follows:

$y = c + i + g$

$y = 100 + 0.75(y - 150) + 1{,}000 - 25r + 200$

$y = 1{,}187.5 + 0.75y - 25r$

$y = 4{,}750 - 100r.$

(b) Calculate the slope of the *IS* curve.

The *IS* curve is

$$y = 4{,}750 - 100r. \quad (6.1)$$

The slope of the *IS* curve is $\Delta r/\Delta y$ as the economy moves along its *IS* curve. From Equation (6.1), as $r$ increases to $r + \Delta r$, y changes to $y + \Delta y$ such that

$$y + \Delta y = 4{,}750 - 100(r + \Delta r). \quad (6.2)$$

Subtracting Equation (6.1) from Equation (6.2) gives

$\Delta y = -100\Delta r.$

The slope of the *IS* curve is

$\Delta r/\Delta y = -1/100 = -0.01.$

(c) Rose Land's demand for money is

$M^d = (100 + 0.2y - 5r)P.$

If Rose Land's supply of money is 1,000 and its price level is 1, what is the equation to Rose Land's *LM* curve?

Along the *LM* curve, the quantity of money demanded equals the quantity supplied. That is,

$$1{,}000 = 100 + 0.2y - 5r \quad (6.3)$$

Rearranging Equation (6.3) gives the equation to Rose Land's *LM* curve:

$$y = 4{,}500 + 25r. \quad (6.4)$$

(d) What is the slope of Rose Land's *LM* curve?

The *LM* curve is

$$y = 4{,}500 + 25r. \quad (6.4)$$

The slope of the *LM* curve is $\Delta r/\Delta y$ as the economy moves along its *LM* curve. From Equation (6.4), as $r$ increases to $r + \Delta r$, y changes to $y + \Delta y$ such that

$$y + \Delta y = 4{,}500 + 25(r + \Delta r). \quad (6.5)$$

Subtracting Equation (6.4) from Equation (6.5) gives

$\Delta y = 25\Delta r.$

The slope of the *LM* curve is

$\Delta r/\Delta y = 1/25 = 0.04.$

(e) Calculate Rose Land's equilibrium interest rate and equilibrium real GDP.

Rose Land's *IS* and *LM* curves are:

$$y = 4{,}750 - 100r \quad (6.1)$$

$$y = 4{,}500 + 25r \quad (6.4)$$

To solve these equation for $r$, subtract Equation (6.4) from Equation (6.1), which gives

$0 = 250 - 125r$

$r = 2.$

To find the value of $y$, substitute 2 for $r$ in either Equation (6.1) or Equation (6.4), which gives

$y = 4{,}550.$

(f) Find the equation to Rose Land's aggregate demand curve.

Rose Land's *IS* and *LM* curves are

$$y = 4{,}750 - 100r \quad (6.1)$$

$$y = 4{,}500 + 25r \quad (6.4)$$

The aggregate demand curve traces out the quantity of real GDP demanded as the price level varies. The quantity of real GDP demanded is equilibrium real GDP as determined by the intersection of the *IS* curve and the *LM* curve.

To find how real GDP is related to the price level, we need to go back to the *LM* curve and find the equation to it that includes the price level. Above we substituted the particular value (1) for the price level. Now we must go back and replace the price level with *P*.

The equation to the *LM* curve is

$$1{,}000 = (100 + 0.2y - 5r)P. \tag{6.6}$$

Re-arranging Equation (6.6) gives

$$y = 5{,}000/\mathrm{P} - 500 + 25r. \tag{6.7}$$

You can see that as the price level changes the *LM* curve shifts and the intersection of the *LM* and *IS* curves traces out the level of real GDP.

To find the equation to the *AD* curve, use the *IS* and *LM* curves, eliminate the interest rate *r* and get the relationship between the price level and real GDP. That is, from the *IS* curve, Equation (6.1), the interest rate is equal to

$$r = 47.5 - 0.01y.$$

Substitute for *r* in the *LM* curve, Equation (6.7), which gives

$$y = 4{,}000/P + 550. \tag{6.8}$$

Equation (6.8) is Rose Land's aggregate demand curve.

## Problems to Solve

1. In Star Kingdom, the consumption function in billions of dollars is

$$c = 50 + 0.6(y - t_0).$$

Autonomous taxes are $8 billion and planned government expenditures are $10 billion. Star Kingdom is a closed economy and there are no induced taxes. It investment function is

$$i = 750 - 15r.$$

(a) What is the equation to Star Kingdom's *IS* curve?

(b) What is the slope of the *IS* curve?

(c) What is aggregate expenditure when the interest rate is 4 percent a year?

(d) What is real GDP when the interest rate is 2 percent a year?

2. On Green Island, the consumption function in billions of dollars is

$$c = 100 + 0.75(y - t_0).$$

The investment function in billions of dollars is

$$i = 1{,}000 - 75r.$$

Government expenditures are $400 billion and autonomous taxes are $400 billion. Green Island is a closed economy, and there are no induced taxes.

(a) What is the equation to Green Island's *IS* curve?

(b) The government of Green Island cuts its expenditures on goods and services by $100 billion. Calculate the shift of the *IS* curve.

(c) The government of Green Island makes a balanced budget cut of $100 billion. Calculate the shift of the *IS* curve.

3. Shark Island is a closed economy and its *IS* and *LM* curves are as follows:

*IS* curve: $y = 600 - 30r$

*LM* curve: $y = 520 + 48r$.

(a) Calculate Shark Island's equilibrium interest rate.

(b) Calculate Shark Island's equilibrium real GDP.

(c) Calculate the slope of Shark Island's *IS* curve.

(d) Calculate the slope of Shark Island's *LM* curve.

4. You are given the following data about the economy of Fish Point:

*IS* curve: $y = 1{,}400 - 25r$

Demand for money: $M^d/P = 200 + 0.4y - 10r$

Supply of money: $M = 1{,}000$.

The price level at Fish Point is 2.

(a) What is the equilibrium quantity of real money demanded?

(b) Calculate the equilibrium real GDP and the interest rate.

(c) Calculate the slope of the *IS* curve.

(d) Calculate the equation to the aggregate demand curve.

5. You have the following data about Coral Island, a closed economy:

$c = 100 + 0.75(y - t_0)$

$i = 50 - 25r$

$g = 200$

$t_0 = 200$.

(a) What is the equation to Coral Island's *IS* curve?

(b) Calculate the slope of Coral Island's *IS* curve.

(c) Calculate the shift of the *IS* curve if government expenditures increase by 100.

(d) Calculate the shift of the *IS* curve if taxes increase by 100.

(e) Calculate the shift of the *IS* curve if government expenditures and taxes each increase by 100.

6. Silly Isle's *LM* curve is

$y = 3{,}500 + 25r$.

(a) Calculate the slope of Silly Isle's *LM* curve.

(b) Silly Isle's real money supply increases by 100. Calculate the change in the slope of its *LM* curve.

(c) Silly Isle's interest rate increases by 1 percentage point. Calculate the change in the quantity of money demanded.

7. Heron Island is a closed economy and its *IS* and *LM* curves are as follows:

*IS* curve: $y = 1{,}300 - 30r$

*LM* curve: $y = 520 + 48r$.

(a) Calculate Heron Island's equilibrium interest rate.

(b) Calculate Heron Island's equilibrium real GDP.

8. Shark Island's investment function is given by:

$i = 750 - 250r$.

Calculate the slope of Shark Island's investment function.

9. On Heron Island, the marginal propensity to consume is 0.75. Autonomous consumption is 100. Investment is less than or equal to 500 and decreases by 25 if the interest rate increases 1 percentage point. Government expenditures are 300, the government's budget is balanced, and all taxes are autonomous.

(a) What is the equation to Heron Island's *IS* curve?

(b) Calculate the slope of Heron Island's *IS* curve.

(c) Compare the slopes of Heron Island's *IS* curve and investment function.

10. You are given the following data about the economy of Sail Island:

*IS* curve: $y = 2{,}400 - 50r$

Demand for money: $M^d/P = 200 + 0.5y - 10r$

Supply of money: $M = 2{,}000$.

The price level at Sail Island is 2.

(a) What is the equilibrium quantity of real money demanded?

(b) Calculate the equilibrium real GDP and the interest rate.

(c) Calculate the slope of the *IS* curve.

(d) Calculate the equation to the aggregate demand curve.

## Answers

### Fill in the Blanks

1. real, nominal
2. nominal
3. Investment demand
4. net income, price
5. investment, interest rate
6. real GDP, real GDP
7. rightward, greater than
8. money demanded
9. real money
10. higher, lower
11. real income, interest rate
12. real income, real money
13. propensity to hold money
14. money
15. leftward

### True or False

1F 5F 9T 13T 17F

2T 6T 10F 14T 18T

3T 7F 11T 15F 19T

4T 8T 12F 16T 20F

### Multiple Choice

1e 5c 9b 13d 17b

2c 6d 10e 14c 18d

3a 7a 11a 15c 19b

4b 8a 12b 16a 20c

### Short Answer Questions

1. The nominal interest rate is also called the market interest rate and includes an inflation component. This is the interest rate actually paid in dollar terms. The real interest rate is the nominal interest rate minus the inflation rate. This is the interest rate that is really paid and received after taking inflation into account.
2. The quantity of money demanded depends on the price level, real income, and the interest rate.
3. (a)The *IS* curve shifts to the right.

   (b)The *IS* curve shifts to the right.

   (c)The *IS* curve does not shift.
4. (a) The two main determinants of investment are the interest rate and the rate of return on capital.

   (b) Investment demand is the planned rate of purchase of new capital—the planned rate of investment.
5. (a) The rate of return on a piece of capital equipment is equal to the net income received from using the capital equipment expressed as a percentage of the equipment's price.

   (b) To determine whether a particular investment is worthwhile, we compare its rate of return with the interest rate. Investment projects are undertaken if the rate of return is greater than or equal to the interest rate.
6. (a) The *LM* curve does not change.

   (b) The *LM* curve shifts to the right.
7. Changes in the interest rate result in a movement along the investment function. Anything that changes the rate of return on capital shifts the investment function.
8. Along the *IS* curve aggregate expenditure equals real GDP. As an economy moves down its *IS* curve real GDP increases, so aggregate expenditure also increases.
9. Along the *IS* curve leakages equal injections. An increase in government expenditures increases injections, so leakages must increase. In order for saving, a leakage, to increase, real GDP must increase. Real GDP increases at a given interest rate, so the *IS* curve shifts rightward.
10. A decrease in the price level shifts the *LM* curve to the right. The new intersection point of the *IS* and *LM* curves occurs at a greater real GDP. That is, a decrease in the price level increases the level of aggregate expenditure and increases the level of aggregate demand. The aggregate demand curve slopes downward.

### Problem Solving

1. (a) $y = 2{,}013 - 37.5r$

   (b) –0.0267

   (c) \$1,863 billion

   (d) \$1,938 billion
2. (a) $y = 4{,}800 - 300r$

(b) 400 to the left
(c) 100 to the left
3. (a) 1.03
(b) 569
(c) –0.033
(d) 0.021
4. (a) 500
(b) $r = 13$, $y = 1{,}075$
(c) –0.04
(d) $y = 1{,}250/P + 450$
5. (a) $y = 800 - 100r$
(b) –0.01
(c) 400 to the right
(d) 300 to the left
(e) 100 to the right
6. (a) 0.04
(b) no change
(c) no change
7. (a) 10
(b) 1,000
8. –0.004
9. (a) $y = 2{,}700 - 100r$
(b) –0.01
(c) The slope of the investment function is –0.04. The *IS* curve is flatter than the investment function.
10. (a) 1,000
(b) $r = 11.43$, $y = 1{,}828$
(c) –0.02
(d) $y = 2{,}857.14/P + 400$

**Chapter 7**

# Monetary and Fiscal Policy Influences on Aggregate Demand

## Perspective and Focus

This chapter puts the *IS-LM* model of aggregate demand to work and studies the effects of changes in monetary policy and fiscal policy on the equilibrium interest rate and level of real GDP at a given price level. In other words it studies how the aggregate demand curves shifts when the money supply changes (monetary policy) and when government expenditures or taxes (fiscal policy) change.

If you find you are having difficulties with this chapter, your problems could arise from the fact that you did not take our advice seriously enough concerning the need to study the previous chapter extremely thoroughly. You may find it necessary, from time to time, to go back to Chapter 6 and review and refresh your memory and understanding of certain key things.

Although this chapter deals with monetary and fiscal policy, do not be mislead into regarding the results you will be finding as telling you the full and final effects of policy. They tell you how policy shifts the aggregate demand curve. To work out the ultimate effects of policy we have to see how the shifted aggregate demand curve interacts the aggregate supply curve. That is, we have to place the effects of policy on the aggregate demand curve in the context of the *AD-AS* analysis of Chapter 4.

## Learning Objectives

*After studying this chapter, you will be able to:*

- Describe the fluctuations in money supply growth, government expenditures, and taxes in Canada in recent years
- Explain how a change in the money supply influences interest rates, real GDP, and the price level
- Describe how monetary policy has been used to slow down the Canadian economy
- Explain how changes in government expenditures influence interest rates, real GDP, and the price level
- Describe the shifts in the Canadian investment function between 1970 and 1998
- Explain how changes in taxes influence interest rates, real GDP, and the price level

## Increasing Your Productivity

One of the neatest things about the *IS-LM* model is the way in which it helps us to understand the impacts of monetary and fiscal policy. The key thing to notice is that fiscal policy influences the *IS* curve but not the *LM* curve while monetary policy influences the *LM* curve but not the *IS* curve. These facts enable us to analyze the effects of monetary and fiscal policy and to obtain clear predictions about the outcome of various policy actions.

Work hard first of all to understand why a change in the money supply shifts the *LM* curve. An increase in the money supply shifts the *LM* curve to the right and a decrease shifts the *LM* curve to the left. Work at understanding why this occurs. Similarly work hard to understand why a decrease in taxes shifts the *IS* curve to the right, while an increase in government expenditures on goods and services shifts the *IS* curve to the right. Similarly, an increase in taxes shifts the *IS* curve to the left and a decrease in government expenditures shifts the *IS* curve to the left.

Once you have understood these shifts in the *IS* and *LM* curves you are ready to analysis how monetary and fiscal policy influences interests rates and real GDP at a given price level—how they shift the aggregate demand curve.

In studying these influences of monetary and fiscal policy, *always draw the diagram*. Don't try to work things out in your head. It is not that they are impossible to work out in your head, but it is just that much easier to work them out with a diagram. A diagram lets you check with your eyes as well as your reasoning that you are getting the right answers.

Once you have learnt how changes in monetary and fiscal policy shift the aggregate demand curve, you are ready to integrate the aggregate demand analysis back into the *AD-AS* analysis. There is nothing fundamentally new here, just a richer understanding of the forces that make the aggregate demand curve shift.

This chapter contains an appendix on the algebra of fiscal and monetary policy multipliers. It is worth spending some time trying to understand the material in this appendix. *It is not* worth spending one second trying to *memorize* the formulas. The way to study this material is to begin with the appendix of Chapter 6 and then build on that set of results by changing the equilibrium.

To change an equilibrium we change some exogenous variables—in this case the money supply, government expenditures on goods and services, or taxes. We then work out the new equilibrium and find out the multiplier effects on the endogenous variables—*in this case* real GDP and the interest rate. Work through these formulas and check that you can understand how they are derived. Once you understand their derivation, work to understand the intuition behind the multipliers and connect them back to the shifts in the *IS* and *LM* curves. Then go onto convince yourself that you understand the story about what is happening in a real economy when these forces are at work. Also check that you can interpret these equations in terms of the forces at work. Once you have done all this you will be able to derive these equations whenever you need them and understand and interpret the results that you obtain from them.

## Self Test

### Fill in the Blanks

1. The _______ _______ _______ is a monetary arrangement in which Canada kept its monetary policy in close harmony with the policies of other countries in a system of fixed exchange rates.
2. In the years following World War II, the world operated a gold exchange standard during the _______.
3. The world monetary order that had prevailed since World War II collapsed in _______.
4. A policy of announcing a target growth rate for the money supply and then attempting to deliver a growth rate inside the announced target range is _______ _______.
5. During the late 1970s the Bank of Canada targeted the growth rate of _______.
6. Between 1975 and 1997 tax revenue in Canada was _______ _______ government spending and the government had a budget _______.
7. When the money supply increases, the _______ curve shifts _______ and the _______ curve shifts _______.
8. The _______ the *IS* curve, the larger is the effect of a change in the money supply on equilibrium real GDP.
9. During 1980-1982 and 1989-1994 the real money supply growth rate in Canada decreased and real GDP growth _______.
10. When the real interest rate rises, investment _______.
11. When the government increases its expenditures on goods and services, the *IS* curve shifts _______ and the *LM* curve shifts _______.
12. The _______ the *LM* curve, the larger is the effect of fiscal policy on real GDP.
13. _______ _______ is the effect of an increase in government expenditures on investment.
14. _______ _______ _______ occurs when government expenditures increase in an economy at full employment.
15. When an economy is below its full-employment level, the *LM* curve is upward sloping, and the *IS* curve is downward sloping, an increase in government expenditures results in _______ _______ _______.

### True or False

1. When the Bank of Canada targeted the money supply in the 1970s, it chose as its target M2+.
2. The most obvious and dramatic feature of Canadian fiscal policy is the large deficit that emerged between government spending and the tax revenue in 1975 and persisted until 1997.
3. The flatter the *IS* curve, the less the rightward shift in the aggregate demand curve for any given increase in the money supply.

4. The steeper the *LM* curve, the larger is the effect of a change in the money supply on aggregate demand.
5. A flatter *LM* curve makes monetary policy less potent because the demand for money is more sensitive to interest rates.
6. Two periods of unusually slow real M2+ growth in Canada are 1980-1982 and 1989-1994.
7. An increase in government expenditures on goods and services will shift the *IS* curve to the left.
8. The combination of the rightward shift of the *IS* curve and the leftward shift of the *LM* curve increases the interest rate.
9. Crowding out is the name for the effect of an increase in investment on government expenditures.
10. In the *IS-LM* model, an increase in autonomous taxes changes real GDP in a similar manner as an increase in government expenditures does, but the magnitude of the change in real GDP resulting from a 1 unit increase in autonomous taxes is greater.
11. Fiscal policy is any policy that changes aggregate demand.
12. Fiscal policy is any government policy that shifts the *IS* curve.
13. Fiscal policy is not very effective if the *IS* curve is fairly steep.
14. Fiscal policy is more effective, the more sensitive investment is to the interest rate.
15. Complete crowding out occurs when investment is not very sensitive to a change in the interest rate.
16. Expansionary monetary policy lowers interest rates, increases investment, and increases aggregate demand.
17. An increase in government expenditures increases aggregate demand for goods and services and shifts the *IS* curve to the right. The interest rate increases. As a result, investment decreases and aggregate demand for goods and services decreases. The *IS* curve shifts to the left.
18. A decrease in the money supply shifts the *LM* curve to the left. Interest rates increase. As a result, investment decreases, and aggregate expenditure decreases.
19. An increase in the money supply increases aggregate demand only because it results in an increase in government expenditures.
20. If investment is insensitive to changes in the interest rates, then an increase in government expenditures does not result in crowding out.

## Multiple Choice

1. During the 1960s, Canada kept its monetary policy in close harmony with policies of other countries in a system of fixed exchange rates by using
(a) special drawing rights.
(b) a silver exchange standard.
(c) a gold exchange standard.
(d) a fiat exchange standard.
(e) none of the above.

2. In the second half of the 1970s the Bank of Canada committed itself to
(a) fiscal targeting.
(b) gold targeting.
(c) silver targeting.
(d) fiat targeting.
(e) monetary targeting.

3. In the late 1970s, the Bank of Canada targeted
(a) M1+.
(b) M1.
(c) M2+.
(d) (b) and (c).
(e) all of the above.

4. The flatter the *IS* curve, then the larger is the
(a) leftward shift in the aggregate demand curve for any increase in the money supply.
(b) rightward shift in the aggregate demand curve for any decrease in the money supply.
(c) rightward shift in the aggregate demand curve for any given increase in the money supply.
(d) leftward shift in the aggregate demand curve

for an absence of change in the money supply.

(e) movement up along the aggregate demand curve for any given increase in the money supply.

5. Monetary policy is less potent, the

(a) steeper *IS* curve.

(b) steeper *LM* curve.

(c) flatter *IS* curve.

(d) flatter *LM* curve.

(e) both (a) and (d).

6. Which of the following are *incorrect* with respect to an increase in government expenditures on goods and services?

(a) The *IS* curve shifts to the left.

(b) The aggregate demand curve shifts to the right.

(c) Equilibrium real GDP increases.

(d) The equilibrium price level increases.

(e) The higher price level shifts the *LM* curve to the left.

7. The slope of the *IS* curve depends on the sensitivity of

(a) the money demand to the interest rate.

(b) saving to the interest rate.

(c) government expenditures on goods and services to the interest rate.

(d) investment to the interest rate.

(e) the money supply to the interest rate.

8. The effect of an increase in government expenditures on investment is known as

(a) expulsion.

(b) arbitrage.

(c) crowding out.

(d) overshadowing.

(e) restructuring.

9. A complete crowding out occurs at less than full employment provided that the *LM* curve

(a) and *IS* curve are vertical.

(b) and *IS* curve are horizontal.

(c) is horizontal or the *IS* curve is vertical.

(d) is vertical or the *IS* curve is horizontal.

(e) and *IS* curve are negatively sloped.

10. The economy is approaching full employment. If government expenditures have increased and the investment function has shifted to the right, there will be

(a) downward pressure on interest rates, which will, to some degree, choke off additional investment.

(b) upward pressure on interest rates, which will not have any effect on additional investment.

(c) downward pressure on interest rates, which will not have any effect on additional investment.

(d) upward pressure on interest rates, which will, to some degree, choke off additional investment.

(e) no pressure on interest rates, but additional investment will be chocked off to some degree.

11. On Green Island, the quantity of real money demanded is independent of interest rates. As a result

(a) monetary policy will be effective in changing output.

(b) monetary policy will not be very effective in changing output.

(c) both fiscal and monetary policy will be very effective in changing output.

(d) only fiscal policy will be effective in changing output.

(e) none of the above.

12. The government of Lizard Island is considering the following expansionary policies: Policy 1 removes an investment tax and Policy 2 increases the money supply. Which of the following statements best describes the outcome of these policies?

(a) Each policy increases aggregate demand, interest rates, and investment.

(b) Each policy increases aggregate demand and investment but interest rates increase under Policy 1 and decrease under Policy 2.

(c) Each policy increases aggregate demand and investment but decreases interest rates.

(d) Each policy increases aggregate demand but interest rates increase and investment decreases under Policy 1 and interest rates decrease and investment increases under Policy 2.

(e) None of the above.

**Fact 7.1** You are given the following data about Sandy Island, a closed economy:

$c = 100 + 0.8(y - t)$

$i = 500 - 50r$

$g = 200$

$t = 250$

$M^d/P = 0.5y + 200 - 10r$

$M = 1{,}000$

$P = 1$

13. Use Fact 7.1. The equation to the *IS* curve is

(a) $y = 1{,}600 - 60r$.

(b) $y = 3{,}000 - 250r$.

(c) $y = 1{,}600 + 100r$.

(d) $y = 1{,}800 - 100r$.

(e) $y = 4{,}250 - 250r$.

14. Use Fact 7.1. The equation to the *LM* curve is

(a) $y = 1{,}600 + 20r$.

(b) $y = 1{,}425 + 10r$.

(c) $y = 2{,}800 - 100r$.

(d) $y = 600 + 30r$.

(e) $y = 1{,}600 - 60r$.

15. Use Fact 7.1. Sandy Island's equilibrium real GDP and interest rate are

(a) 877 and 9.2 percent respectively.

(b) 1,459 and 3.41 percent respectively.

(c) 1,800and 10 percent respectively.

(d) 1,704and 5.19 percent respectively.

(e) 1,450and 2.5 percent respectively.

16. Use Fact 7.1. The government of Sandy Island increases its expenditures on goods and services by 100. As a result,

(a) the *IS* curve shifts right by 100 and the *LM* curve remains constant.

(b) the *IS* curve shifts right by 500 and the *LM* curve remains constant.

(c) the *IS* curve shifts right by 100 and the *LM* curve shifts right by 100.

(d) the *IS* curve shifts right by 500 and the *LM* curve shifts right by 400.

(e) the *IS* curve shifts right by 800 and the *LM* curve shifts right by 100.

17. Use Fact 7.1. The government of Sandy Island increases its expenditures on goods and services by 100. As a result, investment

(a) increases by 100.

(b) increases by more than 100.

(c) decreases by 100.

(d) decreases by less than 100.

(e) none of the above.

18.Use Fact 7.1. If the government of Sandy Island increases its expenditures on goods and services

(a) by 100, complete crowding out results.

(b )by more than 100, complete crowding out results.

(c) by 100, partial crowding out results.

(d) no crowding out occurs.

(e) none of the above.

19. Use Fact 7.1. An increase in the money supply of 100,

(a) increases the equilibrium interest rate to 6 percent.

(b) increases the equilibrium interest rate to more than 6 percent.

(c) increases real GDP by less than 200.

(d) both (a) and (c)

(e) none of the above.

20.Use Fact 7.1. An increase in the money supply of 100,

(a) increases the investment by 100.

(b) decreases the investment by 100.

(c) increases investment by less than 100.

(d) decreases investment by less than 100.

(e) none of the above.

## Short Answer Questions

1. How does the slope of the *IS* curve and the slope of the *LM* curve affect the potency of a change in the money supply?.

2. How does the slope of the *IS* curve and *LM* curve affect equilibrium real GDP when there is a change in government expenditures?

3. Why is monetary policy less potent with a flatter *LM* curve?

4. What monetary arrangement did Canada use during the 1960s?

5. What is crowding out? Explain why crowding out arises.

6. Explain the effect of an increase in taxes on investment.

7. An economy is at a below full-employment equilibrium. Explain the effects of an increase in government expenditures on real GDP, the price level, and the interest rate.

8. An economy is at a below full-employment equilibrium. Explain the effects of an increase in the money supply on real GDP, the price level, and the interest rate.

9. Describe the relationship between tax revenue and government spending in Canada between 1975 and 1997.

10. Can complete crowding out occur when real GDP is below its full-employment level?

## Problem Solving

### Practice Problems

You are given the following information about Stony Island:

$c = 100 + 0.75(y - t)$

$i = 900 - 20r$

$g = 100$

$t = 100$

$M^d/P = 0.2y + 150 - 75r$

$M = 500$

$P = 1$

(a) Calculate equilibrium real GDP and the interest rate.

**(b) Calculate the equilibrium level of investment.**

**(c) If the money supply increases by 100, how far does the *LM* curve shift?**

**(d) Calculate the change in aggregate demand resulting from an increase in the money supply of 100.**

**(e) Calculate the change in investment that results from an increase in the money supply of 100.**

**(f) Calculate the shift of the *IS* curve that results from an increase in government expenditures of 100.**

**(g) Calculate the change in investment resulting from an increase in government expenditures of 100.**

**(h) Has the increase in government expenditures crowded out investment?**

### Solutions to Practice Problems

(a) Calculate equilibrium real GDP and the interest rate.

Equilibrium real GDP and the interest rate are determined at the intersection of the *IS* and *LM* curves. By using the method set out in Chapter 6, the *IS* and *LM* curves are as follows:

*IS* curve: $y = 4{,}100 - 80r$

*LM* curve: $y = 1{,}750 + 375r$

Equilibrium real GDP equals 3,686.8 and the equilibrium interest rate equals 5.165 percent a year.

(b) Calculate the equilibrium level of investment.

The investment function tells us the level of investment:

$i = 900 - (20 \times 5.165)$

$i = 796.7.$

(c) If the money supply increases by 100, how far does the *LM* curve shift?

The increase in the money supply shifts the

*LM* curve to the right.

The equation to the new *LM* curve is derived by equating the quantities of real money demanded and supplied:

$600 = 0.2y + 150 - 75r$

which is

$y = 2250 + 375r$.

The *LM* curve shifts to the right by 2250 – 1750, which is 500.

(d) Calculate the change in aggregate demand resulting from an increase in the money supply of 100.

When the money supply increases by 100, the *LM* curve shifts to the right and becomes

$y = 2250 + 375r$.

The increase in aggregate demand is equal to the increase in equilibrium real GDP. Solve the equations to the *IS* and *LM* curves for real GDP—the new level of aggregate demand.

Equilibrium real GDP is equal to 3,774.7. Therefore the increase in aggregate demand is equal to 87.9.

(e) Calculate the change in investment that results from an increase in the money supply of 100.

When the money supply increases by 100, the *LM* curve shifts to the right and real GDP increases to 3,774.7. By substituting for $y$ in the *IS* curve, you can calculate the new equilibrium interest rate. It is 4.066.

With an interest rate of 4.066, investment, from the investment function, increases to $i = 900 - (20 \times 4.066)$, which is 818.7.

The increase in the money supply decreases the interest rate and increases investment by 818.7 – 796.7, which is 22.

(f) Calculate the shift of the *IS* curve that results from an increase in government expenditures of 100.

The increase in government expenditures shifts the *IS* curve to the right by $1/(1 - b)$ times the increase in government expenditures. That is, the *IS* curve shifts by $1/(1 - 0.75) \times 100$, which is 400.

(g) Calculate the change in investment resulting from an increase in government expenditures of 100.

The new *IS* curve is

$y = 4500 - 80r$.

The new interest rate, at the intersection of the new *IS* curve and the *LM* curve is found by solving the equations to the new *IS* curve and the *LM* curve. It is 6.044.

Investment, from the investment demand function, is

$i = 900 - (20 \times 6.044)$

$= 779.1$.

The increase in government expenditures increases the interest rate and decreases investment by

796.7 – 779.1, which is 17.6.

(h) Has the increase in government expenditures crowded out investment?

The increase in government expenditures increases the interest rate from 5.165 to 6.044. As a result, investment decreases from 796.7 to 779.1, a decrease of 17.6. The decrease in investment is less than the increase in government expenditures so there is partial crowding out.

## Problems to Solve

1. On Lizard Island:

$c = 100 + 0.7(y - t)$

$i = 900 - 25r$

$g = 100$

$t = 100$

$M^d/P = 0.2y + 100 - 50r$

$M = 500$

$P = 1$.

Calculate the equilibrium value of

(a) real GDP.

(b) the interest rate.

2. You are given the following data about Green Island:

$c = 200 + 0.6(y - t)$

$i = 500 - 100r$

$g = 300$

$t = 400$

$M^d/P = 0.2y + 500 - 50r$

$M = 700$

$P = 1.$

(a) Calculate the equilibrium real GDP.

(b) Calculate the equilibrium value of consumption.

(c) Calculate the equilibrium value of investment.

(d) Calculate the equilibrium interest rate.

(e) Calculate the effect on equilibrium real GDP of a unit increase in the money supply.

(f) Calculate the effect on equilibrium real GDP of a unit increase in taxes.

(g) Calculate the effect on equilibrium real GDP of a unit increase in government expenditures.

3. On Easter Island:

$c = 150 + 0.75(y - t)$

$i = 900 - 40r$

$g = 100$

$t = 100$

$M^d/P = 0.2y + 100 - 5r$

$M = 500.$

$P = 1.$

(a) Calculate Easter Island's equilibrium real GDP.

(b) Calculate Easter Island's equilibrium real interest rate.

(c) Calculate Easter Island's equilibrium consumption.

(d) Calculate Easter Island's equilibrium investment.

4. In Problem 3, the government of Easter increases taxes by 50.

(a) Calculate the change in Easter Island's real GDP.

(b) Calculate the change in Easter Island's real interest rate.

In Problem 3, the government of Easter increases government expenditures by 50.

(c) Calculate the change in Easter Island's real GDP.

(d) Calculate the change in Easter Island's real interest rate.

In Problem 3, the government of Easter increases government expenditures by 50 and also increases taxes by 50.

(e) Calculate the change in Easter Island's real GDP.

(f) Calculate the change in Easter Island's real interest rate.

5. You are given the following data about the closed economy of Windy Isle:

*IS* curve: $y = 2000 - 25r$

Demand for money: $M^d/P = 200 + 0.4y - 10r$

Supply of money: $M = 800$.

Price level is 2 and the marginal propensity to consume is 0.85.

The government of Windy Isle increases its expenditures by 150.

(a) Calculate the change in Windy Isle's real GDP.

(b) Calculate Windy Isle's new interest rate.

(c) Calculate the change in Windy Isle's investment.

(d) Is there crowding out? Explain.

## Answers

### Fill in the Blanks

1. gold exchange standard
2. 1960s
3. 1971
4. monetary targeting
5. M1
6. less than, deficit
7. *LM*, rightward, *AD*, rightward
8. flatter
9. decreased
10. decreases
11. rightward, leftward
12. flatter
13. Crowding out
14. Complete crowding out
15. Partial crowding out

### True or False

1F 5T 9F 13F 17F
2T 6T 10F 14F 18T
3F 7F 11F 15F 19F
4T 8T 12T 16T 20T

### Multiple Choice

1c 5e 9b 13b 17d
2e 6a 10d 14a 18c
3b 7d 11a 15d 19c
4c 8c 12b 16b 20c

### Short Answer Questions

1. The flatter the *IS* curve, the larger is the effect of a change in the money supply on equilibrium real GDP.

   The steeper the *LM* curve, the larger is the effect of a change in the money supply on equilibrium real GDP.

2. The steeper the *IS* curve, the larger is the effect of a change in government expenditures on real GDP.

   The flatter the *LM* curve, the larger is the effect of a change in government expenditures on real GDP.

3. The flatter the *LM* curve, the more sensitive is the demand for money to interest rates. When the money supply increases, interest rates fall, but how far they fall depends on the demand for money.

   If the demand for money is highly responsive to changes in the interest rate, then a large increase in the money supply brings only a small fall in interest rates.

   The smaller the fall in the interest rate, the smaller is the increase in investment and the smaller the increase in aggregate demand.

4. During the 1960s, the world operated on a gold exchange standard, a monetary arrangement in which Canada kept its monetary policy in close harmony with the policies of other countries in a system of fixed exchange rates.

   The value of the U.S. dollar was fixed in terms of gold. Thirty-five U.S. dollars bought one fine ounce of gold. The Canadian dollar was fixed against the U.S. dollar

5. Crowding out results when an increase in government expenditures decreases investment. Crowding out arises because an increase in government expenditures shifts the *IS* curve to the right and increases the interest rate. When the interest rate rises, investment decreases.
6. An increase in taxes shifts the *IS* curve to the left. The interest rate decreases, and investment increases.
7. When government expenditures increase, real GDP increases, the price level rises, and the interest rate rises.
8. When the money supply increases, real GDP increases, the price level rises, and the interest rate falls.
9. Between 1975 and 1977 government spending exceeded tax revenues and a persistent deficit emerged.
10. Complete crowding out will occur if the *LM* curve is vertical or the *IS* curve is horizontal. In reality, neither of these extremes occurs.

### Problem Solving

1. (a) 3,075

   (b) 4.3 percent

2. (a) 1,450

(b) 830
(c) 320
(d) 1.8 percent
(e) increases by 2.5 units
(f) decreases by 0.75 units
(g) increases by 1.25 units

3. (a) 2,311
(b) 12.43 percent
(c) 1,808
(d) 403

4. (a) –20 units
(b) –0.81 percentage points
(c) 27
(d) 1.08 percentage points
(e) 7 units
(f) 0.27 percentage points

5. (a) 500
(b) 50 percent a year
(c) –75
(d) There is partial crowding out because investment falls by 75 which is less than the increase in government expenditures of 150

**Chapter 8**

# World Influences on Aggregate Demand

## Perspective and Focus

Up to now we have been studying a "closed" economy. The only "closed economy" is the world economy. This economy is an important one and it is very worthwhile studying how a closed economy operates. But national economies are the ones which focus most of our interest and attention, especially when it comes to discussing and evaluating the effects of macroeconomic policy.

This chapter takes the step of expanding the model of aggregate demand to include features of the open economy—of the linkages between the Canadian economy and the rest of the world.

## Learning Objectives

*After studying this chapter, you will be able to:*

- Describe the trends in Canadian international accounts
- Describe the balance of payments accounts
- Explain how net exports are determined
- Explain the behaviour of net exports during the 1980s and 1990s
- Explain how foreign exchange markets work and how the foreign currency value of the Canadian dollar is determined
- Describe the behaviour of interest rates around the world during the 1980s and 1990s
- Explain why interest rates vary from one country to another and why they are really equal
- Explain the open economy *IS-LM* model
- Explain how fiscal policy operates with a fixed exchange rate
- Explain how fiscal and monetary policy operate with a flexible exchange rate

## Increasing Your Productivity

The key part of this chapter on which you will spent most of your time is the open economy *IS-LM* model. However, it is important that you spend enough time before getting to the open economy *IS-LM* model to ensure that you understand thoroughly the concepts of the real exchange rate, the determination of the net exports, and the concept of interest rate parity. Work hard to thoroughly master these topics.

The open economy *IS-LM* model has three relationships between the interest rate and real GDP—the *IS* curve, the *LM* curve, and the interest rate parity condition *IRP*. But only two of these relationships operate to determine real GDP and the interest rate. The two in question depend on the exchange rate regime.

With a fixed exchange rate, equilibrium is determined at the intersection of the *IS* and *IRP* curves, the money supply adjusting to shift the *LM* curve to satisfy the equilibrium. With a flexible exchange rate, equilibrium is determined at the intersection of the *IS* and *LM* curves, the interest rate and expected exchange rate adjusting to shift the *IRP* curve to satisfy the equilibrium.

It is the fundamental difference in the determination of equilibrium under fixed and flexible exchange rates that lies at the heart of the differences in the monetary policy and the fiscal policy multipliers under the two exchange rate regimes. You will discover that monetary policy has no effect under fixed exchange rates. The reason is that the monetary authority has tied its hands by fixing the exchange rate and cannot control the quantity of money supplied. Like a monopoly producer of any kind of good or service, the monetary authority can only pick one—the exchange rate or the quantity of money supplied. Having chosen the exchange rate, the monetary authority must let the market determine the quantity of money that will be held at that exchange rate. If there is any change in the money supply, it immediately sets off a balance of payments movement that offsets the initial change.

Conversely, under a flexible exchange rate regime the monetary authority can determine the money supply and its actions do indeed influence domestic interest rates and the exchange rate, as well as the expected future exchange rate.

Under fixed exchange rates, fiscal policy is highly potent. Its potency arises from the fact that the interest rate is determined on world markets and there is no crowding out (or much less crowding out, in general) than under a flexible exchange rate regime.

Like its two predecessors, this chapter has an algebraic appendix. This appendix on the algebra of the open economy *IS-LM* model is a little more intensive in notation than the two previous ones. It is not vital that you study this appendix and we suggest that unless you genuinely enjoy and easily gain insights from an algebraic approach that you do not devote a large amount of time to this material.

## Self Test

### Fill in the Blanks

1. The ________ economy model is a model in which there are no international transactions between the domestic economy and the rest of the world. The ________ economy model is a model that takes into account linkages between the domestic economy and the rest of the world.
2. Net foreign investment income is recorded in the ________ account.
3. The account that records the receipts from nonresidents and payments made to nonresidents arising from the issuing of new debt or the repayment of old debt is the ________ account.
4. Investments by Canadian residents in the rest of the world are called ________ ________. New investments flowing into Canada from the rest of the world are called ________ ________.
5. The three balance of payments accounts are the ________ account, the ________ account, and the ________ ________ account. The sum of the balances of these three accounts equals ________.
6. Unilateral transfers are transactions that are included in the ________ account.
7. The account that records the net receipts and payments of gold and foreign currency is the ________ ________ account.
8. The ________ exchange rate measures the number of units of a foreign good that can be obtained for one unit of a domestic good. The ________ exchange rate is the number of units of a foreign currency that can be obtained with one unit of domestic currency.
9. The relationship between net exports and Canadian real GDP, income in the rest of the world, and the real exchange rate is the ________ ________.
10. The net exports curve shows the relationship between net exports and ________ ________, holding the ________ exchange rate constant.
11. A decrease in the number of yen that one dollar buys is ________ of the yen and ________ of the dollar.
12. An index that is the weighted average of the value of the Canadian dollar in terms of all other currencies, where the weight on each currency is the proportion of Canadian international trade undertaken in that currency is called the ________ exchange rate.
13. An exchange rate that is market determined is called a ________ exchange rate. An exchange rate that is declared and maintained by the central bank is called a ________ exchange rate regime.
14. The equality of the value of money in all countries is called ________ ________.
15. The exchange rate between two currencies for immediate delivery is the ________ exchange rate. The price at which one currency is traded for another for delivery at a specified future date is the ________ exchange rate.
16. The equality of rate of return on assets, independent of the currency in which they are denominated is ________ ________.
17. ________ are U.S. dollars deposited in foreign banks outside the United States.
18. The equality of rates of return where the investor takes the risk is called ________ ________ ________.
19. The equality of rates of return when no risk is taken is called ________ ________

__________.

20. A forward contract is a contract entered into today to buy or sell an agreed quantity at an agreed future __________ and an agreed __________.

## True or False

1. Net foreign investment income is the earnings of Canadian residents on assets held in the rest of the world minus the earnings of foreigners on assets held in Canada.
2. Gifts from Canadians to people in the rest of the world minus gifts to Canadians from people in other countries are known as bilateral transfers.
3. The real exchange rate is the price of domestic goods and services relative to the price of foreign goods and services.
4. A managed floating exchange rate is an exchange rate whose value is determined by market forces.
5. Purchasing power parity explains day-to-day fluctuations in the exchange rate.
6. Since the early 1970s, the Canadian economy has operated with a flexible exchange rate.
7. The exchange rate between two currencies for immediate delivery is called the forward exchange rate.
8. In an economy with a fixed exchange rate, fiscal policy has no influence on aggregate demand.
9. A country's capital account balance is its capital imports minus its capital exports.
10. The net exports function is the relationship between net exports and the variables that influence it—real GDP, real GDP in the rest of the world, and the real exchange rate.
11. An increase in real GDP in the rest of the world shifts the *IS* curve to the right.
12. As an economy moves up its *LM* curve, net exports decrease.
13. As domestic interest rates increase the *LM* curve shifts because the demand for money decreases.
14. A depreciation of the domestic currency does not shift the *IS* curve.
15. The *IS* curve in an open economy with a flexible exchange rate is flatter than the *IS* curve in an economy with a fixed exchange rate because a change in the interest rate also changes the real exchange rate.
16. In a fixed exchange rate regime, an increase in foreign real income increases interest rates and increases the capital account.
17. In a fixed exchange rate regime, an increase in foreign real income increases exports and increases the domestic money supply.
18. An increase in real GDP in the rest of the world when the exchange rate is flexible has no effect on net exports but appreciates the domestic currency.
19. A rise in foreign interest rates decreases the money supply and decreases domestic real income if the exchange rate is fixed.
20. A rise in foreign interest rates depreciates the domestic currency and increases net exports if the exchange rate is flexible.

## Multiple Choice

1. Since 1993 Canada's

(a) net exports have been negative.
(b) net exports have been positive.
(c) net exports have shown a downward trend.
(d) net exports have decreased and the real exchange rate has decreased.
(e) both (a) and (d).

2. The capital account

(a) records new investments by Canadian residents in some specified countries.
(b) records new investments by Canadian residents in the rest of the world and foreign investments in Canada.
(c) shows capital imports as investments by Canadian residents in the rest of the world.
(d) balance is obtained by subtracting capital imports from capital exports.
(e) records gifts from Canadians to people in the rest of the world.

3. Expansionary fiscal policy
(a) decreases interest rates and, to some degree, crowds out investment.
(b) increases interest rates and, to some degree, increases investment.
(c) increases interest rates and, to some degree, crowds out investment.
(d) decreases interest rates and, to some degree, decreases investment.
(e) none of the above.

4. The government budget deficit and the Canadian deficit with the rest of the world are known as the
(a) bilateral deficit.
(b) twin deficits.
(c) unilateral deficit.
(d) structural deficit.
(e) multilateral deficit.

5. The equality of rates of return when no risk is taken and when the investor covers the transaction by taking out a forward contract is known as
(a) spot interest parity.
(b) forward interest parity.
(c) uncovered interest parity.
(d) covered interest parity.
(e) real interest parity.

6. With a fixed exchange rate, the
(a) *IS* curve is flatter than in a closed economy.
(b) *LM* curve is flatter than in a closed economy; but because the money supply is endogenous, so is the position of the *LM* curve.
(c) *IS* curve is vertical in both a closed and an open economy.
(d) *LM* curve is steeper than in the closed economy; but because the money supply is exogenous, so is the position of the *LM* curve.
(e) *IS* curve is steeper than in a closed economy.

7. The equality of rates of return when the investor takes a risk and does not cover the transaction by taking out a forward contract is referred to as
(a) entrepreneurial parity.
(b) managed floating interest parity.
(c) nominal exchange parity.
(d) uncovered interest parity.
(e) official settlements parity.

8. The relationship between net exports and real GDP, holding the real exchange rate constant, is known as the
(a) fixed exchange rate curve.
(b) current account curve.
(c) capital exports curve.
(d) real dollar curve.
(e) net exports curve.

9. An index number calculated as a weighted average of the value of the Canadian dollar in terms of all other currencies, where the weight on each currency is a proportion of Canadian international trade undertaken in that currency is known as
(a) dollar exchange rate.
(b) appreciation exchange rate.
(c) depreciation exchange rate.
(d) current exchange rate.
(e) effective exchange rate.

10. The position of the open economy *IS* curve depends on
(a) government expenditures on goods and services.
(b) taxes.
(c) real income in the rest of the world.
(d) interest rates in the rest of the world.
(e) all of the above.

11. The Bretton Woods system
(a) pegged the national currencies to the U.S. dollar.
(b) established a system of flexible exchange rates.
(c) required nations with deficits to revalue their currencies.
(d) pegged the world's currency to silver.
(e) required nation's with serious inflation to revalue their currencies.

12. The Bretton Woods system collapsed
(a) at the end of World War II.
(b) during the Korean War.
(c) during the Great Depression.
(d) in the early 1970s.
(e) in the early 1980s.

13. If the German demand for Japanese cars increases, then
(a) the supply of German marks decreases.
(b) the supply of Japanese yen increases.
(c) a smaller quantity of German marks will be bought and sold.
(d) the Japanese yen will appreciate relative to the German mark.
(e) the demand for German marks will decrease.

14. In an open economy, an increase in the real income in the rest of the world shifts
(a) the *IS* curve.
(b) the *LM* curve.
(c) the *IRP* curve.
(d) both (a) and (c).
(e) none of the above.

15. An increase in the money supply in a flexible exchange rate economy moves down its *IS* curve and
(a) increases its capital account.
(b) appreciates its currency.
(c) depreciates its currency.
(d) both (a) and (c).
(e) none of the above.

16. As a flexible-exchange rate economy moves down its *IS* curve,
(a) its currency appreciates.
(b) its net exports remain constant.
(c) its net exports decrease.
(d) its currency depreciates.
(e) both (a) and (d).

17. In an open economy, as real income in the rest of the world decreases the domestic economy's
(a) *LM* curve shifts.
(b) *IS* curve shifts to the right.
(c) *IS* curve shifts to the left.
(d) both (a) and (b).
(e) both (a) and (c).

18. If the Canadian interest rate is lower than the U.S. interest rate
(a) Canadian currency is expected to appreciate.
(b) Canadian currency is expected to depreciate.
(c) rational economic agents will always invest in Canada.
(d) rational economic agents will always borrow funds in the United States.
(e) inflation in Canada must be higher than inflation in the United States.

19. A fax machine costs $1,295.00 and the current exchange between the dollar and the Japanese yen is 180 yen per dollar. The price of the fax machine in yen is
(a) 7.194 yen.
(b) 180 yen.
(c) 1,295 yen.
(d) 233,100 yen.
(e) none of the above.

20. As an economy moves up its *LM* curve
(a) its current account balance becomes larger.
(b) its capital account becomes smaller.
(c) its current account balance becomes smaller.
(d) its balance of payments becomes smaller.
(e) both (c) and (d).

## Short Answer Questions

1. Briefly explain the difference between an open economy model and a closed economy model.

2. What are the main influences on exports and imports?

3. Briefly explain the difference between a flexible exchange rate and a managed floating exchange rate.

4. (a) What does the interest rate parity theory predict?

(b) When does interest rate parity prevail?

5. (a) What are the balance of payments accounts?

   (b) What do they record?

6. What is the net exports function?

7. What is an effective exchange rate?

8. What is meant by a forward contract?

9. What is meant by purchasing power parity.

10. Explain why a central bank does not have control of the money supply if the exchange rate is fixed.

## Problem Solving

### Practice Problems

1. Last year, Rose Island had the following international transactions:

| Item | Dollars |
|---|---|
| Exports of goods and services | 6,000 |
| Imports of goods and services | 5,000 |
| Dividends paid by Rose Islanders to the rest of the world | 2,000 |
| Dividends received by Rose Islanders from the rest of the world | 1,000 |
| Rose Islanders' gifts to residents of the rest of the world | 700 |
| Gifts to Rose Islanders from the rest of the world | 500 |
| Rose Islanders' purchases of debt issued by the rest of the world | 4,000 |
| Purchases of Rose Island debt by residents of the rest of the world | 3,000 |

(a) Calculate the current account balance.

(b) Calculate the capital account balance.

(c) Calculate the official settlements balance.

2. The price of a television set in Japan is 26,250 yen. The spot exchange rate is 75 yen per dollar. Calculate the price of a television set in Canada.

### Solutions to Practice Problems

1. (a) Calculate the current account balance.

The current account balance is equal to (exports + dividends received from the rest of the world + gifts received from the rest of the world) minus (imports + dividends paid to the rest of the world + gifts to the rest of the world).

That is,

(6,000 + 1,000 + 500) – (5,000 + 2,000 + 700)

which equals –$200.

(b) Calculate the capital account balance.

The capital account balance equals purchases of Rose Island debt minus debt purchased by Rose Islanders.

That is,

(3,000 – 4,000)

which equals –$1,000.

(c) Calculate the official settlements balance.

The official settlements balance is the negative of the sum of the current account and capital account balances.

The sum of the current account and capital account balances is

–200 –1,000 = –1,200.

The official settlements balances is $1,200.

2. Calculate the price of the television set in Canada.

The price of the television set in Canada is equal to the price in yen converted to dollars at the spot exchange rate. That is,

26,250/75 dollars,

which is $350.

## Problems to Solve

1. A Honda sells for 1,200,000 yen in Japan and for 10,000 dollars in Canada. The exchange rate is 120 yen per dollar.

   (a) What is the Canadian real exchange rate.

   (b) In which country is the Honda cheaper?

2. Seal Island had the following international transactions in 1991:

| Item | Dollars |
|---|---|
| Exports of goods and services | 3,000 |
| Imports of goods and services | 4,000 |
| Dividends and interest paid by Seal Islanders to the rest of the world | 500 |
| Dividends and interest received by Seal Islanders from the rest of the world | 1,000 |
| Seal Islanders' gifts to residents of the rest of the world | 250 |
| Gifts to Seal Islanders from the rest of the world | 500 |
| Seal Islanders' purchases of debt issued by the rest of the world | 1,500 |
| Purchases of Seal Island debt by residents of the rest of the world | 2,000 |

   Calculate Seal Island's

   (a) current account balance.

   (b) capital account balance.

   (c) net exports.

   (d) official settlements balance.

3. You are considering buying a bond. The interest rate on dollar-denominated bonds is 10 percent per year and on pound-denominated bonds is 20 percent per year. Today's spot exchange rate is £1.20 per dollar and the expected exchange rate in one year is £1.32 per dollar. Which bond will you buy? Explain your answer.

4. Big Wave Island has a fixed exchange rate. Its *IS* curve and demand for money are

   *IS* curve: $y = 10{,}550 - 15r + (200/P)$

   Demand for money: $M^d/P = 0.2y + 200 - 10r$.

   The price level in Big Wave Island is 4 and the interest rate in the rest of the world is 2 percent a year.

   (a) Calculate equilibrium real income and interest rate in Big Wave Island.

   (b) Calculate the equilibrium money supply in Big Wave Island.

   (c) The government of Big Wave Island decreases its expenditures on goods and services and as a result the *IS* curve shifts to the left by 100. Calculate the immediate change in the interest rate.

   (d) In (c), calculate real GDP in the long run.

   (e) In (d), calculate the change in the money supply in the long run.

5. Big Wave Island has a fixed exchange rate. Its *IS* curve and demand for money are

   *IS* curve: $y = 10{,}550 - 15r + (200/P)$

   Demand for money: $M^d/P = 0.2y + 200 - 10r$.

   The price level in Big Wave Island is 4 and the interest rate in the rest of the world is 2 percent a year.

   (a) The government of Big Wave Island increases the money supply and as a result the *LM* curve shifts to the right by 50. Calculate the immediate change in the interest rate.

   (b) In (a), calculate real GDP in the long run.

   (c) In (b), calculate the interest rate in the long run.

## Answers

### Fill in the Blanks

1. closed, open
2. current
3. capital
4. capital exports, capital imports
5. current, capital, official settlements, zero
6. current
7. official settlements
8. real, nominal
9. net exports function
10. Canadian real GDP, real
11. appreciation, depreciation
12. effective
13. flexible, fixed
14. purchasing power parity
15. spot, forward
16. interest rate parity
17. Eurodollars
18. uncovered interest parity
19. covered interest parity
20. date, price

### True or False

1T 5F 9T 13F 17T
2F 6T 10T 14T 18F
3T 7F 11T 15T 19T
4F 8F 12F 16F 20T

### Multiple Choice

1b 5d 9e 13d 17c
2b 6e 10e 14a 18a
3c 7d 11a 15c 19d
4b 8e 12d 16d 20c

### Short Answer Questions

1. A closed economy model is a model in which there are no international transactions between the domestic economy and the rest of the world.

   An open economy model takes into account linkages between the domestic economy and the rest of the world.
2. The main influences on exports are the real exchange rate and real GDP in the rest of the world.

   The main influences on imports are the real exchange rate and Canadian real GDP.
3. A flexible exchange rate is a foreign exchange rate whose value is determined by market forces. The central bank does not declare a target value for the exchange rate and has no direct interest in the value of the exchange rate. The central bank does not intervene and manipulate the relative price of its currency in the foreign exchange market.

   A managed floating exchange rate is one that is manipulated but is not necessarily held constant by the central bank. Usually the central bank announces that it is floating but does not tell the market what course it would like to see the exchange rate follow.
4. (a) The interest rate parity theory predicts that rates of return on assets denominated in different currencies are equal once the expected rate of currency depreciation or appreciation is taken into account.

   The theory also predicts that the exchange rate will adjust from hour to hour and day to day to ensure that interest rate parity prevails.

   (b) Interest parity prevails when investors make the same rate of return regardless of the currency in which they borrow and lend.
5. (a) The balance of payment accounts are the current account, the capital account, and the official settlements account.

   (b) The current account records the values of net exports, net foreign investment income, and unilateral transfers.

   The capital account records the new investments by Canadian residents in the rest of the world and foreign investments in Canada.

   The official settlements account records the net receipts and payments of gold and foreign currency resulting form all transactions recorded in the current and capital accounts.
6. The net exports function is the relationship between net exports and Canadian real GDP, income in the rest of the world, and the real exchange rate.
7. An effective exchange rate is an index number

calculated as a weighted average of the value of the Canadian dollar in terms of all other currencies, where the weight on each currency is the proportion of Canadian international trade undertaken in that currency.

8. A forward contract is a contract entered into today to buy or sell an agreed quantity at an agreed future date and at an agreed price.
9. Purchasing power parity is a condition that exists when the value of money in one country is the same as its value in another country. Purchasing power parity holds in the long run.
10. In a fixed exchange rate regime, the money supply is endogenous. Central bank monetary policy is conducted to maintain the chosen value of the exchange rate.

    The quantity of Canadian dollars in existence depends on the demand for Canadian dollars. If people can get a better return on Canadian dollars than on other currencies then the quantity of Canadian dollars will increase. If a higher rate of return can be obtained on foreign currencies than on Canadian dollars, people will move their money out of Canadian dollars into these other currencies and the quantity of Canadian dollars will decrease. Thus with a fixed exchange rate, the Bank of Canada loses control of the quantity of Canadian dollars in existence.

## Problem Solving

1. (a) 1

   (b) The prices are the same.
2. (a) –$250

   (b) $500

   (c) –$1,000

   (d) –$250
3. If you buy the dollar-denominated bond, you lend $100 and a year later you receive $110. Your rate of return is 10 percent per year.

   If you buy the pound-denominated bond, you have to buy pounds first. You receive £120 for your $100 and lend it at an interest rate of 20 percent a year. You receive £144 at the end of the year. Converting £144 into dollars, you expect to receive $109.09.

   Your return is greatest if you buy the dollar-denominated bond.
4. (a) $y$ = 10,570, $r$ = 2 percent a year

   (b) $9,176

   (c) falls by 1.54 percentage points to 0.46 percent a year

   (d) 10,470

   (e) decreases by $80 to $9,096
5. (a) decreases by 0.77 percentage points to 1.23 percent a year

   (b) 10,570

   (c) 2 percent a year

**Chapter 9**

# Capital, Technology, and Economic Growth

## Perspective and Focus

You have now completed your study of the details of aggregate demand. It is time to move on to probing details of aggregate supply. This chapter and the next two do just that.

In macroeconomics the terms *short run* and *long run* have ambiguous meanings. In microeconomics, the term *short run* always means a period in which some factors of production are fixed in quantity. Sometimes in macroeconomics, the stock of capital is fixed and so is the state of technology. The only factor of production whose quantity varies is the labour employed. This is the *microeconomic* short-run. But macroeconomics makes another kind of distinction between short-run and long-run which is really part of the microeconomic short-run. The *macroeconomic short-run* is a period in which not only are the capital stock and technology fixed but so are factor prices. The *macroeconomic long-run* is a *microeconomic short-run* in which wage rates and other factor prices are flexible so that full employment prevails.

In this chapter, we study the *microeconomic* long-run—the period in which the quantities of all factors of production can be varied. This chapter explains how economies grow.

## Learning Objectives

*After studying this chapter, you will be able to:*

- Describe the main features of the expansion of Canadian output from 1926 to 1998
- Describe the sources of economic growth
- Explain the neoclassical model of economic growth
- Explain how the saving rate influences the rate of economic growth
- Explain how technological change influences economic growth
- Explain new growth theory and the *Ak* model of economic growth
- Describe the convergence test of neoclassical and new growth theory

## Increasing Your Productivity

The key to understanding the theory of neoclassical economic growth is to understand Figures 9.4, 9.5, and 9.6. Focus your attention on these figures and be sure you understand exactly what is going on in them. Once you have got it you will be able to do the rest of the chapter with ease. The key to Figure 9.4 is that it explains a steady-state relationship. It does not describe someone's behavior. Figure 9.4 tells you the rate at which the economy must save *and invest* if the level of capital per person is to remain constant. The text explains how the steady-state investment line is derived.

Figure 9.5 explains behavior. It tells us the amount of saving *and investment* that will take place at each level of capital per person.

Figure 9.6 brings Figure 9.4 and Figure 9.5 together. It tells us that if capital per person is below its steady-state level ($60,000 in Figure 9.6), actual saving and investment exceeds that required to keep the capital per person constant. Capital per person increases. If capital per person exceeds its steady-state level, then the amount of saving and investment falls short of that required to keep the capital per person constant. In this case, capital per person decreases. In either case, whether the capital per person is initially below or above its steady-state level, the process of adjustment forces the economy's capital per person back to its steady-state level.

With your understanding of Figures 9.4, 9.5, and 9.6 and the analysis that surrounds them you are ready to study the effects of changes in the population growth rate, the saving rate, and the rate of technological change. These are the key exogenous influences on steady-state output per person and the rate of economic growth.

## Self Test

### Fill in the Blanks

1. The ________ ________ ________ ________ shows the relationship between output per person and capital per person.
2. The marginal product of capital is the increase in ________ ________ per person resulting from a one-unit increase in ________ per person.
3. The marginal product of capital ________ as capital per person increases.
4. The ________ ________ ________ determines real GDP per person, consumption and saving per person, capital per person, and the economic growth rate.
5. When the relevant variables are constant over time, the economy is in a ________ ________.
6. The ________ ________ is the situation in which consumption per person is maximized in the steady state.
7. ________ ________ are the decreases in the marginal product of a factor of production as more of the factor is employed, other inputs held constant.
8. An externality is a ________ or ________ experienced by one economic agent that results from the actions of another agent or agents.
9. Increasing returns occurs when the ________ ________ of a factor of production increases as the quantity of the factor employed increases, other inputs held constant.
10. Neoclassical growth theory predicts that countries with the lowest levels of real GDP per person will have the ________ growth rates of real GDP per person. New endogenous growth theory predicts the absence of significant ________ between the initial level and subsequent growth rate of real GDP.

### True or False

1. The increase of real GDP per person that results from a one-unit increase in capital per person is known as the marginal technical change of capital.
2. When capital per person is constant, the economy is said to be in a variable state—a situation in which the relevant variables are constant over time.
3. The situation in which consumption per person is maximized in the steady state is called the golden rule.
4. When technological change occurs, the per capita production function shifts downward.
5. Diminishing returns are the increases in the marginal product of a factor of production as more of the factor is employed, other inputs held constant.
6. According to the neoclassical growth theory, in the steady state the marginal product of capital always equals the population growth rate.
7. In the *Ak* model of endogenous growth, the growth rate of real GDP is proportional to the saving rate.
8. The neoclassical growth model determines real GDP per person, consumption and saving per person, capital per person, and the economic growth rate.
9. Canada and other major industrial countries spend close to 10 percent of GDP on research and development every year.
10. The presence of externalities and increasing returns to knowledge make it impossible for a large and wealthy economy to grow indefinitely at a faster pace than a small and poor economy.
11. Capital per person increases if investment per person exceeds the population growth rate.
12. A technological advance moves the economy down along its per capita production function.
13. Economywide knowledge is an externality—when one firm invests resources in advancing its own knowledge, it is at the same time expanding the production possibilities of all

the other firms in the economy.

14. Romer's model of the economy does not include the economywide technological knowledge in the economy.

15. The slope of the steady-state investment line is equal to saving per person.

16. Neoclassical growth theory predicts that growth rates of real GDP diverge among countries because saving rates and population growth rates diverge.

17. The steady-state rate of growth of output increases if the population growth rate increases.

18. The government can increase the steady-state growth rate by persuading everyone to save more.

19. An increase in the growth rate of population rotates the steady-state investment line upward.

20. In the steady-state, the capital-labour ratio increases at a constant rate.

## Multiple Choice

1. Which of the following determines real GDP per person, consumption and saving per person, capital per person, and the economic growth rate? The
(a) Keynesian growth model.
(b) Malthus growth model.
(c) monetarist growth model.
(d) neoclassical growth model.
(e) classical growth model.

2. Romer's model of the economy has a large number of competitive firms. Each firm is small relative to the size of the economy and uses four factors of production to produce its output. These factors include
(a) labour.
(b) capital.
(c) its own technological knowledge.
(d) economywide (aggregate) technological knowledge.
(e) all of the above.

3. Between 1926 and 1998, the average growth rate of Canadian real GDP was
(a) equal to the average population growth rate and less than the saving rate.
(b) less than the average population growth rate and greater than the saving rate.
(c) always positive.
(d) greatest during the 1960s.
(e) greater than the average population growth rate.

4. Capital accumulation leads to economic growth by moving the economy
(a) to a higher per capita production function.
(b) to a situation of maximum consumption.
(c) to a situation of maximum investment per person.
(d) along the per capita production function with increasing returns.
(e) along the per capita production function.

5. Capital accumulation alone cannot bring sustained growth in real GDP per person because the marginal product of capital
(a) increases.
(b) remains constant.
(c) diminishes.
(d) is normally negative.
(e) none of the above.

6. According to the *Ak* model of endogenous growth, if the exogenous population growth rate is greater than $A(1 - b)$, then
(a) real GDP decreases persistently.
(b) the saving rate is negative.
(c) the saving rate decreases persistently.
(d) real GDP per person decreases persistently.
(e) real GDP per person remains constant.

7. Which of the following occurs when the marginal product of a factor of production increases as the quantity of the factor employed increases, other inputs held constant?
(a) Diminishing returns.
(b) Variable returns.
(c) Increasing returns.

(d) Constant returns.
(e) Negative returns.

8. A situation in which capital per person and real GDP per person are constant is known as the
(a) golden state.
(b) normal state.
(c) neoclassical state.
(d) steady state.
(e) classical state.

9. Which of the following equations tells us that the capital stock per person will be constant if investment per person equals the growth rate of the population multiplied by capital per person?
(a) $\Delta k/n = \Delta k/n/(n/k)$.
(b) $\Delta k/n = \Delta k/k/(k/n)$.
(c) $\Delta k/n = \Delta n/n/(k/n)$.
(d) $\Delta k/n = \Delta n/n$.
(e) $\Delta n/k = \Delta k/n$.

10. According to the neoclassical model, consumption per person is maximized when the marginal product of
(a) labour equals the population growth rate.
(b) capital equals the population growth rate.
(c) labour is greater than the population growth rate.
(d) capital is greater than the population growth rate.
(e) capital equals the marginal product of labour.

11. Capital per person increases if investment per person
(a) is less than the population growth rate.
(b) exceeds the population growth rate.
(c) exceeds saving per person.
(d) is less than saving per person.
(e) is more than consumption per person.

12. A technological advance
(a) shifts the economy's steady-state investment line.
(b) shifts the per capita consumption function upward.
(c) shifts the per capita saving function downward.
(d) shifts the per capita production function downward.
(e) moves the economy down along its per capita production function.

13. If the population growth rate in the $Ak$ model of endogenous growth equals $A(1 - b)$, then
(a) the equilibrium is unique.
(b) the steady-state investment function is steeper than the per capita production function.
(c) the saving function is steeper than the per capital production function.
(d) the steady-state investment function is flatter than the saving function.
(e) no unique equilibrium exists.

14. The per capita production function shifts up over time as a result of
(a) saving.
(b) labour productivity increasing as the population grows.
(c) the quantity of labour employed increasing.
(d) technological advances.
(e) capital per person employed increasing.

15. The steady-state rate of growth of output increases if
(a) investment per person increases.
(b) saving per person increases.
(c) the population growth rate increases.
(d) both (b) and (c).
(e) all of the above.

16. At the golden rule:
(a) investment per person equals saving per person.
(b) consumption per person equals output per person.
(c) investment per person equals the population growth rate.
(d) the marginal product of capital equals the population growth rate.
(e) both (a) and (d).

**Fact 9.1** On Heron Island, the per capita production function is:

$y/n = (k/n) - 0.15(k/n)^2$.

The population growth rate is 0.03. The saving rate is 0.2.

17. Use Fact 9.1. The steady-state growth rate is
(a) between 11 and 15 percent a year.
(b) between 8 and 10 percent a year.
(c) between 2 and 7 percent a year.
(d) less than 2 percent a year.
(e) none of the above.

18. Use Fact 9.1. The steady-state saving per person is greater than
(a) 0 and less than or equal to 0.02.
(b) 0.02 and less than or equal 0.03.
(c) 0.03 and less than or equal to 0.05.
(d) 0.05 and less than or equal to 1.
(e) 1.

19. Use Fact 9.1. The steady-state investment per person is greater than
(a) 0 and less than or equal to 0.01.
(b) 0.01 and less than or equal 0.03.
(c) 0.03 and less than or equal to 0.08.
(d) 0.08 and less than or equal to 1.
(e) 1.

20. Use Fact 9.1. The golden rule capital per person is greater than
(a) 0 and less than or equal to 0.5.
(b) 0.5 and less than or equal 0.9.
(c) 0.9 and less than or equal to 1.5
(d) 1.5 and less than or equal to 2.
(e) 2.

21. Use Fact 9.1. The golden rule consumption per person is greater than
(a) 0 and less than or equal to 1.
(b) 1 and less than or equal 1.5.
(c) 1.5 and less than or equal to 1.7.
(d) 1.7 and less than or equal to 2.
(e) 2.

22. Use Fact 9.1. The golden rule saving per person is greater than
(a) 0 and less than or equal to 0.5.
(b) 0.5 and less than or equal 0.6.
(c) 0.6 and less than or equal to 0.9.
(d) 0.9 and less than or equal to 1.2.
(e) 1.2.

23. Use Fact 9.1. The golden rule output growth rate
(a) between 11 and 15 percent a year.
(b) between 8 and 10 percent a year.
(c) between 5 and 7 percent a year.
(d) less than 5 percent a year.
(e) none of the above.

24. Use Fact 9.1. The golden rule marginal product of capital is
(a) between 0.11 and 0.15.
(b) between 0.08 and 0.10.
(c) between 0.05 and 0.07.
(d) less than 0.05.
(e) none of the above.

25. Use Fact 9.1. Heron Island experiences a technological advance. The golden rule capital per person
(a) increases and the golden rule marginal product of capital does not change.
(b) increases and the golden rule marginal product of capital increases.
(c) does not change.
(d) increases and the golden rule marginal product of capital decreases.
(e) increases and so does the population growth rate.

## Short Answer Questions

1. Briefly explain the per capita production function.
2. What is determined by the neoclassical growth model?
3. What are the four factors of production used by firms in Romer's endogenous technology model?

4. Define the steady state.
5. What is meant by the golden rule?
6. What are the two main sources of economic growth?
7. Which country or group of countries has the highest saving rate in the world and where does Canada fit in?
8. When does capital per person increase?
9. Technological change increases income per person for two reasons. What are they?
10. Explain why an increase in the saving rate does not increase the steady-state growth rate.

## Problem Solving

### Practice Problems

1. Wetland has the following per capita production function:

$(y/n) = (k/n) - 0.2(k/n)^2$ (9.1)

Wetland's saving rate is 0.2 and its population growth rate is 0.03.

(a) Calculate Wetland's steady-state investment line.

(b) Calculate Wetland's per capita saving function.

(c) Calculate Wetland's steady-state capital per person.

(d) Calculate Wetland's steady-state real GDP per person.

(e) Calculate Wetland's steady-state consumption per person.

### Solutions to Practice Problems

1. (a) Calculate Wetland's steady-state investment line.

The steady-state investment line shows the relationship between capital per person $(k/n)$ and investment per person $(\Delta k/n)$, such that the stock of capital per person is constant.

The population is growing at 3 percent a year, so the equation of the steady-state investment line is

$(\Delta k/n) = 0.03(k/n)$.

(b) Calculate Wetland's per capita saving function.

Because the saving rate is 0.2, the per capita saving function is

$(s/n) = 0.2(y/n)$ (9.2)

$(s/n) = 0.2[(k/n) - .2(k/n)^2]$

$(s/n) = 0.2(k/n) - .04(k/n)^2$

(c) Calculate Wetland's steady-state capital per person.

The steady-state capital per person is the capital stock per person that generates the amount of saving and in turn investment to keep the capital stock per person constant. The saving line tells us saving per person and the steady-state investment line tells us the relationship between investment per person and the capital stock per person. These two lines together determine the steady-state capital per person.

$(\Delta k/n) = 0.03(k/n)$ (9.3)

Because saving equals investment,

$(s/n) = (\Delta k/n)$. (9.4)

Substituting Equations (9.2) and (9.3) into Equation (9.4) and solving for $(k/n)$ gives steady-state capital per person:

$(k/n) = 4.25$.

(d) Calculate Wetland's steady-state real GDP per person.

Steady-state real GDP per person is found by substituting the steady-state capital per person in the per capita production function. Steady-state capital per person is 4.25. Real GDP per person is

$(y/n) = (k/n) - 0.2(k/n)^2$ (9.1)

$(y/n) = 0.6375$

(e) Calculate Wetland's consumption per person.

The marginal propensity to consume is 0.8, so

steady-state consumption per person is $0.8(y/n)$, which is 0.51.

## Problems to Solve

1. An economy's per capita production function is

   $(y/n) = (k/n) - 0.25(k/n)^2$.

   The marginal propensity to consume is 0.9 and the population growth rate is 4 percent per year.

   (a) What is the steady-state investment line?

   (b) What is the per capita saving function?

   (c) What is the steady-state per capita capital?

   (d) What is the steady-state per capita output?

   (e) What is the steady-state per consumption?

2. In problem 1, the population growth decreases to 2 percent per year.

   (a) What is the steady-state investment line?

   (b) What is the per capita saving function?

   (c) What is the steady-state per capita capital?

   (d) What is the steady-state per capita output?

   (e) What is the steady-state per consumption?

   (f) Compare the steady state in problem 1 and problem 2.

3. Sunny Isle's per capita production function is

   $(y/n) = (k/n) - 0.1(k/n)^2$.

   Sunny Isle's marginal propensity to consume is 0.75 and its population growth rate is 8 percent a year.

   (a) Calculate Sunny Isle's steady-state capital per person.

   (b) Calculate Sunny Isle's steady-state output per person.

   (c) Calculate Sunny Isle's steady-state consumption per person.

   (d) Calculate Sunny Isle's steady-state saving per person.

4. An economy's per capita production function is

   $(y/n) = (k/n) - 0.7(k/n)^2$.

   Its marginal propensity to consume is 0.6 and its population growth rate is 10 percent a year.

   (a) Calculate the slope of the steady-state investment line.

   (b) Calculate the steady-state output per person.

   (c) Calculate the steady-state saving per person.

   (d) Calculate the golden rule level of consumption per person.

   (e) Calculate the golden rule investment per person.

   (f) Technological change increases output per person by 10 percent. What is the new steady-state capital per person?

5. An economy's per capita production function is

   $y = 0.25k$.

   The marginal propensity to consume is 0.80 and the population growth rate is 5 percent a year.

   (a) What is the saving curve?

   (b) What is the growth rate of real GDP?

   (c) What is the growth rate of real GDP per person?

## Answers

### Fill in the Blanks

1. per capital production function
2. real GDP, capital
3. diminishes
4. neoclassical growth model
5. steady state
6. golden rule
7. Diminishing returns
8. cost, benefit
9. marginal product
10. highest, correlation

### True or False

1F 5F 9F 13T 17F
2F 6F 10F 14F 18F
3T 7T 11T 13F 19T
4F 8T 12F 16T 20F

### Multiple Choice

1d 6d 11b 16e 21b
2e 7c 12b 17c 22a
3e 8d 13e 18d 23d
4e 9c 14d 19d 24d
5c 10b 15c 20e 25a

### Short Answer Questions

1. The per capita production function is the relationship between output per person and capital per person. Output per person is equal to income per person and these two equivalent concepts are measured as real GDP per person.
2. The neoclassical growth model determines real GDP per person, consumption and saving per person, capital per person and the economic growth rate.
3. The four factors of production in Romer's endogenous technology model are labour, capital, the firm's own technological knowledge, and economywide (aggregate) technological knowledge.
4. The steady state is defined as a situation in which relevant variables are constant over time. In our analysis of the neoclassical growth model, the relevant variables are real GDP per person, capital per person, and consumption, saving, and investment per person.
5. The golden rule is the situation in which consumption per person is maximized in the steady state.
6. The two main sources of economic growth are capital accumulation and technological change.
7. Other Europe (the combined countries of Cypress, Greece, Iceland, Luxembourg, Malta, Portugal, Romania, Turkey, the former USSR, Yugoslavia, and the Czech Republic) have the highest saving rate at 34 percent of GDP and Canada fits into the intermediate saving rate of between 20 and 26 percent of GDP.
8. Capital per person increases if investment per person exceeds the population growth rate.
9. First, with the new technology we are able to produce more output from given inputs. Furthermore, with more real income, we save more and accumulate more capital.
10. An increase in the saving rate increases steady-state capital per person and increases steady-state output per person. It does not increase the steady-state rate of growth because output grows at a rate equal to the population growth rate and it has not changed.

### Problem Solving

1. (a) $(\Delta k/n) = 0.04(k/n)$
   (b) $(s/n) = 0.1(k/n) - 0.025(k/n)^2$
   (c) 2.4
   (d) 0.96
   (e) 0.864
2. (a) $(\Delta k/n) = 0.02(k/n)$
   (b) $(0s/n) = 0.1(k/n) - 0.025(k/n)^2$
   (c) 3.2
   (d) 0.64
   (e) 0.576
   (f) In problem 1, the steady-state per capita capital is less than in problem 2 but the steady-state per capita output is greater in problem 1 than in problem 2.

3. (a) 6.8
   (b) 2.176
   (c) 1.632
   (d) 0.544
4. (a) 0.1
   (b) 0.27
   (c) 0.11
   (d) 0.21
   (e) 0.14
   (f) 1.10
5. (a) $(s/n) = 0.05k$
   (b) 0.05
   (c) Real GDP per person remains constant.

**Chapter 10**

# Productivity Growth and the Real Business Cycle

## Perspective and Focus

In Chapter 9 you studied economic growth in the neoclassical growth model with no technological change. In Chapter 10, you are studying real business cycle theory and the implications of technological change on the economy.

Real business cycle theory explains the business cycle as the response to changes in productivity driven by the uneven pace of technological change. This chapter uses the steady-state equilibrium of the neoclassical growth model and shows the effects of a technological advance that makes the capital stock more productive.

## Learning Objectives

*After studying this chapter, you will be able to:*

- Describe the key features of the postwar business cycle
- Explain the main ideas of real business cycle theory
- Explain how the labour market behaves over a real business cycle
- Explain how a dynamic general equilibrium model is calibrated
- Describe the importance of the contribution of technological change to Canadian economic growth
- Describe the Canadian productivity slowdown of the 1980s and 1990s and explain its origins

## Increasing Your Productivity

The key to understanding business cycle theory is a firm grasp of the neoclassical growth theory presented in Chapter 9. There is a brief review on p.254, but if you are unsure of the neoclassical growth theory it is probably a good idea to go Chapter 9 now and do some review.

Let's start our study of Chapter 10 by focusing on some of the figures. Figure 10.1 presents the initial steady state and figure 10.2 shows the real business cycle expansion. Make sure you understand why an increase in productivity shifts the production function and the saving curve upward and why capital per person, saving per person, and real GDP per person increase.

When you are sure that you understand Figure 10.2 look at figures 10.3, 10.4, and 10.5. Figure 10.3 tracks the capital market in a real business cycle expansion while figures 10.4 and 10.5 track the labour market in a real business cycle expansion.

Figure 10.3 shows that in a real business cycle expansion, an increase in productivity increases investment demand and saving supply. The interest rate rises. Rising income brings a further increase in saving supply and the interest rate falls. Overall saving and investment per person increase and the real interest rate remains unchanged.

Figure 10.4 shows that initially the increase in productivity which increases the marginal product of labour increases the demand for labour. The same increase in productivity increases the marginal product of capital and increases the real interest rate. The supply of labour increases through the intertemporal substitution effect. The quantity of labour employed increases and the real wage rate rises.

Figure 10.5 shows that as capital accumulates and the real interest rate falls, the supply of labour decreases. The marginal product of labour and the demand for labour increase further as the capital stock per person increases. Overall, employment may be unchanged, but the real wage rate increases.

Now focus on putting it all together! Check that you can work your way through a business cycle expansion and a business cycle recession and read the summaries presented on pages 259 and 260.

## Self Test

### Fill in the Blanks

1. In the Canadian postwar business cycle, ________ and ________ fluctuate more than real GDP. ________ fluctuates over a similar range to real GDP.
2. The effects of fluctuations in the pace of technological change are changes in the pace of ________ and saving and the ________ ________ ________, changes in the demand for and supply of labour, employment, and the ________ ________ ________.
3. Capital stock per person is constant when saving and investment per person equals the growth rate of the ________ multiplied by ________ ________ ________.
4. During a real business cycle expansion, the production function shifts ________ and the saving curve shifts ________. Investment ________, capital ________, and real GDP ________.
5. The slope of the production function is the ________ ________ ________ ________.
6. During an expansion, the real interest rate initially ________ and then ________.
7. Firms maximize profit when the real wage rate equals the ________ ________ ________.
8. A technological advance initially increases the supply of labour because of ________ ________.
9. Comparing the new steady state following a business cycle expansion with the original steady state, the capital stock per person ________, real GDP per person ________, and the real wage rate ________.
10. In the production function, the variable $Z$ summarizes all influences on the productivity of capital and labour include the state of technology, ________ ________, and ________ and ________ ________.
11. A ________ productivity shock occurs when a technological advance has a sufficiently large effect on the depreciation of human capital.
12. The ________ ________ is an estimate of the contribution of productivity change to the change in output.
13. To estimate $Z$, Solow assumes that the production function is a ________ production function.
14. The Solow residual ________ the contribution of technological change to economic growth because it does not recognize the fact that the pace of capital accumulation is ________ with technological change than without it.
15. In Canada since 1930, the ________ was the decade of slowest growth and the ________ was the decade of fastest growth.

### True or False

1. The classical model can explain economic conditions leading to the Great Depression but it cannot explain the less extreme business fluctuations that have occurred in Canada since 1960.
2. Adam Smith's idea of the invisible hand is a cornerstone of the Keynesian *IS—LM* model.
3. There is no regularity in the timing of the fluctuations of the business cycle.
4. Saving and investment are more volatile than capital stock, aggregate hours, productivity, and consumption.
5. Real business theory is an application of dynamic programming, an advanced mathematical tool.
6. The pace of technology and productivity grow at a constant rate.
7. In a steady state, real GDP per person is constant, but capital per person can be increasing or decreasing depending on the growth rate of the population.
8. A technological advance that makes the capital stock more productive is shown as a movement along the per capita production function.
9. When an increase in productivity occurs, the saving curve shifts upward.

10. In a real business cycle expansion, an increase in productivity increases the marginal product of labour and decreases the real wage rate.

11. When a negative productivity shock occurs, the production function shifts downward, the marginal product of capital decreases, and the marginal product of labour decreases.

12. Human capital can depreciate because of an advance in technology.

13. A source of negative productivity shocks is the state of technology.

14. Fluctuations in real GDP are associated with fluctuations in the Solow residual.

15. Productivity growth in Canada in the 1990s was slower than in the 1970s.

## Multiple Choice

1. The regularity in the business cycle is the
(a) predictable fluctuations in real GDP.
(b) predictable length of expansions but not contractions.
(c) variables that move up and down with real GDP in a systematic way.
(d) predictable length of contractions but not expansions.
(e) (a) and (c).

2. The equation that best shows that saving per person is a fraction of output per person is

(a) $\frac{s}{n} = (1-b)f\left(\frac{k}{n}\right)$.

(b) $\frac{s}{n} = bf\left(\frac{k}{n}\right)$.

(c) $s = (1-b)f\left(\frac{y}{n}\right)$.

(d) $s = (b)f\left(\frac{k}{n}\right)$.

(e) $\frac{s}{n} = (1-b)f\left(\frac{y}{n}\right)$.

3. When a technological advance occurs, the equation of the new production function is

(a) $y = Zf\left(\frac{k}{n}\right)$, $Z<1$.

(b) $y = Zf\left(\frac{k}{n}\right)$, $Z>1$.

(c) $k = Zf\left(\frac{y}{n}\right)$, $Z>1$.

(d) $\frac{y}{n} = Zf\left(\frac{k}{n}\right)$, $Z>1$.

(e) $\frac{y}{n} = Zf\left(\frac{k}{n}\right)$, $Z<1$.

4. In a real business cycle expansion,
(a) the production function shifts upward, there is a movement along the saving curve, and investment does not change.
(b) the production function and saving curve shift upward and capital per person and real GDP per person increase to a new steady state.
(c) the production function does not shift but there is a movement along the production function as capital per person and real GDP per person increase to a new steady state.
(d) the marginal product of capital decreases and the marginal product of labour increases.
(e) the marginal product of capital increases and the marginal product of labour decreases.

5. The slope of the production function is the
(a) real interest rate.
(b) marginal product of labour.
(c) marginal product of capital.
(d) (a) and (c).
(e) (a), (b), and (c).

6. The initial influences of a technological advance include
(a) an increase in investment demand, a decrease in saving supply, and a fall in the real interest rate.
(b) a decrease in investment demand, a decrease in saving supply, and a fall in the real interest rate.

(c) an increase in investment demand, an increase in saving supply, and a fall in the real interest rate.
(d) a decrease in investment demand, a decrease in saving supply, and a rise in the real interest rate.
(e) an increase in investment demand, an increase in saving supply, and a rise in the real interest rate.

7. When the real interest rate is high following a technological advance,
(a) the supply of labour increases, the labour supply curve shifts rightward, and the level of employment increases.
(b) the marginal product of capital increases, the quantity of capital demanded increases, and the quantity of labour employed decreases.
(c) the marginal product of capital decreases, the quantity of capital demanded decreases, and the quantity of labour employed increases.
(d) the price of capital is too high so production becomes more labour intensive.
(e) the supply of labour increases, the demand for labour decreases, and the real wage rate rises, falls, or remains the same.

8. If the influence of technological change on the marginal product of labour is greater than on intertemporal substitution, then the
(a) production function shifts upward.
(b) real wage rate rises.
(c) production function does not shift.
(d) real wage rate falls.
(e) (a) and (b).

9. When a negative productivity shock occurs,
(a) investment demand decreases, saving supply increases, and the real interest rate rises.
(b) employment decreases and the real wage rate change is ambiguous.
(c) the marginal product of capital decreases and the marginal product of labour increases.
(d) the marginal product of capital increases and the marginal product of labour decreases.
(e) (b) and (c)

10. A technological advance destroys some firms and networks of firms bringing a temporary decrease in productivity. The result is a
(a) decrease in the quantity of labour supplied.
(b) decrease in the quantity of physical capital.
(c) negative productivity shock.
(d) (a) and (b).
(e) (a), (b), and (c).

11. The Solow residual is an estimate of the contribution of
(a) productivity change to the change in capital per person.
(b) the change in capital to productivity change.
(c) change in capital to the change in output.
(d) the change in capital per person to the change in output per person.
(e) productivity change to the change in output.

12. In the Cobb-Douglas production function $y=Zk^{a}n^{1-a}$, the coefficient $a$ is equal to the
(a) the share of real GDP accounted for by income from an increase in labour.
(b) percentage increase in capital arising from a 1 percent increase in labour.
(c) the marginal product of labour.
(d) share of real GDP accounted for by income from capital.
(e) percentage increase in real GDP arising from a 1 percent increase in labour and capital.

13. The Solow residual overestimates the importance of technological change for all of the following reasons except it
(a) includes effects from changes in the composition of the labour force.
(b) includes effects from changes in the composition of output.
(c) does not recognize the fact that the pace of capital accumulation is faster with technological change than without it.
(d) includes effects from variations in the capital utilization rate.
(e) combines many separate influences.

14. Most fluctuations in real GDP per person come from fluctuations in
(a) the Solow residual.
(b) the pace of capital accumulation.

(c) the quantity of labour employed.
(d) the capital utilization rate.
(e) human capital.

15. The more important factors accounting for the decrease in the growth rate of Canadian real GDP during the 1980s and 1990s include all of the following except
(a) composition of output.
(b) population growth.
(c) energy price shocks.
(d) inflation.
(e) composition of the labour force.

## Short Answer Questions

1. What does real business cycle theory seek to explain?
2. How does the pace of technological change effect the capital market and the labour market?
3. Describe what happens to the production function and the saving curve in a real business cycle contraction. Describe capital per person and real GDP per person in the new steady state.
4. Explain why changes in the real interest rate occur during a real business cycle expansion.
5. Why does the supply of labour decrease during a real business cycle contraction?
6. Describe the new steady state following a business cycle expansion.
7. Describe the events that occur when a negative productivity shock occurs.
8. Why does real income per person change?
9. What are the effects of the Solow residual and capital accumulation on real GDP per person?
10. What are two requirements for the real business cycle theory to have merit?

## Problem Solving

### Practice Problems

1. An economy's production function is

$$y = Zk^{a}n^{(1-a)}. \qquad (10.1)$$

Its saving rate is 5 percent and its population is growing at 1 percent a year. $Z$ is 5.

(a) Find the per capita production function.

(b) Find the per capita saving function.

(c) Find the steady-state saving line.

(d) Calculate the steady-state level of capital per person.

(e) Calculate the steady-state level of saving per person.

(f) Calculate the steady-state level of output per person.

### Solutions to Practice Problems

1. (a) Find the per capita production function.
To obtain the per capita production function, divide both sides of equation 10.1 by $n$.

The per capita production function is

$$\frac{y}{n} = Z\left(\frac{k}{n}\right)^{a} = 5\left(\frac{k}{n}\right)^{a}.$$

(b) Find the per capita saving function.

The saving rate is 0.05 so the per capita saving function is

$$\frac{s}{n} = 0.05\frac{y}{n}$$

$$\frac{s}{n} = (0.05)(5)\left(\frac{k}{n}\right)^{a}$$

$$\frac{s}{n} = 0.25\left(\frac{k}{n}\right)^{a}.$$

(c) Find the steady-state saving line.

In a steady state, capital per person is constant. To maintain the capital per person, the saving must be:

$$\frac{s}{n} = \frac{\Delta n}{n}\left(\frac{k}{n}\right).$$

The population growth rate is 1 percent a year, so the steady-state saving line is

$$\frac{s}{n} = 0.01\left(\frac{k}{n}\right).$$

(d) Calculate the steady-state level of capital per person.

The steady-state level of capital is determined where the per capita saving function interests the steady-state saving line.

The per capita saving function is

$$\frac{s}{n} = 0.25\left(\frac{k}{n}\right)^{a}.$$

The steady-state saving line is

$$\frac{s}{n} = 0.01\left(\frac{k}{n}\right).$$

Equating these two formulas gives

$$0.25\left(\frac{k}{n}\right)^{a} = 0.01\left(\frac{k}{n}\right)$$

$$25 = \left(\frac{k}{n}\right)^{1-a}$$

$$\frac{k}{n} = 25^{\frac{1}{1-a}}.$$

(e) Calculate the steady-state level of saving per person.

The steady-state level of saving is the level of saving at the steady-state level of capital. The steady-state level of capital is

$$\frac{k}{n} = 25^{\frac{1}{1-a}}.$$

The per capita saving function is

$$\frac{s}{n} = 0.25\left(\frac{k}{n}\right)^{a}.$$

Substituting the steady-state level of capital into the per capita saving function gives

$$\frac{s}{n} = 0.25(25)^{\frac{a}{1-a}}.$$

(f) Calculate the steady-state level of output per person.

The steady-state level of output per person is the level of output produced by the steady-state level of capital. The steady-state level of capital is

$$\frac{k}{n} = 25^{\frac{1}{1-a}}.$$

The per capita production function is

$$\frac{y}{n} = 5\left(\frac{k}{n}\right)^{a}.$$

Substituting the steady-state level of capital into the per capita production function gives the steady-state level of output.

$$\frac{y}{n} = 5(25)^{\frac{a}{1-a}}.$$

## Problems to Solve

1. An economy's production function is

$$y = Zk^{a}n^{(1-a)}.$$

Its saving rate is 5 percent and its population is growing at 2 percent a year. $Z$ is 10.

(a) Find the per capita production function.

(b) Find the per capita saving function.

(c) Find the steady-state saving line.

(d) Calculate the steady-state level of capital per person.

(e) Calculate the steady-state level of saving per person.

(f) Calculate the steady-state level of output per person.

2. In the economy described in problem 1, $Z$ increases by 10 percent.

(a) Calculate the steady-state level of capital per person.

(b) Calculate the steady-state level of saving

per person.

(c) Calculate the steady-state level of consumption per person.

(d) Calculate the steady-state level of output per person.

(e) What happens to the interest rate when $Z$ increases by 10 percent?

3. In the economy described in problem 1, $Z$ increases by 20 percent and at the same time the population growth rate increases to 5 percent a year. Capital earns one-third of real GDP.

(a) Calculate the steady-state level of capital per person.

(b) Calculate the steady-state level of saving per person.

(c) Calculate the steady-state level of consumption per person.

(d) Calculate the steady-state level of output per person.

4. You are given the following information about an economy:

| Year | Real GDP | Employment | Capital Stock |
|---|---|---|---|
| 1990 | 7.05 | 13.2 | 40 |
| 1991 | 6.92 | 12.9 | 43 |
| 1992 | 7.15 | 12.8 | 46 |
| 1993 | 7.48 | 13.0 | 49 |
| 1994 | 7.69 | 13.3 | 53 |
| 1995 | 7.82 | 13.5 | 57 |
| 1996 | 8.13 | 13.7 | 61 |
| 1997 | 8.38 | 13.9 | 66 |
| 1998 | 8.60 | 14.3 | 71 |

The production function is Cobb-Douglas with constant returns to scale and capital earns one-third of real GDP.

(a) Find the Solow residual for this economy for each year shown in the table.

(b) Describe the contribution of productivity change to the change in output for the years shown in the table.

5. In the economy described in problem 4, the production function is Cobb-Douglas with constant returns to scale and capital earns one- quarter of GDP.

(a) Find the Solow residual for this economy for each year shown in the table.

(b) Compare the Solow residuals calculated in problem 4 and problem 5.

## Answers

### Fill in the Blanks

1. saving, investment, consumption
2. investment, real interest rate, real wage rate
3. population, capital per person
4. upward, upward, increases, increases, increases
5. marginal product of capital
6. rises, falls
7. marginal product of labour
8. intertemporal substitution
9. increases, increases, increases
10. human capital, institutional, network capital
11. negative
12. Solow residual
13. Cobb-Douglas
14. underestimates, faster
15. 1930s, 1940s

### True or False

1F 4T 7F 10F 13F

2F 5T 8F 11T 14T

3T 6F 9T 12T 15F

### Multiple Choice

1c 4b 7a 10c 13c

2a 5d 8b 11e 14a

3d 6e 9b 12d 15b

### Short Answer Questions

1. Real business theory seeks to explain the patterns in real variables such as real GDP, consumption, saving, investment, capital, aggregate hours, and productivity as the consequence of real disturbances.
2. Fluctuations in the pace of technological change occur through the capital market by changing the pace of saving and investment and influencing the real interest and through the labour market by changing the demand for and the supply of labour, employment and the real wage rate.
3. In a real business cycle contraction the production function shifts downward and the saving curve shifts downward. Saving and investment decrease and capital per person and real GDP per person decrease to a new steady state.
4. When the advance in technology occurs, investment demand increases. Because real GDP increases, saving also increases. The saving supply curve and the investment demand curve both shift rightward. The interest rate rises. As real GDP continues to increase, saving supply increases further and the saving supply curve shifts further rightward. During this phase of adjustment the interest rate falls. Eventually the new steady state is reached and the real interest rate is back at its initial level.
5. The source of the decrease in the supply of labour is intertemporal substitution. The real interest rate is low relative to its average level when a negative productivity shock has decreased the marginal product of capital. So working less now and more in the future is a more efficient use of time.
6. The capital stock per person, real GDP per person, and the real wage rate have increased. The real interest rate is unchanged and (possibly) employment is unchanged.
7. The production function shifts downward and the marginal product of capital and marginal product of labour decrease. Investment demand decreases, saving supply decreases, and the real interest rate falls. The demand for labour decreases, the supply of labour decreases, employment decreases, and the real wage rate change is ambiguous.
8. Real income per person can change because capital per person changes or because productivity changes.
9. Most of the fluctuations in real GDP per person come from fluctuations in the Solow residual. Fluctuations arising from fluctuations in the pace of capital accumulation are very small. Capital accumulation has accounted for the ongoing, steady upward drift in real GDP per person.
10. For the real business cycle theory to have merit, it must be the case that

    i. the Solow residual can generate not only the fluctuations in real GDP but also the other features of the cycle and

ii. the Solow residual must be exogenous. It must cause real GDP fluctuations and not itself be caused by real GDP fluctuations.

## Problem Solving

1. (a) $\frac{y}{n} = 10\left(\frac{k}{n}\right)^a$

(b) $\frac{s}{n} = 0.5\left(\frac{k}{n}\right)^a$

(c) $\frac{s}{n} = 0.02\left(\frac{k}{n}\right)$

(d) $\frac{k}{n} = 25^{\frac{1}{1-a}}$

(e) $\frac{s}{n} = 0.5(25)^{\frac{a}{1-a}}$

(f) $\frac{y}{n} = 10(25)^{\frac{a}{1-a}}$

2. (a) $\frac{k}{n} = (27.5)^{\frac{1}{1-a}}$

(b) $\frac{s}{n} = 0.55(27.5)^{\frac{a}{1-a}}$

(c) $\frac{c}{n} = 10.45(27.5)^{\frac{a}{1-a}}$

(d) $\frac{y}{n} = 11(27.5)^{\frac{a}{1-a}}$

(e) When $Z$ increases by 10 percent, the interest rate increases by $a$ times 10 percent.

3. (a) 41.6
(b) 2.08
(c) 39.52
(d) 41.6

4. (a) The Solow residuals for the years 1990 through 1998 are 0.369, 0.359, 0.365, 0.369, 0.365, 0.358, 0.361, 0.358, and 0.352.

(b) The contribution of productivity change to the change in output for the years shown in the table is almost constant, ranging from a low of 0.352 to a high of 0.369.

5. (a) The Solow residuals for the years 1990 through 1998 are 0.404, 0.397, 0.405, 0.413, 0.409, 0.404, 0.409, 0.408, and 0.403.

(b) The Solow residuals calculated in problem 5 are greater than the Solow residuals calculated in problem 4.

**Chapter 11**

# Nominal Rigidity and Short-Run Aggregate Supply

## Perspective and Focus

This chapter studies the microeconomic foundations of aggregate supply and the microeconomic decisions that lie behind the short-run aggregate supply curve.

Macroeconomics is a living science and is in a constant state of change. Most of the research of the past decade has concentrated on the aggregate supply side of the economy and, naturally, economists have tried a variety of alternative approaches. This chapter describes the new classical research program and the new Keynesian research program.

## Learning Objectives

*After studying this chapter, you will be able to:*

- Describe the correlation between real GDP and inflation
- Derive the short-run aggregate supply curve
- Explain the new classical theory of the labour market and the Lucas aggregate supply curve
- Explain the new Keynesian theory of the labour market
- Compare the behaviour of wages over the business cycle with the competing theories of wage determination

## Increasing Your Productivity

In the new classical theory of the labour market, focus on understanding the idea of rational expectations.

The idea of rational expectations lies at the heart of the whole of economics. It was first developed, however, in the context of the new classical theory and the output-inflation tradeoff. However, do not get hung up on the lack of realism of the concept of rational expectations. At one level, it is the only realistic theory there is. People simply do not throw away information. They use information as efficiently as they use any other scarce resource. At another level, the theory is unrealistic. People do not go through the mental processes that you as a student of economics are capable of going through to predict the macroeconomic equilibrium and the price level. But performing that exercise is just the economists way of attempting to *build a model* of the process of expectations formation. A model is a conscious abstraction from reality.

The key to understanding the new Keynesian theory of the labour market is to maintain a sharp distinction between the time at which wage rates are set and the time at which employment is determined. Wage rates are set on the basis of expectations about the demand for and supply of labour. Employment is determined after wage rates have been set and based on the actual state of the economy at the time of the labour demand decision. Keep this distinction in your mind and you will have no trouble understanding the new Keynesian theory. This labour market is set out in section 11.7.

To reinforce your understanding of both the new Keynesian theory of the labour market and the new classical theory of the labour market, it is worth spending a good deal of time studying the differences between the two approaches.

## Self Test

### Fill in the Blanks

1. The output-inflation tradeoff is the relationship between deviations of real GDP from ______ ______ and ______ from its expected level.
2. The ______ the output-inflation tradeoff curve, the larger is the cost of reducing inflation in terms of lost real GDP.
3. The effect of the ______ ______ on the real wage rate makes the short-run aggregate supply curve slope upward.
4. An increase in the money wage rate shifts the short-run aggregate supply curve ______ and an increase in potential GDP shifts the short-run aggregate supply curve ______.
5. The new classical theory of the labour market assumes that the quantity of labour demanded depends on the ______ real wage rate

and the quantity of labour supplied depends on the __________ real wage rate.

6. According to the new classical theory of the labour market, if the actual price level is lower than expected, the money wage rate __________, employment __________, and the real wage rate __________.
7. The __________ __________ shows the maximum real GDP supplied at each price level when, given the expected price level, the labour market is in equilibrium.
8. The __________ expectation of the price level is the price level that is expected on the basis of all __________ __________ available at the time the expectation is formed.
9. The policy ineffectiveness proposition is the proposition that __________ changes in __________ __________ have no effect on real GDP or any other real variable.
10. The new Keynesian theory assumes that money wage rates are set to make the __________ quantity of labour demanded equal the __________ quantity of labour supplied.
11. In the new Keynesian theory, __________ determine the level of employment and employment equals the quantity of labour __________.
12. __________ is the distinct annual round of wage negotiations that occurs each spring in Japan.
13. The Lucas aggregate supply curve is __________ than the new Keynesian aggregate supply curve.
14. The key difference between the new Keynesian and new classical theories of aggregate supply is the behaviour of the __________ __________.
15. A COLA is the component of a wage agreement that makes the rate of wage change over the term of a contract depend on the __________ __________ __________.

### True or False

1. The output-inflation tradeoff is the loss of real GDP resulting from a given percentage increase in inflation.
2. The short-run aggregate supply curve shows the relationship between the quantity of real GDP supplied and the price level when the wage rate and other factor prices are fixed.
3. The relevant price for calculating the real wage rate is the same on both the supply side and demand side of the market in the new classical theory of the labour market.
4. Once incomplete information is introduced into the new classical theory of the labour market, equilibrium in the labour market depends on the price level relative to the expected price level.
5. In the new classical labour market, the money wage rate depends only on the expected price level.
6. If the actual price level is less than the expected price level, then in a new classical labour market, employment exceeds full employment.
7. In the new classical labour market, price level expectations that turn out to be wrong are immediately changed to keep the labour market at a full-employment equilibrium.
8. Along the Lucas aggregate supply curve, the labour market is in equilibrium, given the expected price level.
9. The rational expectation of the price level is the price level that is expected on the basis of all relevant information available at the time the expectation is formed.
10. As an economy moves down along its Lucas aggregate supply curve, the money wage rate decreases and the actual real wage rate increases.
11. As an economy moves up along its Lucas aggregate supply curve, the actual real wage rate decreases and the expected real wage rate increases.
12. The policy ineffectiveness proposition applies to the new Keynesian theory.
13. According to new Keynesian theory, labour markets act like continuous auction markets, with wage rates being frequently adjusted to achieve an ongoing equality between the

quantities of labour supplied and demanded.

14. *Shunto* translates into English as "spring wage defensive."

15. Money wage rates are set in a contract for an agreed period of time before the quantity of labour supplied and demanded is known.

16. If the actual price level is less than the expected price level, then the actual real wage rate in a new Keynesian labour market is higher than in a new classical labour market.

17. In a new Keynesian labour market, the economy can never be at full employment.

18. In the new Keynesian labour market, the economy can never have less than the natural rate of unemployment.

19. The economy is initially at a full-employment equilibrium. An unanticipated increase in aggregate demand decreases the actual real wage rate and by a larger amount if the labour market is new Keynesian rather than new classical.

20. If wage contracts are overlapping, the new Keynesian short-run aggregate supply curve depends on current price expectations, not past price expectations.

## Multiple Choice

1. The slope of the output-inflation tradeoff
(a) is the same in all countries.
(b) shows little variation from country to country.
(c) does not vary from one time period to another.
(d) varies from one time period to another.
(e) (a), (b), and (d).

2. The short-run aggregate supply curve lies to the right of the long-run aggregate supply curve at higher price levels because the
(a) real wage rate is below its full-employment equilibrium level.
(b) real wage rate is above its full-employment equilibrium level.
(c) money wage rate increases as the price level increases.
(d) money wage rate decreases as the price level increases.
(e) (a) and (d)

3. The new classical theory of the labour market assumes that the
(a) quantity of labour demanded depends on the actual real wage rate.
(b) quantity of labour supplied depends on the expected real wage rate.
(c) average money wage rate continually adjusts to achieve labour market equilibrium.
(d) both (a) and (b).
(e) all the above.

4. The proposition that anticipated changes in monetary policy do not have an effect on employment, real GDP, or any other real variable is known as the policy
(a) effectiveness proposition.
(b) anticipation proposition.
(c) ineffectiveness proposition.
(d) defect proposition.
(e) diversion proposition.

**Fact 11.1** Consider an economy with a new classical labour market. Its production function is

$$y = 50 + 13n - 0.1n^2.$$

Its demand for and supply of labour are given by

$$n^d = 65 - 5(W/P)$$

$$n^s = 15 + 7(W/P^e).$$

5. Use Fact 11.1. Full-employment output is
(a) less than 100.
(b) between 101 and 200.
(c) between 201 and 300.
(d) between 301 and 400.
(e) more than 400.

6. Use Fact 11.1. Full-employment level of employment is
(a) less than 15.
(b) between 16 and 25.
(c) between 26 and 40.

(d) between 41 and 50.

(e) more than 50.

7. Use Fact 11.1. The expected price level is 2 and the actual price level is 1. The money wage rate is

(a) less than $2.00.

(b) between $2.10 and $4.00.

(c) between $4.10 and $5.50.

(d) between $5.51 and $6.50.

(e) more than $6.50.

8. Use Fact 11.1. The expected price level is 2 and the actual price level is 1. Employment is

(a) less than 20.

(b) between 21 and 34.

(c) between 35 and 45.

(d) between 46 and 50.

(e) more than 50.

9. Use Fact 11.1. The expected price level is 2 and the actual price level is 1. The expected real wage rate is

(a) less than 3.

(b) between 4 and 6.

(c) between 7 and 10.

(d) between 11 and 15.

(e) more than 15.

**Fact 11.2** Caribou Country has a labour market that is new classical and described by the following equations:

$$n^d = 2{,}000 - 60(W/P)$$

$$n^s = 1{,}000 + 60(W/P).$$

10. Use Fact 11.2. Workers expect the price level to be 2 and the actual price level is 2.5. The money wage rate is

(a )between $10.00 and $12.00.

(b) between $12.00 and $14.00.

(c) between $14.00 and $16.00.

(d) between $16.00 and $18.00.

(e) above $18.00.

11. Use Fact 11.2. Workers expect the price level to be 2 and the actual price level is 2.5. The employment level is

(a) less than 1,400.

(b) between 1,400 and 2,000.

(c) between 2,000 and 2,600.

(d) between 2,600 and 3,400.

(e) more than 3,400.

12. Use Fact 11.2. Workers expect the price level to be 2 and the actual price level is 2.5. The unemployment rate

(a) equals the natural rate of unemployment.

(b) exceeds the natural rate of unemployment.

(c) is less than the natural rate of unemployment.

(d) equals zero.

(e) cannot be determined with the given information.

13. Use Fact 11.2. Workers expect the price level to be 2 and the actual price level is 2.5. The real wage rate

(a) equals its full-employment level.

(b) exceeds its full-employment level.

(c) is less than its full-employment level.

(d) exceeds the expected real wage rate.

(e) both (c) and (d).

14. Which of the following represent the three key assumptions in the new Keynesian theory of the labour market?

(a) Money wage rates are set on a yearly basis, money wage rates are set to make the actual quantity of labour demanded equal to the actual quantity of labour supplied, and the level of employment is determined by the actual demand for labour.

(b) Money wage rates are set for a fixed contract period, money wage rates are set to make the expected quantity of labour demanded equal to the expected quantity of labour supplied, and the level of employment is determined the expected demand for labour.

(c) Money wage rates are set for a fixed contract period, money wage rates are set to make the expected quantity of labour demanded equal to the expected quantity of labour supplied, and the level of employment is determined by the actual demand for labour.

(d) Money wage rates are set every year, money wage rates are set to make the expected quantity of labour demanded equal to the actual quantity of labour supplied, and the level of employment is determined by the actual demand for labour.

(e) Money wage rates are set for a fixed contract period, money wage rates are set to make the actual quantity of labour demanded equal to the expected quantity of labour supplied, and the level of employment is determined by the expected demand for labour.

15. Choose the best statement.

(a) The Lucas aggregate supply curve is steeper than the new Keynesian aggregate supply curve.

(b) The Lucas aggregate supply curve is less steep than the new Keynesian aggregate supply curve.

(c) The Lucas aggregate supply curve is as steep as the new Keynesian aggregate supply curve.

(d) The new Keynesian aggregate supply curve is steeper than the Lucas aggregate supply curve.

(e) none of the above.

16. In the new Keynesian labour market, the money wage rate is set so as to achieve

(a) full employment.

(b) expected labour market equilibrium.

(c) actual labour market equilibrium.

(d) both (a) and (c).

(e) all the above.

**Fact 11.3** Consider an economy with a new Keynesian labour market. The expected price level is 1. The production function, demand for labour, and supply of labour curves are

$$y = 75 + 13n - 0.1n^2$$

$$n^d = 65 - 5\,(W/P)$$

$$n^s = 15 + 7(W/P).$$

17. Use Fact 11.3. Full-employment output is

(a) less than 100.

(b) between 101 and 200.

(c) between 201 and 300.

(d) between 301 and 400.

(e) more than 400.

18. Use Fact 11.3. Full-employment level of employment is

(a) less than 15.

(b) between 16 and 25.

(c) between 26 and 35.

(d) between 36 and 45.

(e) more than 45.

19. Use Fact 11.3. The contracted money wage rate is

(a) less than $1.00.

(b) between $1.10 and $3.00.

(c) between $3.10 and $4.50.

(d) between $4.51 and $5.50.

(e) more than $5.50.

20. Use Fact 11.3. The actual price level turns out to be 2. Employment is

(a) less than 20.

(b) between 21 and 36.

(c) between 37 and 51.

(d) between 52 and 56.

(e) more than 56.

21. Use Fact 11.3. The actual price level turns out to be 2. The actual real wage rate paid is

(a) less than 5.

(b) between 6 and 11.

(c) between 12 and 15.

(d) between 16 and 20.

(e) more than 20.

22. Use Fact 11.3. The actual price level turns out to be 2. The expected real wage rate is

(a) less than 3.

(b) between 4 and 6.

(c) between 7 and 11.

(d) between 12 and 15.

(e) more than 15.

23. Use Fact 11.3. The actual price level turns out to be 0.5. Employment is
(a) less than 20.
(b) between 21 and 26.
(c) between 27 and 31.
(d) between 32 and 35.
(e) more than 35.

24. Use Fact 11.3. The actual price level turns out to be 0.5. The actual real wage rate paid is
(a) less than 5.
(b) between 6 and 11.
(c) between 12 and 15.
(d) between 16 and 20.
(e) more than 20.

25. Use Fact 11.3. The actual price level turns out to be 0.5. The expected real wage rate is
(a) less than 5.
(b) between 6 and 11.
(c) between 12 and 15.
(d) between 16 and 20.
(e) more than 20.

## Short Answer Questions

1. What are the assumptions of the new classical theory of the labour market?
2. What causes the short-run aggregate supply curve to shift?
3. What is the policy ineffectiveness proposition?
4. Explain why the Lucas aggregate supply curve is upward sloping.
5. Explain how an output-inflation tradeoff is generated.
6. What are the three key assumptions in the new Keynesian theory of the labour market?
7. Why is the Lucas aggregate supply curve steeper than the new Keynesian supply curve?
8. Does the policy ineffectiveness proposition apply to the new Keynesian model?
9. What is the relationship between the deviation of real GDP from potential GDP and the inflation rate?
10. What is the role of overlapping wage contracts in the new Keynesian theory?

## Problem Solving

### Practice Problems

1. Sandy Island has a new classical labour market, as described by the following equations:

$$n^d = 200 - 2.5(W/P)$$

$$n^s = 100 + 2.5(W/P).$$

The actual price level is 1 and the expected price level is 0.5.

(a) Calculate the money wage rate.

(b) Calculate the number of people employed.

(c) Calculate the expected real wage rate.

2. Sunny Island has a new Keynesian labour market, as described by the following equations:

$$n^d = 200 - 2.5(W/P)$$

$$n^s = 100 + 2.5(W/P).$$

The actual price level is 1 and the expected price level is 0.5.

(a) Calculate the money wage rate.

(b) Calculate the number of people employed when the price level is 1.

(c) Calculate the expected real wage rate.

### Solutions to Practice Problems

1. (a) Calculate the money wage rate.

Each firm's demand for labour depends on the actual price of its output. So the aggregate demand for labour depends on the actual price level. The supply of labour depends on the expected price level. The equilibrium money wage rate ($W$) is determined by the demand for and supply of labour. That is, it is the money wage rate determined at the intersection of:

$n^d = 200 - 2.5(W/P)$ (11.1)

$n^s = 100 + 2.5(W/P^e)$ (11.2)

where $P$ is the actual price level, and $P^e$ is the expected price level.

But the actual price level is 1, and the expected price level is 0.5. Substituting these values into Equations (11.1) and (11.2) gives

$n^d = 200 - 2.5(W)$ (11.3)

$n^s = 100 + 2.5(W/0.5)$ (11.4)

Solving Equations (11.3) and (11.4) gives $W = \$13.33$.

(b) Calculate the number of people employed.

To calculate the number of people employed ($n$), substitute 13.33 for $W$ in the demand for labour curve—Equation (11.3). That is,

$n = 166.67$.

(c) Calculate the expected real wage rate.

The expected real wage rate equals the money wage rate divided by the expected price level. That is, the

expected wage rate = $W/P^e$

= \$13.33/0.5

= \$26.67.

2. (a) Calculate the money wage rate.

The contract money wage rate ($W$) is determined by the expected demand for labour and the expected supply of labour. That is, it is the money wage rate determined at the intersection of:

$n^d = 200 - 2.5(W/P^e)$ (11.5)

$n^s = 100 + 2.5(W/P^e)$ (11.6)

where $P^e$ is the expected price level.

The expected price level is 0.5. Substituting this value into equations (11.6) and (11.6) gives

$n^d = 200 - 2.5(W/0.5)$ (11.7)

$n^s = 100 + 2.5(W/0.5)$ (11.8)

Solving Equations (11.7) and (11.8) gives $W = \$10$.

(b) Calculate the number of people employed when the price level is 1.

To calculate the number of people employed ($n$), substitute 10 for $W$ in the actual demand for labour curve. That is,

$n^d = 200 - 2.5(W/P)$

$n^d = 200 - 2.5(10)$

$n^d = 175$.

(c) Calculate the expected real wage rate.

The expected real wage rate equals the money wage rate divided by the expected price level. That is, the

expected real wage rate = $W/P^e$

= \$10/0.5

= \$20.

## Problems to Solve

1. Sail Island has a new classical labour market, as described by the following equations:

$n^d = 250 - 2.5(W/P)$

$n^s = 100 + 2.5(W/P)$.

The actual price level is 1.5 and the expected price level is 1.

Calculate the

(a) money wage rate.

(b) expected real wage rate.

(c) actual real wage rate.

(d) number of people employed.

2. Big Wave Island has a new classical labour market, as described by the following equations:

$$n^d = 100 - 5(W/P)$$

$$n^s = 5(W/P).$$

The actual price level is 1.2 and the expected price level is 1.

Calculate the

(a) money wage rate.

(b) expected real wage rate.

(c) actual real wage rate.

(d) number of persons employed.

3. Silly Isle's Lucas aggregate supply curve is

$$y^s = 800 - 250(P^e/P)^2$$

and its aggregate demand curve is

$$y^d = M/P.$$

Calculate

(a) the rational expectation of the price level if the expected money supply is 1,512.5.

(b) the actual price level if the money supply turns out to be 1,769.80.

4. Heron Island's Lucas aggregate supply curve is

$$y^s = 1{,}250 - 50(P^e/P)^2$$

and its aggregate demand curve is

$$y^d = 500 + M/P.$$

Calculate

(a) the rational expectation of the price level if the expected money supply is 500.

(b) the actual real GDP if the money supply turns out to be 400.

**Fact 11.4** Sunny Island has a new classical labour market. It production function is

$$y = 100n - 0.2n^2.$$

Its supply of labour is

$$n^s = 200 + 2.5(W/P).$$

The expected price level is 2.

5. Use Fact 11.4. What is the equation to the demand for labour curve?

6. Use Fact 11.4. Calculate money wage rate and the level of employment if the actual price level is 1.5.

7. Use Fact 11.4. Calculate real GDP if the actual price level is 1.5.

8. Use Fact 11.4. What is the equation to the Lucas aggregate supply curve?

**Fact 11.5** An economy has the following new Keynesian labour market where the demand for labour and the supply of labour are

$$n^d = 250 - 2.5(W/P)$$

$$n^s = 100 + 2.5(W/P).$$

The expected price level is 1.

9. Use Fact 11.5. Calculate the

(a) contract money wage rate.

(b) expected real wage rate.

(c) employment level if the price level turns out to be 1.5.

**Fact 11.6** Sandy Island has a new Keynesian labour market. It production function is

$$y = 100n - 0.2n^2.$$

Its supply of labour is

$$n^s = 200 + 2.5(W/P).$$

The expected price level is 2.

10. Use Fact 11.6. Calculate

(a) the money wage rate if the actual price level is 1.5.

(b) the level of employment if the actual price level is 1.5.

(c) real GDP if the actual price level is 1.5.

(d) the equation to the new Keynesian aggregate supply curve.

## Answers

### Fill in the Blanks

1. potential GDP, inflation
2. flatter
3. price level
4. leftward, rightward
5. actual, expected
6. falls, decreases, rises
7. Lucas aggregate supply curve
8. rational, relevant information
9. anticipated, monetary policy
10. expected, expected
11. firms, demanded
12. *Shunto*
13. steeper
14. money wage rate
15. actual inflation rate

### True or False

1F 5F 9T 13F 17F
2T 6F 10T 14F 18F
3F 7F 11T 15T 19T
4T 8T 12F 16T 20F

### Multiple Choice

1d 6d 11b 16b 21a
2a 7d 12c 17e 22b
3e 8c 13c 18d 23b
4c 9a 14c 19c 24b
5e 10e 15a 20d 25a

### Short Answer Questions

1. The new classical theory of the labour market assumes that the quantity of labour demanded depends on the actual real wage rate; the quantity of labour supplied depends on the expected real wage rate; and the average money wage rate continually adjusts to achieve labour market equilibrium.
2. The short-run aggregate supply curve shifts when the money wage rate changes and when potential GDP changes.
3. The policy ineffectiveness proposition is that

anticipated changes in monetary policy have no effect on real variables, such as real GDP, employment and unemployment. Anticipated policy affects nominal variables only, such as the price level and money wage rate. Their ineffectiveness arises from the fact that although the policy changes the aggregate demand curve, anticipated policy also shifts the short-run aggregate supply curve.

4. The new classical labour market is always in equilibrium, but the equilibrium is only at full employment when the expected price level turns out to be correct. If the actual price level exceeds the expected price level, the actual real wage rate is below its full-employment level and employment exceeds its full-employment level. And as a result, real GDP exceeds its full-employment level. That is, the Lucas aggregate supply curve slopes upward.
5. Suppose that the expected aggregate demand curve shifts upward at a constant rate. A constant inflation rate is expected. Suppose also that the actual aggregate demand curve shifts upward at a varying rate but at an average rate equal to the expected inflation rate. The actual inflation rate will fluctuate around its expected rate. An output-inflation tradeoff is generated along the Lucas aggregate supply curve as aggregate demand fluctuates around its expected level.
6. The three key assumptions in the new Keynesian theory of the labour market are money wage rates are set for a fixed contract period; money wage rates are set to make the expected quantity of labour demanded equal to the expected quantity of labour supplied; and the level of employment is determined by the actual demand for labour.
7. The Lucas aggregate supply curve is steeper than the new Keynesian supply curve because in the new classical model money wage rates adjust to clear the labour market while in the new Keynesian model money wage rates are fixed by contracts.
8. The policy ineffectiveness proposition does not apply to a new Keynesian model because a change in aggregate demand occurring after the wage contract has been signed but before all existing contracts come up for renewal can be reacted to with a policy change in aggregate demand that will take the economy back towards full employment.
9. Other things remaining the same, the greater the deviation of real GDP from potential GDP, the higher is the inflation rate. There is a positive relationship between deviation of real GDP from potential GDP and the inflation rate
10. In the new Keynesian theory, wage contracts overlap so that in any given year, new contracts are being negotiated that cover only a part of the labour force. For this reason, the money wage rate responds to new aggregate demand and the expected price level only slowly.

## Problem Solving

1. (a) \$36
   (b) \$36
   (c) \$24
   (d) 190
2. (a) \$10.91
   (b) \$10.91
   (c) \$9.90
   (d) 54.55
3. (a) 2.75
   (b) 3
4. (a) 0.71
   (b) 1,177
5. $n^d = 250 - 2.5(W/P)$
6. \$17.12, 221.4
7. 12,336
8. $12{,}500 - 2{,}000/(2 + P)^2$
9. (a) \$30
   (b) \$30
   (c) 200
10. (a) \$20
    (b) 216.67
    (c) 12,277
    (d) $y = 12{,}500 - 500/P^2$

## Chapter 12

# Unemployment

## Perspective and Focus

In Chapter 11, you studied the classical theory of the labour market and the Keynesian theory of the labour market and how each theory determines the real wage rate and the level of *employment*. Implicitly, there is a level of *unemployment* lying behind the labour market but in Chapter 11, we did not bring the level of unemployment to the forefront.

Chapter 12 focuses on unemployment. This chapter expands the theory of demand and supply in the labour market and the key feature of the chapter that you need to pay attention to is the distinction between the supply of labour and the labour force.

## Learning Objectives

*After studying this chapter, you will be able to:*

- Describe the patterns in unemployment in Canada and around the world
- Describe Okun's Law
- Explain exactly what unemployment is and how it is measured
- Describe how employment, unemployment, and average work hours fluctuate over the business cycle
- Explain why average work hours fluctuate much less than employment and unemployment
- Explain the meaning of the natural rate of employment and the reasons it fluctuates
- Describe the variations in the natural rate of unemployment since 1970
- Explain why unemployment fluctuates and sometimes rises above its natural rate
- Explain the unemployment during the recession of the early 1990s

## Increasing Your Productivity

One of the key diagrams in this chapter to focus on is Figure 12.7(a). Be sure that you understand how that diagram works. Once you have got it you are ready to race through the analysis in the rest of the chapter. But until you understand how Figure 12.7(a) works you will be wasting your time to move forward. Be sure that you know what the distances *DB* and *AC* mean.

You learnt in Chapter 11 that economists disagree about how the labour market works. But bear in mind when studying this chapter is that although economists do not agree on how quickly wage rates adjust to achieve equilibrium, they do agree about the facts. Nobody denies that there is, on occasion, a high and persistently high unemployment rate. Economists disagree about how to interpret that phenomenon. Those who emphasize wage stickiness believe that to some degree the phenomenon results from the fact that wages are indeed sticky and that they do not always clear the labour market. Economists who emphasize wage flexibility believe that such a phenomenon rises from other real underlying forces that change the natural rate of unemployment.

Although a lot is going on in Figures 12.11(a) and 12.11(b), these figures are two alternative ways of looking at the same phenomenon. They reinforce the point that we have just made about what economists agree and disagree on. Economists agree that the amount of unemployment in 1992 is the amount indicated by the double headed arrow labeled "92" in both parts of the figure. What economists disagree about is exactly how much of that unemployment was "natural" and how much resulted from wages being at a non-market clearing level.

In reviewing this material and understanding it, try to think critically about the two alternative theories and ask yourself the question: what would we have to observe in a real world labour market to reject one or other of these two theories? Nobody has yet found a satisfactory (truly satisfactory) answer to this question but that might not prevent you from putting your mind to it. Students have often found answers to problems that professors have been struggling with for years. In fact, almost all major scientific advance is made by young people whose minds are less rigid than those who have been steeped in the subject for some years.

## Self Test

### Fill in the Blanks

1. People who have no jobs, are willing to work, and are available for work but have stopped searching for work because of their discouraging experience are called ________________.
2. The percentage of the labour force that is ________, ________, and ________ unemployed is the natural rate of unemployment.
3. The ________ ________ is the number of people who are employed and unemployed.
4. When a person is able and willing to work and is available for work but does not have work, that person is ________.
5. The unemployment rate is the number of unemployed people expressed as a percentage of the ________ ________.
6. The number of unemployed people who are searching for a job is ________ unemployment.
7. The number of people who are in the wrong location and have the wrong skills for the available jobs is ________ unemployment.
8. Unemployment that arises because the number of jobs available has decreased because of the season is ________ unemployment.
9. The actual unemployment rate minus its natural rate equals the ________ ________ rate.
10. The ________ ________ is the scale of unemployment benefits divided by the wage rate that a worker can earn.

### True or False

1. During the 1980s and early 1990s, unemployment was not considered to be a serious problem in Canada.
2. Unemployment in the United States and Canada fluctuates in a similar manner but Canadian unemployment became significantly higher than U.S. unemployment in the early 1980s.
3. The unemployment rate in Japan barely fluctuated in the 1980s. It began the decade at 2 percent, rose to a peak of 2.8 percent in 1987, and then fell to 2.1 percent in 1991. During the 1990s Japan's unemployment rate rose to 4.6 percent.
4. The unemployment rate is the number of people unemployed expressed as a percentage of the labour force, where the labour force is the number of people employed plus the number of people unemployed.
5. Discouraged workers are people who do not have jobs, are willing to work, and are available for work but have stopped searching for work because of their discouraging experience.
6. Frictional unemployment is the number of people who are in the wrong location and have the wrong skills for the available jobs.
7. The cyclical unemployment rate is the actual unemployment rate minus its natural rate.
8. The scale of unemployment benefits multiplied by the wage rate a worker can earn is known as the replacement ratio.
9. Minimum wages influence the rate at which unemployed workers can find jobs by increasing the total number of jobs available.
10. The natural rate of unemployment is equal to the sum of frictional unemployment and structural unemployment.
11. Labour market equilibrium is determined where the actual rate of unemployment is equal to the natural rate of unemployment.
12. The actual unemployment rate minus its natural rate is the frictional unemployment rate.
13. The actual unemployment rate minus its natural rate is the structural unemployment rate.
14. Actual unemployment minus the frictional, structural, and seasonal unemployment is cyclical unemployment.
15. Students attending university are counted as being unemployed.
16. Over the business cycle, the number of

persons employed and the average hours they work fluctuate together and fluctuations in the number of people employed account for most of the fluctuations in total hours worked.

17. Households prefer stable work hours because it enables them to use their time efficiently and reduces uncertainty about future income.

18. On Shell Island, the rate of job loss is 1 percent and the rate of finding a job is 24 percent. Shell Island's natural rate of unemployment is 4 percent.

19. On Turtle Island more people are employed than are unemployed, and the rate at which jobs are being lost is less than the rate at which jobs are being found. Turtle Island's natural rate of unemployment is decreasing.

20. An increase in unemployment benefits decreases the value placed on job search by each person in the labour force because the opportunity cost of searching for a job has decreased.

## Multiple Choice

1. The types of unemployment include:

(a) frictional unemployment.
(b) structural unemployment.
(c) cyclical unemployment.
(d) discouraged unemployment.
(e) (a), (b), and (c).

2. The number of people counted as unemployed increases as a result of

(a) new entrants.
(b) job losers.
(c) job finders.
(d) discouraged workers.
(e) both (a) and (b).

3. Which of the following equations represents the change in unemployment ($\Delta U$)?

(a) $U = \ell E + fU$.
(b) $U = \ell E / fU$.
(c) $U = \ell E \times fU$.
(d) $U = \ell E - fU$.
(e) $U = fU - \ell E$.

4. In Canada, fluctuations in average work hours are

(a) smaller and their relationship to fluctuations in real GDP stronger than fluctuations in the number of persons employed.
(b) larger and their relationship to fluctuations in real GDP weaker than fluctuations in the number of persons employed.
(c) smaller and their relationship to fluctuations in real GDP weaker than fluctuations in the number of persons employed.
(d) larger and their relationship to fluctuations in real GDP stronger than fluctuations in the number of persons employed.
(e) none of the above.

5. Which of the following factors influence the outcome of job search and determine the rate at which unemployed workers find jobs? The

(a) scale of unemployment benefits.
(b) minimum wage.
(c) degree of structural mismatch between the skills of the unemployed and of the jobs available.
(d) Social security benefits.
(e) (a), (b), and (c).

6. Between 1990 and 1992, the Canadian economy contracted severely because of

(a) widespread and severe shocks to aggregate supply.
(b) restrictive monetary policy.
(c) expansionary monetary policy.
(d) a favourable supply shock (a decline in the oil price).
(e) both (a) and (b).

7. Craig Riddell of the University of British Columbia and David Card of Princeton University believe that

(a) easier eligibility of unemployment insurance in Canada accounts for most of the unemployment gap between Canada and the United States.
(b) the natural rate of unemployment in Canada and the United States should be equal.
(c) aggregate supply shocks are responsible for a higher rate of employment in Canada than in

the United States.

(d) a higher real exchange rate in Canada than in the United States in the 1980s is responsible for Canada's higher unemployment rate today.

(e) unemployment benefits in Canada are partly but not wholly responsible for the unemployment gap between Canada and the United States.

8. The rate of job loss is influenced by all of the following factors *except*

(a) the scale of unemployment benefits.

(b) technological change.

(c) the phase of the business cycle.

(d) changes in international competitiveness.

(e) changes in regional effects.

9. At the natural rate of unemployment, all unemployment is

(a) frictional.

(b) cyclical.

(c) structural.

(d) seasonal

(e) (a), (c), and (d)

10. Which of the following publishes standardized unemployment rates for the major countries?

(a) International Bank for Reconstruction and Development.

(b) International Monetary Fund.

(c) Organization for Economic Cooperation and Development.

(d) Bank of Canada.

(e) Statistics Canada.

11. When a discouraged worker starts to look for work again and becomes unemployed the

(a) unemployment rate increases.

(b) unemployment rate decreases.

(c) unemployment rate does not change.

(d) size of the labour force decreases.

(e) number of job losers increases.

12. A decrease in aggregate demand when money wage rates are sticky

(a) increases employment and decreases unemployment.

(b) decreases employment and increases unemployment.

(c) increases both employment and unemployment.

(d) decreases both employment and unemployment.

(e) has no effect on employment and unemployment.

13. A decrease in productivity decreases the demand for labour. If money wage rates are flexible, then

(a) employment and unemployment decrease.

(b) the real wage rate and employment increase and unemployment decreases.

(c) the real wage rate decreases and employment decreases.

(d) the real wage rate is unchanged.

(e) employment and unemployment are unchanged.

14. The value placed on job search

(a) by the marginal person employed is less than the value placed on job search by the marginal person in the labour force.

(b) by the marginal person employed is more than the value placed on job search by the marginal person in the labour force.

(c) by the marginal person employed increases as the labour force grows.

(d) by the marginal person in the labour force decreases as the labour force grows.

(e) none of the above.

15. Unemployment decreases if

(a) the flow of new entrants and job losers is less than the flow of retirees and job finders.

(b) more people become discouraged about the prospect of finding a job.

(c) the rate of job loss decreases and the rate at which jobs are found increases.

(d) the rate of job changers is greater than the sum of the rate of job loss and the rate at which jobs are found.

(e) both (b) and (c).

16. All the following people are in the labour force *except*

(a) A person who is not looking for a job, but has a new job starting in one week from now.

(b) A person who is not looking for a job, but already has a job.

(c) A person who does not have a job, but has been looking for a job for the past six months.

(d) A person who has a job.

(e) A person who wants a job but has given up looking because the wage rate is too low.

17. The natural rate of unemployment is equal to the rate at which people

(a) lose jobs plus the rate at which people find jobs.

(b) find jobs minus the rate at which people lose jobs.

(c) find and lose jobs divided by the rate at which people find jobs.

(d) lose jobs divided by the rate at which people lose and find jobs.

(e) none of the above.

18. The horizontal distance between the labour force curve and the labour supply curve measures

(a) unemployment of discouraged workers.

(b) cyclical unemployment.

(c) natural unemployment.

(d) structural unemployment.

(e) actual unemployment.

19. The vertical distance between the labour force curve and the labour supply curve measures

(a) the real wage rate.

(b) the value placed on job search.

(c) unemployment benefits.

(d) the cost of job search plus unemployment benefits.

(e) actual unemployment.

20. The labour force curve describes how the

(a) number of persons willing to work remains constant as the real wage rate varies.

(b) number of persons working or seeking work varies as the real wage rate varies.

(c) number of people willing to search for a job varies as the real wage rate varies.

(d) the number of people willing to search for a job varies as the real wage rate remains constant.

(e) none of the above.

## Short Answer Questions

1. In general, why are stable hours preferred by

   (a) households?

   (b) firms?

2. Explain Okun's Law.

3. Explain the difference between frictional unemployment and structural unemployment.

4. Why does unemployment fluctuate and sometimes rise above its natural rate?

5. What factors influence the rate of job loss?

6. What is meant by "startup costs?"

7. How does Statistics Canada define people as being unemployed?

8. (a) How is the job-finding rate determined?

   (b) What is the cost of job search?

   (c) What is the benefit from job search?

   (d) What are the three factors that influence the outcome of job search and determine the rate at which unemployed workers find jobs?

9. What is the disagreement about how fluctuations in the actual unemployment rate decompose into fluctuations in the natural rate of unemployment and fluctuations in cyclical unemployment?

10. (a) How is unemployment data collected in Canada?

    (b) Who is not included in the measured unemployment rate?

Problem Solving

**Practice Problems**

1. You have the following information about Turtle Island:

Demand for labour: $n^d = 90 - 1.5(W/P)$

Supply of labour: $n^s = 0.75(W/P)$

Supply of job search: $j^s = 0.25(W/P)$.

(a) Calculate the equilibrium real wage rate.

(b) Calculate the equilibrium level of employment.

(c) Calculate the equilibrium labour force.

(d) Calculate the equilibrium level of unemployment.

(e) Calculate the value placed on job search by the last person employed.

(f) Calculate the value placed on job search by the last person to join the labour force.

**Solutions to Practice Problems**

1. (a) Calculate the equilibrium real wage rate.

The equilibrium real wage rate is the $(W/P)$ determined by the intersection of the demand for labour and supply of labour curves.

$$n^d = 90 - 1.5(W/P) \qquad (12.1)$$

$$n^s = 0.75(W/P) \qquad (12.2)$$

Solving Equations (12.1) and (12.2) gives $(W/P) = 40$.

(b) Calculate the equilibrium level of employment.

The number of people employed at the equilibrium real wage rate of 40 can be found by substituting 40 for $(W/P)$ in either Equation (12.1) or (12.2). The equilibrium level of employment is 30.

(c)Calculate the equilibrium labour force.

The number of people in the labour force is equal to the number employed plus the number who are job searching. That is, at any real wage rate the labour force is equal to the quantity of labour supplied (willing to take a job without further search) plus the quantity of job searchers.

The equation to the labour force curve is

$$lf = n^s + j^s$$

$$lf = 0.75(W/P) + 0.25(W/P)$$

$$lf = (W/P).$$

At the equilibrium real wage rate of 40, the labour force is 40.

(d) Calculate the equilibrium level of unemployment.

The equilibrium level of unemployment is the labour force minus the level of employment, which equals the level of job search.

Unemployment = $0.25(W/P)$

Unemployment = 10.

(e) Calculate the value placed on job search by the last person employed.

The last person employed is the 30th person. This person is willing to join the labour force and search for a job at a real wage rate given by the labour force curve. It is the real wage rate that makes the labour force equal to 30. That is,

$$lf = (W/P)$$

$$30 = (W/P).$$

This person is willing to take a job at a real wage rate of 40. So the value placed on job search by the last person employed is equal to 40 – 30, which is 10.

(f) Calculate the value placed on job search by the last person to join the labour force.

The last person in the labour force is the 40th person. This person is willing to join the labour force and search for a job at a real wage rate of 40.

This person is willing to take a job at a real wage rate equal to that which makes the quantity of labour supplied equal to 40. That is,

$$n^s = 0.75(W/P)$$

$$40 = 0.75(W/P)$$

$(W/P) = 53.33.$

This person is willing to take a job at a real wage rate of 53.33. So the value placed on job search by the last person to join the labour force is equal to 53.33 – 40, which is 13.33.

## Problems to Solve

1. You are given the following information concerning the demand for labour, supply of labour, and supply of job search:

$n^d = 10 - 0.5(W/P)$

$n^s = 0.5(W/P)$

$j^s = 0.1(W/P)$.

At the equilibrium, calculate

(a) the real wage rate.

(b) employment.

(c) labour force.

(d) unemployment.

(e) the value placed on job search by the last person employed.

(f) the value placed on job search by the last person to join the labour force.

2. In Problem 1, the government introduces a minimum wage and the real wage rate increases to 12.

At the equilibrium, calculate the

(a) labour force.

(b) quantity of labour supplied.

(c) level of employment.

3. You are given the following information concerning the demand for labour, supply of labour, and labour force:

$n^d = 100 - 4(W/P)$

$n^s = 6(W/P)$

$L = 8(W/P)$.

At the equilibrium, calculate

(a) the real wage rate and the level of employment.

(b) the size of the labour force.

(c) the natural rate of unemployment.

(d) the value placed on job search by the last person employed.

(e) the value placed on job search by the last person to join the labour force.

4. In Problem 3, if the government introduces a minimum wage that has the effect of increasing the economy's average real wage rate by 5 percent, calculate

(a) the equilibrium real wage rate and the level of employment.

(b) the size of the labour force.

(c) the unemployment rate

5. An economy has 100 competitive firms and each firm has the following short-run production function where $n$ is employment and $y$ is real GDP:

| $n$ | 1 | 2 | 3 | 4 | 5 | 6 | 7 |
|---|---|---|---|---|---|---|---|
| $y$ | 50 | 95 | 135 | 170 | 200 | 225 | 245 |

The labour market of an economy is described by the following schedule.

| $(W/P)$ | 8 | 10 | 12 | 15 | 18 | 20 |
|---|---|---|---|---|---|---|
| $n$ | 200 | 300 | 400 | 500 | 600 | 700 |

At the equilibrium, calculate

(a) the real wage rate.

(b) employment.

(c) real GDP.

## Answers

### Fill in the Blanks

1. discouraged workers
2. frictionally, structurally, seasonally
3. labour force
4. unemployed
5. labour force
6. frictional
7. structural
8. seasonal
9. cyclical unemployment
10. replacement rate

### True or False

1F 5T 9F 13F 17T
2T 6F 10F 14T 18T
3T 7T 11F 15F 19F
4T 8F 12F 16T 20F

### Multiple Choice

1e 5e 9e 13c 17d
2e 6e 10c 14e 18c
3d 7e 11a 15e 19b
4c 8a 12b 16e 20b

### Short Answer Questions

1. (a) Stable hours are preferred by households because it enables them to allocate time efficiently, reduce income uncertainty, and minimize startup costs.

   (b) With stable hours, firms are able to obtain optimal work effort and organize team production more efficiently.
2. Okun's Law states that the higher the level of real GDP as a percentage of potential GDP, the lower is the unemployment rate.
3. Frictional unemployment is the number of people who are searching for a job. These people are new entrants into the labour force and those who have re-entered the labour force or voluntarily quit their jobs to search for a better one.

   Structural unemployment is the number of people who are in the wrong location and have the wrong skills for the available jobs.
4. Unemployment can fluctuate either because of a change in the natural rate of unemployment or because of a change in cyclical unemployment. An increase in the rate of job loss or a decrease in the rate of job finding shifts the labour supply curve to the left and the natural rate of unemployment increases.

   A decrease in aggregate demand that decreases the price level increases the real wage rate. If money wage rate is sticky, the real wage rate rises. The quantity of labour demanded is less than the quantity of labour supplied and unemployment increases above the natural rate.
5. The rate of job less is influenced by technological change, changes in international competitiveness, changes in regional effects, and phase of the business cycle.
6. Startup costs are the costs associated with beginning an activity. The startup costs of working include the costs of both time and transportation to and from work. These costs have to be borne whether a person works for one hour or ten hours a day.
7. Statistics Canada defines the following people as being unemployed:

   Those who did not work during a specific week (called the reference week), made specific efforts to find a job within the 4 previous weeks, and were available for work during the reference week.

   Also counted as unemployed are the people who did not work at all during the reference week, were available for work, and were waiting either to be called back to a job from which they had been laid off for 26 weeks or less or to report to a new job within 4 weeks.
8. (a) The job-finding rate is determined by each unemployed worker's decision to stop looking for a better job and accept the best job currently available.

   (b) The cost of job search is the loss of wages while unemployed minus any unemployment benefit received.

   (c) The benefit from job search is the expected higher wage rate that might be obtained from looking longer and harder for a better job than what is currently available.

   (d) The three main factors that influence the outcome of job search and determine the rate at which unemployed workers find jobs are the scale of unemployment benefits, the minimum wage, and the degree of structural mismatch between the unemployed and jobs available.

9. Some economists believe that the natural rate of unemployment fluctuates very little and that most of the fluctuations in actual unemployment are fluctuations in cyclical unemployment.
   Another view is that most of the fluctuations in unemployment are deviations from the natural rate but that the natural rate increased during the 1970s, 1980s, and early 1990s and then decreased during the rest of the 1990s.
10. (a) Unemployment data are based on a survey of households called the Labour Force Survey. Each month about 59,000 households across Canada are interviewed.
   (b) Discouraged workers and part-time workers who want full-time employment are excluded from those counted as unemployed.

## Problem Solving

1. (a) $10
   (b) 5
   (c) 6
   (d) 1
   (e) $1.67
   (f) $2
2. (a) 7.2
   (b) 6
   (c) 4
3. (a) real wage rate = $10
   employment = 60
   (b) 80
   (c) 20
   (d) $2.50
   (e) $3.33
4. (a) real wage rate = $10.50
   employment = 58
   (b) 84
   (c) 0.31
5. (a) $20
   (b) 700
   (c) 24,500

Chapter 13

# Inflation, Interest Rates, and the Exchange Rate

## Perspective and Focus

At this point of your study of macroeconomics you have completed the basic theoretical framework. You now understand the theory of aggregate demand and aggregate supply and much of what lies behind those concepts and relationships. This chapter and the next two begin to apply what you have learnt—to study macroeconomic issues and problems using the tools of macroeconomic theory.

This chapter focuses on inflation at full employment. It studies the determination of the rate of change of the price level, the interest rate, and the exchange rate. It doesn't worry about the simultaneous fluctuation in aggregate activity that may accompany the inflation. You can think of this chapter as explaining the trend in inflation but not the cycles and fluctuations in its rate.

## Learning Objectives

*After studying this chapter, you will be able to:*

- Describe inflation, interest rates, and money growth around the world in the 1990s
- Explain the effects of an anticipated increase in the money supply growth rate on inflation and real GDP
- Illustrate the effects of anticipated inflation with Israel's experience
- Explain the effects of inflation on interest rates
- Illustrate the effects of inflation on interest rates with Switzerland's and Brazil's experiences
- Explain how inflation is determined in a fixed exchange rate economy
- Illustrate inflation in a fixed exchange rate economy with the experiences of the major countries in the 1960s and the countries of the euro area in the 1980s and 1990s
- Explain how inflation is determined in a flexible exchange rate economy
- Illustrate inflation in a flexible exchange rate economy with the world inflationary experience of the 1980s and 1990s

## Increasing Your Productivity

A key thing to keep at the front of your mind when studying this chapter is the fundamental difference between a fixed exchange rate and a flexible exchange rate economy when it comes to understanding the forces that determine inflation and interest rates.

With a fixed exchange rate, a country has no choice but to accept the inflation and interest rates that the rest of the world throws at it. With a flexible exchange rate, a country has complete freedom to set its own course independently of what is happening in the rest of the world.

With this lesson and basic understanding in mind you will have no difficulty in working through the analysis of this chapter. But there is just one other thing that you need to pay attention to—the chapter studies *inflation*, not the determination of the *price level*.

The *AD-AS* model has the price level on the vertical axis and so the process of inflation can only be captured in such a model with the *AD* curve and *AS* curve constantly shifting and intersecting at higher and higher price levels. It is inconvenient, as well as a waste of ink and paper, to draw the *AD* curve forever shifting upward. Therefore in the figures in the text, we shift them just once. This gives the impression that we are talking about only an increase in the price level. You must always remember that this is just a convenience. The process is ongoing. The curves never stop moving in a real-world situation.

## Self Test

### Fill in the Blanks

1. The expected inflation rate is the __________ __________ __________ for some future period.
2. A forecast about the future value of an economic variable made using all available information is a __________ __________.
3. __________ __________ is a process in which the price level is increasing at rates

forecasted by all the economic actors.

4. ___________ ___________ is a process in which the price level increases at a pace that has been incorrectly forecast to some degree.

5. The proposition that a change in the growth rate of the money supply brings an equal percentage change in the ___________ is called the ___________ ___________ ___________ ___________.

6. The equation of exchange states that the quantity of money multiplied by the ___________ ___________ equals ___________.

7. Arbitrage is the process of ___________ and ___________ ___________.

8. The ___________ ___________ ___________ was an agreement among some members of the European Union to promote exchange rate stability.

9. The ___________ ___________ ___________ was a system of fixed exchange rates between the currencies of some members of the European Monetary System.

10. The ___________ Agreement was an agreement among ___________ major nations to bring national monetary policies into closer harmony, thereby reducing the amount of exchange rate volatility.

True or False

1. Inflation is a process of rising prices and the inflation rate is measured as the percentage change in a price index.

2. The actual inflation rate plays an important role in determining the rate of wage increase and wage increases influence the expected inflation rate.

3. By definition, the money supply growth rate plus the velocity growth rate equals the inflation rate plus the real GDP growth rate.

4. The Plaza Agreement was an agreement to bring national monetary policies into closer harmony with each other, thereby lowering the degree of exchange rate volatility.

5. With unanticipated inflation, the actual inflation rate is equal to the expected inflation rate.

6. The equilibrium real wage rate is the real wage rate when the unemployment rate equals the natural rate of unemployment.

7. The higher the expected inflation rate, the higher is the equilibrium quantity of real money balances.

8. A country with a fixed exchange rate is able to control its money supply growth rate.

9. The fundamental relationship that influences inflation in a fixed exchange rate economy is purchasing power parity.

10. The United Kingdom was one of the main members of the European Monetary System.

11. An equal percentage increase in the money supply and the price level shifts the *LM* curve to the right.

12. A rational expectation is a forecast made about the future value of an economic variable that is correct.

13. The equation of exchange states that the quantity of money multiplied by the velocity of circulation equals total expenditure.

14. The European Monetary System was a system of managed floating exchange rates.

15. Suppose that a slice of cheesecake can be purchased for £2.50 in England and for 480 yen in Japan. Purchasing parity holds if the exchange rate is 192 yen per pound.

16. The inflation rate in an open economy is determined by the domestic money supply growth if the exchange rate is fixed.

17. If the price level on Sandy Island is increasing at 10 percent a year and the price level in the rest of the world is increasing at 8 percent a year, then the value of the Sandy Island dollar against all other currencies is appreciating by 2 percent a year.

18. Christmas Island has a fixed exchange rate. Therefore it cannot choose its money supply growth rate and inflation rate independent of the rest of the world.

19. When a country has a flexible exchange rate,

other things remaining the same, an increase in the money supply growth rate increases the inflation rate and decreases the rate of depreciation of the country's currency.

20. The overshooting proposition holds because an increase in the money supply growth rate shifts the *LM* curve to the right, increases aggregate demand and increases the inflation rate. The inflation rate increases quickly and returns the *LM* curve to its original position.

## Multiple Choice

1. Inflation is a process of rising prices and the inflation rate is measured as the percentage change in a price index such as the
(a) Consumer Price Index.
(b) GDP deflator.
(c) Producer Price Index.
(d) Real Price Index.
(e) both (a) and (b).

2. The point of intersection of the *IS* and *LM* curves determines the equilibrium
(a) interest rate and equilibrium level of real GDP at various price levels.
(b) price level and equilibrium level of real GDP at various interest rates.
(c) interest rate and equilibrium price level at various equilibrium levels of real GDP.
(d) interest rate and equilibrium level of real GDP at a given price level.
(e) interest rate for various levels of real GDP and price levels.

3. The money wage rate is the real wage rate
(a) multiplied by the price level.
(b) divided by the price level.
(c) minus the price level.
(d) plus the price level.
(e) factored by the price level.

4. A forecast about the future value of an economic variable made using all the available information is called
(a) an adaptive expectation.
(b) a random expectation.
(c) an irrational expectation.
(d) a rational expectation.
(e) a steady-state expectation.

5. A process in which the price level increases at a pace that has been incorrectly forecast to some degree is known as
(a) anticipated inflation.
(b) unanticipated inflation.
(c) hyperinflation.
(d) autocorrelated inflation.
(e) erroneous inflation.

6. The equation stating that the quantity of money multiplied by the velocity of circulation equals total expenditure is called the
(a) Liquidity Equation.
(b) Speculative Equation.
(c) Transactions Equation.
(d) Equation of Exchange.
(e) Oxford Equation.

7. Planned investment depends not only on the
(a) interest rate but also on the unanticipated inflation rate.
(b) unemployment rate but also on the unanticipated inflation rate.
(c) exchange rate but also on the anticipated inflation rate.
(d) interest rate but also on the anticipated inflation rate.
(e) saving rate but also on the unanticipated inflation rate.

8. If the money supply growth rate exceeds the inflation rate, the
(a) *IS* curve is shifting to the left.
(b) *IS* curve is shifting to the right.
(c) *LM* curve is shifting to the left.
(d) *LM* curve is shifting to the right.
(e) *LM* curve is not shifting to the right or the left.

9. If goods are cheaper in one country than in another, it will pay people to purchase goods in the country where they are cheap and sell goods in the country where they are more expensive. Such a process known as

(a) arbitrage.
(b) circulation.
(c) trade targeting.
(d) quota circumvention.
(e) none of the above.

10. A system of fixed exchange rates between the currencies of some members of the EMS was known as the
(a) International Monetary System.
(b) Plaza Monetary System.
(c) Rational Agreement.
(d) Exchange Rate Mechanism.
(e) International Monetary Fund Agreement.

11. If the price level increases by the same percentage rate as the increase in the money supply, then the *LM* curve
(a) shifts to the right.
(b) shifts to the left.
(c) becomes vertical.
(d) becomes horizontal.
(e) does not shift.

12. Seal Isle's inflation rate is 10 percent a year, while inflation in the rest of the world is 12 percent a year. Seal Isle's currency is
(a) appreciating by 2 percent a year.
(b) depreciating by more than 2 percent a year.
(c) depreciating by 2 percent a year.
(d) appreciating by more than 2 percent a year.
(e) none of the above.

13. A country with a flexible exchange rate
(a) cannot choose its money supply and inflation rate independent of the rest of the world.
(b) cannot choose its inflation rate but it can choose its money supply growth rate independent of the rest of the world.
(c) keeps the value of the exchange rate constant and so insulates the domestic economy from inflation in the rest of the world.
(d) can choose its money supply and inflation independent of the rest of the world.
(e) can choose its inflation rate independent of the rest of the world but not its money supply growth rate.

14. In a country with a fixed exchange rate
(a) domestic inflation is equal to inflation in the rest of the world.
(b) the country uses its monetary policy to peg the value of its money in terms of foreign money.
(c) the appreciation of the exchange rate is equal to the inflation rate in the rest of the world minus the inflation rate in the domestic economy.
(d) the value of the exchange rate is determined by domestic monetary policy but not rest-of-world monetary policy.
(e) both (a) and (b).

15. Windy Island's inflation rate is 12 percent a year and its long-run real GDP growth rate is 5 percent a year. A change in Windy Island's money supply growth rate to 9 percent a year changes its inflation rate in the long-run to
(a) less than or equal to 13 percent a year.
(b) more than 13 percent a year and less than or equal to 14 percent a year.
(c) more than 14 percent a year and less than 15 percent a year.
(d) 15 percent a year.
(e) more 15 percent a year.

16. Cactus Country increases its money supply growth rate by 10 percent and everyone anticipates the increase. As a result,
(a) the money wage rate does not change.
(b) the money wage rate increases by 10 percent.
(c) its *LM* curve does not shift.
(d) its *IS* curve shifts to the left.
(e) none of the above.

17. When the money supply growth rate decreases, the inflation rate responds more quickly, the faster
(a) the real money supply increases.
(b) expectations change.
(c) the money wage rate changes.
(d) both (b) and (c).
(e) none of the above.

18. An anticipated increase in the money supply growth rate from 4 percent a year to 10 percent a year, increases the inflation rate in the long run by
(a) 4 percentage points.
(b) more than 6 percentage points.
(c) between 1 and 4 percentage points.
(d) 6 percentage points.
(e) none of the above.

19. The assumptions that turn the equation of exchange into the quantity theory of money include
(a) a constant price level.
(b) a constant velocity of circulation.
(c) real GDP growth independent of money supply growth.
(d) both (b) and (c).
(e) all the above.

20. The position of the *IS* curve depends on the
(a) saving rate.
(b) interest rate.
(c) exchange rate and on the expected inflation rate.
(d) unemployment rate and the unanticipated inflation rate.
(e) expected inflation rate.

## Short Answer Questions

1. Briefly explain the Exchange Rate Mechanism of the European Monetary System.

2. Briefly summarize how inflation is determined

   (a) in a fixed exchange rate regime.

   (b) in a flexible exchange rate regime.

3. What is the difference between anticipated inflation and unanticipated inflation?

4. (a) What is a rational expectation?

   (b) What are two important properties of a rational expectation?

5. What is the difference between the equilibrium real wage rate and the money wage rate?

6. (a) Was inflation in Israel in the 1980s anticipated or unanticipated?

   (b) What happened during the 1980s to real GDP growth in Israel?

7. (a) What is arbitrage?

   (b) How long will arbitrage transpire?

8. From 1945 to the early 1970s, what exchange rate system was adopted by the

   (a) Canada?

   (b) rest of the world?

9. Explain why anticipated inflation affects the *IS* curve.

10. Explain how anticipated inflation affects the *LM* curve.

## Problem Solving

### Practice Problems

1. You are given the following information about Placid Isle's short-run aggregate supply and aggregate demand curves:

   $y^s = -100 + 100P$

   $y^d = 300 - 100P.$

   (a) Calculate real GDP.

   (b) The money supply increases by 5 percent and this increase is expected. Calculate the price level.

   (c) Calculate the equation to the new short-run aggregate supply curve.

2. The money supply growth rate is 6 percent a year and inflation is also 6 percent a year. Now the money supply starts to grow at 10 percent a year and this increase in the money supply growth rate is expected to continue forever.

   (a) How does the increase in the money supply growth rate change the *LM* and *IS* curves?

   (b) What is the path of inflation?

   (c) What is the change in the interest rate?

**Solutions to Practice Problems**

1. (a) Calculate real GDP.

Real GDP is determined at the intersection of aggregate demand curve and the short-run aggregate supply curve. Solving the equations to the *AD* and *SAS* curves for *y* gives real GDP equal to 100.

(b) The money supply increases by 5 percent and this increase is expected. Calculate the price level.

A 5 percent increase in the money supply shifts the *AD* curve upward by 5 percent. But the increase is expected, so the money wage rate increases by 5 percent, shifting the *SAS* curve upward by 5 percent. The price level increases by 5 percent to 2.1.

(c) Calculate the equation to the new short-run aggregate supply curve.

The short-run aggregate supply curve shifts upward by 5 percent. To calculate the equation to the new *SAS* curve, notice that any level of real GDP will now be supplied only at a price level that is 5 percent higher. Begin by writing the equation to the original *SAS* curve as

$P = (y^s + 100)/100.$

The money supply has increased, so the price level at which any value of *y* will now be supplied is 5 percent higher. That is,

$P = 1.05(y^s + 100)/100.$

Re-arranging, the equation to the new *SAS* curve gives

$y^s = -100 + 95.24P.$

2. (a) How does the increase in the money supply growth rate change the *LM* and *IS* curves?

The *LM* curve shifts to the left. An increase in the growth rate of the money supply would shift the *LM* curve to the right. But the increase in the growth rate of the money supply is expected, so inflation increases immediately, and the quantity of real money demanded decreases. But the price level rises, which decreases the quantity of real money supplied. The price level rises to make the quantity of real money supplied equal to the quantity of real money demanded. With the quantity of real money less than initially, the new *LM* curve is to the left of the original *LM* curve.

The *IS* curve shifts to the right. Firms, expecting higher inflation, are now willing to invest at higher interest rates. Firms increase their investment demand. The increase in investment shifts the *IS* curve to the right. If inflation is expected to remain at 10 percent a year, the size of the shift of the *IS* curve, measured in the vertical direction, is 4 percentage points.

(b) What is the path of inflation?

The inflation rate jumps from 6 percent a year to above 10 percent a year, but then decreases to 10 percent a year and then remains at 10 percent a year.

(c) What is the change in the interest rate?

The interest rate rises by 4 percentage points.

## Problems to Solve

1. The money supply is increasing at 5 percent a year and anticipated inflation is 5 percent a year. What is happening to

   (a) real GDP?

   (b) the price level?

   (b) aggregate demand?

   (c) short-run aggregate supply?

2. When the inflation rate is expected to be zero, an investment project is just profitable at an interest rate of 5 percent a year. Would this investment project still be profitable when the interest rate is 10 percent a year and the price level is expected to rise by 5 percent a year?

3. Initially the anticipated inflation rate is 5 percent a year. If expectations are revised—the money supply growth rate is anticipated to be cut by 5 percentage points a year, explain what happens to the interest rate.

4. Windy Isle adopts a fixed exchange rate.

   (a) Explain what determines the inflation rate on Windy Isle.

   (b) Explain the effect of its inflation on the

money supply growth rate on Windy Isle.

5. What is the effect on inflation of an anticipated change in the money supply growth rate of 10 percent.

6. The inflation rate is expected to be 10 percent a year. What is the effect on the *LM* curve of this expected inflation rate.

**Fact 13.1** Shark Island's real GDP growth rate is constant at 4 percent a year. Its inflation rate is constant at 4 percent a year, and its velocity of circulation is constant at 10.

7. Use Fact 13.1. Calculate the growth rate of Shark Island's money supply.

8. Use Fact 13.1. Shark Island doubles its money supply growth rate and the increase is anticipated. Calculate Shark Island's new long-run inflation rate.

9. Use Fact 13.1. Shark Island doubles its money supply growth rate and the increase is anticipated. Describe the path of Shark Island's inflation rate back to equilibrium.

10. Snake Island is an open economy and its exchange rate is flexible. It has the following short-run aggregate supply and aggregate demand curves:

$y^s = -3{,}500 + 250P$

$y^d = 5{,}000 - 250P.$

The government of Snake Island increases its money supply by 6 percent and this increase is expected. What are the equations for the new
(a) *AD* curve?
(b) *SAS* curves?

## Answers

### Fill in the Blanks

1. forecasted inflation rate
2. rational expectation
3. Anticipated inflation
4. Unanticipated inflation
5. inflation rate, quantity theory of money
6. velocity of circulation, total expenditure
7. buying low, selling high
8. European Monetary System
9. Exchange Rate Mechanism
10. Plaza, five

### True or False

1T 5F 9T 13T 17F
2F 6T 10F 14F 18T
3T 7F 11F 15T 19F
4T 8F 12F 16F 20F

### Multiple Choice

1e 5b 9a 13d 17d
2d 6d 10d 14e 18d
3a 7d 11e 15a 19d
4d 8d 12a 16b 20e

### Short Answer Questions

1. The Exchange Rate Mechanism of the European Monetary System was a system of fixed exchange rates between the currencies of some members of the European Community. The main members of the Exchange Rate Mechanism were France, Germany, Belgium, and the Netherlands.

2. (a) When a country has a fixed exchange rate, its inflation is determined by world inflation. Money supply growth adjusts to accommodate that inflation.

   (b) When a country has a flexible exchange rate, this country is free to determine its monetary policy and inflation rate.

3. Anticipated inflation is a process in which the price level is increasing at a rates forecasted by all the economic actors. With anticipated inflation, the actual inflation rate is equal to the expected inflation rate.

Unanticipated inflation is a process in which the price level increases at a pace that has been incorrectly forecast to some degree. With unanticipated inflation, the actual rate of inflation is not equal to the expected rate of inflation.

4. (a) A rational expectation is a forecast about the future value of an economic variable made using all available information.

   (b) First, it is unbiased. The expected forecast error is zero. There is as much chance of being wrong on the upside as on the downside and by an equal amount.

   Second, the forecast has the minimum possible range of error. This does not mean that it might not be wildly wrong, but there is no way to reduce the range of error in the forecast.

5. The equilibrium real wage rate is the real wage rate at which the quantity of labour demanded equals the quantity of labour supplied.

   The money wage rate is the real wage rate multiplied by the price level.

6. (a) Inflation in Israel in the 1980s was anticipated. Between 1980 and 1983, inflation was steady but high. In 1984, the money supply growth rate shot up to more than 400 percent a year and inflation increased to almost the same rate. In 1985 and 1986 the money supply growth rate decreased and the inflation rate fell by a similar amount.

   (b) Real GDP growth was undisturbed by these monetary and inflationary developments. The Israeli experience shows that an almost fully anticipated inflation can have little or no effect on economic growth.

7. (a) If goods are cheaper in one country than in another country, it will pay people to buy goods in the country where they are cheap and sell them in the country where the goods are more expensive. This is a process called arbitrage.

   (b) Arbitrage will occur until there are no profit opportunities remaining from buying at the low price and selling at a high price. At that point, the price of an internationally tradeable good will be the same in all countries.

8. (a) From 1945 to the early 1970s, Canada operated on a fixed exchange rate system.

   (b) From 1945 to the early 1970s, the rest of the world operated a fixed exchange rate system.

9. Anticipated inflation increases the cutoff interest rate for any given investment project. This means that the positions of the investment function and the *IS* curve change when the expected inflation rate changes. Specifically, expected inflation shifts both these curves to the right.

10. Anticipated inflation does not affect the *LM* curve because its position depends on the real money supply. With anticipated inflation, the real money supply is constant—the price level increases at the same rate as the money supply does.

## Problem Solving

1. (a) Real GDP remains the same.

   (b) The price level increases by 5 percent.

   (c) The aggregate demand curve shifts upward by 5 percent.

   (d) The short-run aggregate supply curve shifts upward by 5 percent.

2. The same project will just be profitable.
3. The interest rate will fall by 5 percent.
4. (a) Windy Isle's inflation rate is determined by the inflation rate of the world.

   (b) Windy Isle's money supply growth rate adjusts to accommodate the inflation rate.

5. The inflation rate increases by 10 percent.
6. Expected inflation does not shift the *LM* curve.
7. 8 percent a year
8. 12 percent a year.
9. Inflation increases initially above 12 percent a year but then decreases to 12 percent a year.
10. (a) $y^d = 5{,}000 - 235.85P$

    (b) $y^s = -3{,}500 + 235.85P$

**Chapter 14**

# Inflation and the Business Cycle

## Perspective and Focus

This chapter examines how inflation and the business cycle interact with each other. It studies the fluctuations in the inflation rate and the level of economic activity that occur simultaneously as the economy ebbs and flows over the course of the business cycle.

## Learning Objectives

*After studying this chapter, you will be able to:*

- Describe the main features of inflation over the business cycle
- Explain the effects of unanticipated changes in aggregate demand on inflation
- Describe how an unanticipated decrease in aggregate demand brought inflation under control in the early 1980s but also brought recession
- Explain the effects of supply shocks on inflation
- Explain how oil price shocks influenced inflation in the 1970s
- Define the Phillips curve and explain the Phillips curve theory
- Describe the shifts in the Canadian Phillips curve since 1960

## Increasing Your Productivity

The key thing to pay attention to in this chapter is the fact that in order to generate fluctuations in real GDP around its full-employment level and simultaneous fluctuations in the inflation rate, aggregate demand must change in an unanticipated way. Anticipated changes in aggregate demand have the effects that we studied in the Chapter 13—they change the price level (or inflation rate), leaving real GDP unaffected.

The second thing to pay attention to in this chapter is the equivalence of two alternative ways of looking at the determination of real economic activity and the inflation rate. One of these is the *AD-AS* model, with which you now very familiar, and the other is the Phillips curve approach. Figure 14.9 is a crucial one showing you how the *AD-AS* model and the Phillips curve framework are really two ways of looking at the same thing. Be sure to spend a good deal of time working through that figure and the text description and explanation of it. Once you understand how that figure works and are thoroughly familiar with the equivalence of the *AD-AS* and Phillips curve approaches you will have no difficulty in handling any of the material in this chapter.

The "trickiest" thing in this chapter is the analysis of the effects of the shift in the production function on the short-run and long-run aggregate supply curves. This material is summarized in Figure 14.4. Work hard to thoroughly understand this figure.

## Self Test

### Fill in the Blanks

1. A process of rising prices and falling real GDP is called ______________.
2. The Phillips curve is a relationship between the inflation rate and the ______________ ______________, holding constant the natural rate of unemployment and the ______________ ______________.
3. The expectations-augmented Phillips curve is a short-run Phillips curve the position of which depends on the ______________ ______________.
4. A Phillips curve drawn for a particular, given, expected inflation rate is a ______________ Phillips curve.
5. The long-run Phillips curve is the relationship between ______________ and the unemployment rate when ______________ is fully anticipated.

### True or False

1. A process of rising prices and falling real GDP is known as stagflation.
2. A short-run Phillips curve the position of which depends on the expected inflation rate is known as the expectations-augmented Phillips curve.

3. With a high correlation between wage change and inflation, the Phillips curve evolved from the relationship between wage change and unemployment to one between inflation and unemployment.

4. The Phillips curve is a theory of inflation that is quite different from the one based on the aggregate demand-aggregate supply model.

5. The change in the expected inflation rate does not shift the short-run Phillips curve.

6. Between 1966 and 1971, Canadian unemployment was steady and inflation increased. Then, in 1972, unemployment began to increase.

7. Disruptions to the supply of key raw materials from the rest of the world or large increases in the world price of such materials have a positive impact on aggregate supply.

8. Canada was cushioned from the effects of the world-wide OPEC recession by a policy of raising taxes on energy and raising the price of Canadian-produced oil.

9. The Phillips curve provides another way of looking at the relationship between inflation and the business cycle.

10. The long-run Phillips curve is horizontal at the natural rate of unemployment.

11. An unanticipated increase in the money supply increases the price level by the same percentage amount.

12. A negative supply shock decreases long-run and short-run aggregate supply.

13. A positive technology shock increases the demand for labour and increases the real wage rate.

14. An unanticipated slowdown in the rate of inflation increases the real wage rate.

15. An unanticipated increase in the inflation rate shifts the short-run Phillips curve upward.

16. An unanticipated increase in the inflation rate shifts the aggregate demand curve to the right, causes a movement along the short-run aggregate supply curve, and causes a movement along the short-run Phillips curve. Real GDP increases and the unemployment rate decreases.

17. An increase in the natural rate of unemployment decreases the inflation rate.

18. The Canadian Phillips curve has been stable since the 1960s.

19. When inflation expectations increase both inflation and unemployment rise.

20. When inflation expectations increase, the short-run Phillips curve shifts upwards, but the long-run Phillips curve does not change.

## Multiple Choice

1. When an increase in aggregate demand is not anticipated, the money wage rate
(a) rises in anticipation of rising prices.
(b) falls in anticipation of rising prices.
(c) does not rise.
(d) may either rise or fall in anticipation of rising prices.
(e) none of the above.

2. Capital accumulation and technological change
(a) decrease aggregate supply at a constant pace.
(b) do not affect aggregate supply.
(c) decrease aggregate supply.
(d) increase aggregate supply, but their pace is variable.
(e) decrease aggregate demand, but their pace is variable.

3. When the production function shifts down, the long-run aggregate supply curve shifts to the left,
(a) increasing the marginal product of labour and shifting the demand for labour curve to the right.
(b) reducing the marginal product of labour and shifting the demand for labour curve to the right.
(c) increasing the marginal product of labour and shifting the demand for labour curve to the left.
(d) leaving the marginal product of labour constant and the demand for labour curve unchanged.

(e) reducing the marginal product of labour and shifting the demand for labour curve to the left.

4. Choose the best statement.
(a) The steeper the supply of labour curve, the greater is the shift in the long-run aggregate supply curve.
(b) The flatter the supply of labour curve, the greater is the shift in the long-run aggregate supply curve.
(c) The flatter the supply of labour curve, the greater is the shift in the short-run aggregate supply curve.
(d) The steeper the supply of labour curve, the less is the shift in the short-run aggregate supply curve.
(e) None of the above.

5. Which of the following is a short-run Phillips curve, the position of which depends on the expected inflation rate? The
(a) original Phillips curve.
(b) natural-rate Phillips curve.
(c) auction Phillips curve.
(d) expectations-augmented Phillips curve.
(e) rules-augmented Phillips curve.

6. Which of the following will shift a short-run Phillips curve?
(a) A change in the expected inflation rate.
(b) Unanticipated inflation.
(c) The real interest rate.
(d) The market interest rate.
(e) The long-run Phillips curve.

7. Technological change itself
(a) can result in a permanent decrease in aggregate supply when it has a strong sectoral bias.
(b) can bring a temporary decrease in aggregate supply when it has a strong sectoral bias.
(c) has no impact on aggregate supply.
(d) always increases aggregate supply when it has a strong sectoral bias.
(e) none of the above are correct.

8. An economy at full employment experiences an unanticipated decrease in aggregate demand. Real GDP
(a) moves above its full-employment level and inflation accelerates.
(b) moves below its full-employment level and inflation slows.
(c) remains at its full-employment level and inflation accelerates.
(d) remains at its full-employment level and inflation slows down.
(e) moves below its full-employment level and inflation accelerates.

9. The long-run Phillips curve is intersected at any point by which of the following? The
(a) supply of labour curve.
(b) demand for labour curve.
(c) aggregate demand curve.
(d) expectations-augmented Phillips curve.
(e) none of the above.

10. In the United States between 1973 and 1975, massive oil price increases shifted
(a) both the short-run and long-run aggregate supply curves to the right.
(b) both the short-run and long-run aggregate supply curves to the left.
(c) only the short-run aggregate supply curve to the left.
(d) only the long-run aggregate supply curve to the right.
(e) only the short-run aggregate supply curve to the right.

11. A 10 percent unanticipated increase in the money supply
(a) increases aggregate demand to the point at which the new *AD* curve intersects the *LAS* curve at a price level 10 percent higher than the original *AD* curve.
(b) increases the price level by 10 percent.
(c) increases the price level and real GDP because aggregate supply increases.
(d) results in a movement along the short-run aggregate supply curve increasing both the price level and real GDP.
(e) both (a) and (d).

12. A 20 percent increase in the prices of factors of production combined with a 5 percent increase in the money supply, both of which are unanticipated
(a) increases aggregate supply.
(b) decreases real GDP and increases the price level.
(c) increases real GDP and increases the price level.
(d) decreases both real GDP and the price level.
(e) results in inflation but no change in real GDP.

13. A decrease in labour productivity that shifts the short-run production function downward
(a) increases the demand for labour because the existing labour force is less productive.
(b) decreases short-run aggregate supply but not long-run aggregate supply.
(c) decreases long-run aggregate supply but not short-run aggregate supply.
(d) decreases both long-run and short-run aggregate supply by the same amount.
(e) decreases both long-run and short-run aggregate supply but decreases short-run aggregate supply by more than the decrease in long-run aggregate supply.

14. A technological change that increases the marginal productivity of labour
(a) increases employment, increases the real wage rate and increases long-run and short-run aggregate supply.
(b) increases the real wage rate leading to an increase in the supply of labour and an increase in long-run aggregate supply.
(c) increases long-run aggregate supply but does not change short-run aggregate supply.
(d) increases the level of employment but does not change the real wage rate.
(e) increases potential GDP but does not change real GDP in the short run.

15. An increase in prices of factors of production of 10 percent that is unexpected
(a) increases the price level by 10 percent.
(b) decreases real GDP by 10 percent.
(c) increases the price level and decreases real GDP but each by less than 10 percent.
(d) increases short-run aggregate supply.
(e) decreases long-run aggregate supply.

16. As the economy moves down a short-run Phillips curve,
(a) unemployment increases and expected inflation decreases.
(b) unemployment increases and actual inflation decreases but expected inflation remains constant.
(c) actual inflation falls and the natural rate of unemployment increases.
(d) the expected inflation rate falls and the natural rate of unemployment rate increases.
(e) inflation decreases, unemployment increases, but it is not possible to say what happens to either the expected inflation rate or the natural rate of unemployment.

17. Initially the short-run Phillips curve intersects the long-run Phillips curve at an inflation rate of 10 percent a year and an unemployment rate of 5 percent. A change then takes place that results in the short-run Phillips curve intersecting the long-run Phillips curve at the same unemployment rate but at an inflation rate of 5 percent a year.
(a) The natural rate of unemployment has fallen.
(b) The natural rate of unemployment has risen.
(c) The expected inflation rate has fallen.
(d) The expected inflation rate has risen.
(e) The actual inflation rate has fallen.

18. An unexpected increase in the growth rate of the money supply
(a) causes a movement down the short-run Phillips curve increasing the unemployment rate and lowering the inflation rate.
(b) causes a movement up the short-run Phillips curve lowering the unemployment rate and increasing the inflation rate.
(c) shifts the short-run Phillips curve increasing the expected inflation rate.
(d) has no effect on the Phillips curve or the position on the Phillips curve at which the economy operates.
(e) always results in the economy moving to an above full-employment equilibrium.

19. An economy is initially on its long-run and short-run Phillips curve. Then both inflation and unemployment increase. We can infer that
(a) the natural rate of unemployment is increased.
(b) the expected inflation rate has increased.
(c) the natural rate of unemployment has not changed nor has the expected inflation rate.
(d) either the natural rate of unemployment rate has increased or the expected inflation rate has increased but not both.
(e) either the natural rate of unemployment has increased, or the expected inflation rate has increased, or both have increased.

20. During the 1960's
(a) the natural rate of unemployment decreased.
(b) the expected inflation rate increased.
(c) inflation expectations and the natural unemployment rate were constant and there was a movement along the fixed short-run Phillips curve.
(d) the natural rate of unemployment decreased making it possible to keep prices stable even though unemployment was falling.
(e) the short-run Phillips curve and the long-run Phillips curve were identical.

## Short Answer Questions

1. Describe the following Phillips curves.

   (a) An expectations-augmented Phillips curve.

   (b) A long-run Phillips curve.

   (c) A short-run Phillips curve.

2. Briefly summarize the recession of 1981-1982.

3. When looking at inflation, does the Phillips curve have an advantage over the *AD-AS* model? Explain.

4. Is there a correlation between inflation and the business cycle? Explain.

5. What happens to the short-run Phillips curve and the long-run Phillips curve if there is a decrease in the natural rate of unemployment?

6. How did the Phillips curve evolve?

7. What is the effect of an unanticipated increase in the growth rate of the money supply?

8. Describe the Canadian Phillips curve since 1970.

9. How does stagflation arise?

10. (a) What is held constant along the short-run Phillips curve?

    (b) What is held constant along the long-run Phillips curve?

## Problem Solving

### Practice Problems

1. Sun State has the following production function, demand for labour, and supply of labour:

   $y = 20n - 0.1n^2$

   $n^d = 100 - 5(W/P)$

   $n^s = 5(W/P)$.

   (a) What is the full-employment real wage rate?

   (b) What is the full-employment level of employment?

   (c) What is full-employment output?

2. You are given the following data about the economy of Lizard Island:

   $y^d = 300/P$

   $y^s = 250 - 250/P^2$.

   Aggregate demand on Lizard Island unexpectedly increases by 10 percent.

   (a) Calculate the price level.

   (b) Calculate real GDP.

### Solutions to Practice Problems

1. (a) What is the full-employment real wage rate?

   The full-employment real wage rate is determined at the intersection of the demand for labour and supply of labour curves. Substitute $5(W/P)$ for $n$ in the demand for labour curve and solve for $(W/P)$. The full-employment real wage rate is 10.

(b) What is the full-employment level of employment?

At full-employment, the real wage rate is 10. Substitute 10 for ($W/P$) in the supply of labour curve. The full-employment level of employment is 50.

(c) What is full-employment output?

At full employment, the level of employment is 50. Substitute 50 for $n$ in the production function. Full-employment output is 750.

2. (a) Calculate the price level.

The price level is determined at the intersection of the aggregate demand curve and the aggregate supply curve. Real GDP demanded at any price level increases by 10 percent. The new aggregate demand curve is $y^d = 1.1(300/P)$.

The increase in aggregate demand is not expected, so the money wage rate remains the same and so too does the short-run aggregate supply curve. That is, $y^s = 250 - 250/P^2$.

The price level is determined at the intersection of aggregate demand and aggregate supply curves. The price level is 1.86.

(b) Calculate real GDP.

Substitute 1.86 for the price level in either the equation to the aggregate demand or the aggregate supply curves. Real GDP is 177.

## Problems to Solve

**Fact 14.1** An economy has the following aggregate demand and short-run aggregate supply:

$$y^d = 1{,}000 - P$$

$$y^s = 4P.$$

1. Use Fact 14.1. Find the equilibrium level of real GDP.
2. Use Fact 14.1. Find the equilibrium price level.

**Fact 14.2** Given Fact 14.1, aggregate demand now increases unexpectedly by 20 percent.

3. Use Fact 14.2. What is the percentage increase in real GDP?
4. Use Fact 14.2. What is the percentage increase in the price level?

**Fact 14.3** An economy's production function, demand for labour, and supply of labour are described by the following equations:

$$y = 100n - 0.2n^2$$

$$n^d = 250 - 2.5(W_0/P)$$

$$n^s = 100 + 7.5(W_0/P).$$

5. Use Fact 14.3. Calculate full-employment real GDP.
6. Use Fact 14.3. Calculate the full-employment real wage rate.
7. Use Fact 14.3. Calculate the equation for the long-run aggregate supply curve.
8. Use Fact 14.3. Calculate the equation for the short-run aggregate supply curve.

**Fact 14.4** The economy described in Fact 14.3 experiences a 20 percent increase in labour productivity.

9. Use Fact 14.4. Find the new long-run equilibrium real wage rate.
10. Use Fact 14.4. Find the equation for the new long-run aggregate supply curve.
11. Use Fact 14.4. Find the equation for the new short-run aggregate supply curve.
12. Use Fact 14.4. Find the equilibrium level of unemployment.

**Fact 14.5** All the variables are logarithms: $y$ is the log of real GDP, $p$ is the log of the price level and $m$ is the log of the nominal money supply.

You are given the following facts about an economy:

$$y_t^s = 10 + 3(p_t - p_t^e)$$

$$y_t^d = 50 + 1.5(m_t - p_t)$$

$m_t^e = 10$.

13. Use Fact 14.5. Calculate the rational expectation of the price level.

14. Use Fact 14.5. Calculate full-employment level of real GDP.

**Fact 14.6** Refer to Fact 14.5. Suppose there is an unexpected 20 percent increase in the money supply.

15. Use Fact 14.6.

(a) Calculate the new rational expectation of the price level.

(b) Calculate the equilibrium price level.

(c) Calculate the equilibrium level of real GDP.

## Answers

### Fill in the Blanks

1. stagflation
2. unemployment rate, expected inflation rate
3. expected inflation rate
4. short-run
5. inflation, inflation

### True or False

1T 5F 9T 13T 17F
2T 6F 10F 14T 18F
3T 7F 11F 15F 19F
4F 8F 12T 16T 20T

### Multiple Choice

1c 5d 9d 13e 17c
2d 6a 10b 14a 18b
3e 7b 11e 15c 19e
4b 8b 12b 16b 20c

### Short Answer Questions

1. (a) An expectations-augmented Phillips curve is a short-run Phillips curve the position of which depends on the expected inflation rate.

   (b) A long-run Phillips curve shows the relationship between inflation and unemployment when inflation is fully anticipated.

   (c) A short-run Phillips curve is a Phillips curve drawn for a particular, given, expected inflation rate.
2. In the early 1980s, expectations of continuing double-digit inflation were widespread. The short-run aggregate supply curve shifted leftward as costs increased at the expected inflation rate. Aggregate demand growth slowed down as a result of a slowdown in money supply growth and much higher interest rates that brought a large decrease in investment. As a result the economy experienced recession and lower inflation.
3. Yes, because one can keep track of an inflating economy without using curves that constantly shift as the price level increases.
4. No strong, simple correlation exists between

inflation and the business cycle, but there is an important pattern. Inflation tends to increase when real GDP is above potential GDP and decrease when real GDP is below potential GDP.

5. A decrease in the natural rate of unemployment shifts both the long-run Phillips curve and the short-run Phillips curve leftward.
6. A.W. Phillips first proposed the Phillips curve after studying the relationship between unemployment and the rate of change of wages in the United Kingdom. Phillips plotted the rate of change of money wages against the unemployment rate in each year and discovered that the higher the unemployment rate, the lower was the rate of wage change. The Phillips curve evolved from the relationship between wage change and unemployment to one between inflation and unemployment.
7. Aggregate demand increases but long-run aggregate supply and short-run aggregate supply remain the same. With higher aggregate demand, there is a movement along the short-run aggregate supply curve. Real GDP increases and the price level rises.
8. The Canadian Phillips curve shifted up and to the right during the 1970s and 1980s and down and to the left during the 1990s
9. Stagflation arises when short-run aggregate supply decreases by more than aggregate demand increases.
10. (a) Along the short-run Phillips curve the expected inflation rate and the natural rate of unemployment are held constant.

    (b) Along the long-run Phillips curve the natural rate of unemployment is held constant.

## Problem Solving

1. 800
2. 200
3. 15.4 percent
4. 15.4 percent
5. 12,218.75
6. 15
7. $y = 12{,}218.75$
8. $y = 12{,}500 - 281.25(P^e/P)^2$
9. 15.65
10. $y = 14{,}745$
11. $y = 15{,}000 - 255.06(P^e/P)^2$
12. 217.44
13. 36.67
14. 10
15. (a) 36.67

    (b) 37.33

    (c) 12

## Chapter 15

# Public and Private Deficits and Debts

## Perspective and Focus

This chapter focuses on one particular aspect of macroeconomic problems and policy issues—deficits and debts of the government and private sectors. You have met these concepts before when we studied the national income accounts in Chapter 2. There you learnt how the deficit of the government sector is connected with the deficits or surpluses of the private sector and the rest of the world. That is, you learnt that the government deficit (government expenditures minus taxes) equals the private sector surplus (saving minus investment) plus the rest of the world's deficit (imports minus exports).

The goal of this chapter is to focus more detailed attention on these deficits and the way in which they result in the accumulation of debt. The chapter focuses on the dynamic relationships between deficits and debts.

## Learning Objectives

*After studying this chapter, you will be able to:*

- Describe Canadian deficits and debts and place them in their historical and international context
- Explain the relationships between stocks and flows, receipts and expenditures, and borrowing and lending
- Describe the main sources of Canadian government deficits in the 1980s and 1990s
- Explain how inflation distorts the measurement of a deficit (or surplus)
- Explain the limits to the amount that can be borrowed
- Explain how deficits can lead to inflation
- Compare the deficits in Canada, Bolivia, and Israel in the 1980s
- Explain the burden debt places on future generations

## Increasing Your Productivity

The heart of this chapter is the connection between debts and deficits. The key to understanding this connection is the realization that a deficit is a flow while a debt is a stock. Flows change stocks. An ongoing deficit leads to the perpetual accumulation of debt; an ongoing surplus leads to a perpetual accumulation of assets.

The critical feature of the dynamic relationship between deficits and debts is the fact that interest is paid on borrowing or earned on lending. An ongoing deficit not only leads to a rising debt but to an increasing interest burden. Thus an ongoing deficit leads to the accumulation of debt that mushrooms as a result of interest payments.

But if the borrowing is put to productive use, it leads to growth in productive resources and growth in income. Growing incomes enable debt burdens to be carried more readily. Thus the key question that this chapter helps you understand is that of determining how much someone (or a government or a firm) can borrow without running into an ever bigger debt problem and ever larger debt burden in relation to its ability to service the debt.

This chapter uses some simple algebra in the section on budget constraints, borrowing, and lending. The chapter derives those basic relationships especially in Tables 15.1 and 15.2. You do need to spend some time studying this algebra and becoming thoroughly comfortable with it.

## Self Test

### Fill in the Blanks

1. The value of debt outstanding expressed as a percentage of GDP is the ____________ ____________.
2. The debt owed by the private and government sectors of the economy to the rest of the world is ____________ ____________.
3. The __________ deficit is the deficit of the federal government and the total government deficit is the deficit of the ______________, ______________, and ______________

government sectors.

4. The limits to expenditure is called the _____________ _____________.

5. The limits of expenditure at each point in time and the links between spending, ___________, and ___________ is the ___________ ___________ ___________.

6. The real deficit is the change in the real value of outstanding government ___________.

7. Inflation tax is the tax that people implicitly pay when rising prices reduce the real value of ___________ and the ___________ ___________ they hold.

8. The budget deficit excluding debt interest is the _____________ _____________.

9. During the 1920s in Germany, Poland, and Hungary, deficits led to ___________.

10. The Ricardian equivalence theorem is the proposition that government ___________ and ___________ are equivalent to each other and have no effect on interest rates.

## True or False

1. A budget constraint defines the limits of expenditure—the maximum that can be spent given the resources available to finance that spending.
2. Net foreign assets in Canada are equal to government debt minus private debt.
3. The inflation tax is the tax that people implicitly pay when the real value of money and the government debt they hold increases because of rising prices.
4. The government sector's basic deficit is its budget deficit plus debt interest.
5. From the end of World War II through 1976, the debt of the Canadian federal government as a percentage of GDP steadily increased.
6. The balance on the rest of the world's transactions with Canada (viewed from the perspective of residents of the rest of the world) is equal to the value of Canadian imports of goods and services plus the value of Canadian exports of goods and services.
7. People can smooth their expenditure by borrowing when incomes are low and repaying their loans when incomes are high.
8. Between 1980 and 1997 the federal government deficit in Canada accounted for the bulk of the total government sector deficit.
9. The real deficit is the change in the dollar value of outstanding government debt.
10. The proposition that government debt and taxes are equivalent to each other and have no effect on interest rates is known as the Ricardian equivalence theorem.
11. Canada has had a federal government budget deficit every year since 1978.
12. Governments can smooth expenditure by borrowing more when revenue is low and borrowing less when revenue is high. On the average, its deficit is zero and it has no debt.
13. The more a household saves, the faster can its consumption expenditure grow.
14. The government deficit exploded in the 1980s because government expenditure on goods and services as a percentage of GDP grew every year.
15. The presence of inflation makes the government deficit look larger than it really is.
16. If the economy grows at a rate higher than the real interest rate, then there exists a steady-state debt-GDP ratio.
17. If the economy grows at a rate equal to the real interest rate and the government runs a deficit, then the debt-GDP ratio grows without limit.
18. Deficits always lead to inflation.
19. Deficits burden future generations if the present generation ignores the future tax liability created by the present deficit.
20. Inflation reduces the size of the real deficit, making it smaller than the nominal deficit.

## Multiple Choice

1. The sum of the government budget balance, the private sector budget balance, and the rest of the world balance equals

(a) a positive sum.

(b) a negative sum.
(c) zero.
(d) either a positive or a negative sum.
(e) none of the above.

2. Net foreign assets in Canada are equal to
(a) Canadian government sector debt minus Canadian private sector debt.
(b) the ratio of Canadian government sector debt to Canadian private sector debt.
(c) Canadian government sector debt multiplied by Canadian private sector debt.
(d) Canadian government sector debt plus private sector debt.
(e) none of the above.

3. Which of the following states the limits of expenditure at each point in time and the links between spending, borrowing, and lending?
(a) An interdimensional budget constraint.
(b) A multitemporal budget constraint.
(c) An intertemporal budget constraint.
(d) A two-dimensional budget constraint.
(e) None of the above.

4. The equation that states that the change in assets from one year to the next equals income minus expenditure plus interest income is
(a) $A_{t+1} - A_t = Y_t + E_t + r_tA_t$.
(b) $A_{t+1} - A_t = Y_t - E_t + r_tA_t$.
(c) $A_{t+1} - A_t = Y_t - E_t - r_tA_t$.
(d) $A_{t+1} - A_t = Y_t + E_t - r_tA_t$.
(e) $A_{t+1} - A_t = Y_t - E_t - r_tA_{t+1}$.

5. Which of the following equations represents the government's intertemporal budget constraint?
(a) $(D_{t+1} - D_t) = G_t + r_tD_t - T_t$.
(b) $(D_{t-1} + D_t) = G_t + r_tD_t - T_t$.
(c) $(D_{t-1} - D_t) = G_t - r_tD_t - T_t$.
(d) $(D_{t-1} + D_t) = G_t - r_tD_t - T_t$
(e) $(D_{t-1} + D_t) = G_t + r_tD_t + T_t$.

6. Motives for borrowing and lending include
(a) Expenditure smoothing.
(b) Consumption growth.
(c) Saving growth.
(d) Both (a) and (b).
(e) All of the above.

7. An intertemporal budget constraint can be written as
(a) $E_t + A_{t+1} = (1 + r_t)A_t - Y_t$.
(b) $E_t + A_{t+1} = (1 + r_t)A_t/Y_t$.
(c) $E_t + A_{t+1} = (1 + r_t)A_t + Y_t$.
(d) $E_t + A_{t+1} = (1 - r_t)A_t + Y_t$.
(e) $E_t + A_{t+1} = (1/r_t)A_t + Y_t$.

8. The value of debt outstanding expressed as a percentage of GDP is known as the
(a) debt-GDP accelerator.
(b) debt-GDP multiplier.
(c) debt-GDP inflator.
(d) debt-GDP ratio.
(e) debt-GDP deflator.

9. The debt owed by the private and government sectors of the economy to the rest of the world is known as
(a) internal debt.
(b) autonomous debt.
(c) global debt.
(d) endogenous debt.
(e) external debt.

10. In studying debts and deficits and their effects on the macroeconomy, which of the following sectors are distinguished? The
(a) government.
(b) private.
(c) rest of the world.
(d) both (a) and (c).
(e) (a), (b), and (c).

11. The government budget balance is equal to
(a) $T + G$.
(b) $T - G$.
(c) $G - T$.
(d) $T/G$.
(e) $G/T$.

12. A persistent government budget deficit in Canada during the 1980s
(a) had no affect on the real deficit.
(b) increased the debt-GDP ratio.
(c) decreased the debt-GDP ratio.
(d) continued throughout all of the 1990s.
(e) left the debt-GDP ratio unchanged.

13. The federal government's debt as a percentage of GDP has been
(a) growing every year since World War II.
(b) at a higher level during the 1980s than at any other time in history.
(c) on an upward trend since the middle 1970s.
(d) on a declining trend since World War II.
(e) higher in the 1980s than it was in the 1940s.

14. A household has assets of $100, an income from employment of $100, and earns interest at 5 percent a year on its assets. The maximum amount the household can consume in the next time period is
(a) $105.
(b) $100.
(c) $500.
(d) $205.
(e) $200.

15. A government has a debt in year 1 of $1 trillion. Its current years expenditure is $150 billion (excluding interest) and its current period tax receipts are $250 billion. The interest rate is 15 percent a year and the inflation rate is 10 percent a year.
(a) The government has a real surplus but a nominal deficit.
(b) A real surplus and a real deficit.
(c) A nominal surplus and a nominal deficit.
(d) A nominal surplus and a real deficit.
(e) Not enough information to say.

16. The government has a deficit equal to 10 percent of GDP. Real GDP is growing at 5 percent a year and the real interest rate is 4 percent a year. The steady-state debt-GDP ratio is
(a) greater than 20.
(b) less than or equal to 20 but greater than 10.
(c) less than or equal to 10 but greater than 5.
(d) less than or equal to 5 but greater than 2.
(e) less than or equal to 2.

17. A government that has a budget deficit can finance its deficit, no matter how large it is,
(a) by issuing debt.
(b) by printing money.
(c) by any combination of debt issue and money printing it chooses.
(d) by only raising taxes.
(e) by only cutting expenditure.

18. A government that is running a budget deficit and that faces a real interest rate in excess of the economy's growth rate
(a) can keep inflation under control by restricting the rate of money growth.
(b) can keep inflation under control by issuing debt.
(c) cannot keep inflation under control and must accept inflation as an inevitable consequence of its deficit.
(d) will be forced to create a new monetary standard every few years.
(e) will eventually run out of money.

19. The government budget deficit
(a) inevitably poses a burden on future generations.
(b) imposes a burden on foreigners.
(c) imposes a burden on only the current generation.
(d) imposes no burden because the interest payments are somebody's income.
(e) imposes a burden on future generations if investment is crowded out.

20. Sandy Island has a basic deficit of 5 percent of GDP. The interest rate on Sandy Island is 2 percent per year. Government debt at the beginning of the 1998 is $2.5 million. GDP in 1998 is $10 million. GDP growth rate is 2.5 percent a year. In 1999, Sandy Island's debt-GDP ratio is
(a) 5 percent.
(b) 10 percent.

(c) 19 percent.

(d) 30 percent.

(e) 50 percent.

## Short Answer Questions

1. What are the two government deficits?
2. What is the relationship between deficits and debt?
3. Define the budget balance of businesses.
4. Does external debt impose a burden on future generations? Explain.
5. What is a budget constraint?
6. What caused the deficit that persisted in Canada during the 1980s and most of the 1990s?
7. What is meant by an intertemporal budget constraint?
8. (a) What is meant by expenditure smoothing?

   (b) How do governments smooth expenditure?

   (c) How do households smooth expenditure?
9. (a) What is an inflation tax?

   (b) Is this tax a legislated tax?
10. By what amount does the government debt change each year?
11. Describe the trends in the Canadian federal government debt since the end of World War II.
12. What is the relationship between the government budget balance, the private sector budget balance, and the rest of the world balance?
13. Describe the Canadian government sector receipts and expenditure from 1980 to 1998.
14. How is the real deficit calculated?
15. Explain why there is a steady-state debt-GDP ratio if the economic growth rate exceeds the real interest rate.

## Problem Solving

### Practice Problems

1. You are given the following information about Big Wave Island:

| Item | $million |
|---|---|
| GDP | 68 |
| Consumer expenditure | 36 |
| Government expenditures on goods and services | 12 |
| Government transfer payments and subsidies | 4 |
| Total taxes paid | 18 |
| Exports to the rest of the world | 24 |
| Imports from the rest of the world | 28 |

   (a) Calculate the government budget balance.

   (b) Calculate the private sector budget balance.

   (c) Calculate the rest of the world's balance with Big Wave Island.

2. An economy has an interest rate of 3 percent a year and no inflation. The real GDP growth rate is 6 percent a year. Its current debt is $0.25 million and its current GDP is $5 million. The government's basic deficit is equal to 5 percent of GDP.

   (a) Calculate its current debt-GDP ratio.

   (b) Calculate its debt-GDP ratio after one year.

   (c) Calculate the steady-state debt-GDP ratio.

   (d) Calculate the steady-state deficit.

**Solutions to Practice Problems**

1. (a) Calculate the government budget balance.
The government budget balance is defined as $T - G$, where $T$ equals taxes plus government interest income minus transfer payments minus debt interest paid by the government and $G$ equals government expenditures on goods and services:
$T - G = (18 - 4) - 36$
$T - G = -22$

(b) Calculate the private sector budget balance.
The private sector balance is equal to $S - I$, where $S$ equals saving and $I$ equals investment. Neither $S$ nor $I$ is given in the information supplied, but we can calculate $S - I$ as follows:
$(S - I) = -(T - G) + (EX - IM)$
$(S - I) = 22 + (24 - 28)$
$(S - I) = 18.$

(c) Calculate the rest of the world's balance with Big Wave Island.
The rest of the world's balance with Big Wave Island is equal to $IM - EX$, which is
$IM - EX = 28 - 24$
$IM - EX = 4.$

2. (a) Calculate its current debt-GDP ratio.
The current debt-GDP ratio is \$0.25 million/\$5 million, which is 0.05.
(b) Calculate its debt-GDP ratio after one year.
The GDP growth rate is 6 percent a year, so GDP after one year is 1.06 x \$5 million, which is \$5.3 million.
Debt after one year is calculated as
$D_2 = (1 + r)D_1 + zY_1,$
where $r$ is the interest rate, $z$ is the basic deficit as a proportion of GDP, and $Y_1$ is GDP in year 1. Substituting the given values into the equation gives a debt after one year of \$0.51 million. So the debt-GDP ratio at the end of one year is (0.51/5.3), which is 0.096.
(c) Calculate the steady-state debt-GDP ratio.
The steady-state debt-GDP ratio is given by the equation
$d^* = z/(g - r),$
where $z$ is the basic deficit as a proportion of GDP, $r$ is the interest rate, and $g$ is the GDP growth rate. So, the steady-state debt-GDP ratio is 0.05/(0.06 – 0.03), which is 1.67.

(d) Calculate the steady-state deficit.
The steady-state deficit is given by the equation
$(rd^* + z)Y_t,$
where $Y_t$ is GDP in year t.
The steady-state deficit is equal to $0.1Y_t$.

## Problems to Solve

**Fact 15.1** You are given the following information about an economy:

| Item | \$billion |
|---|---|
| GDP | 340 |
| Consumer expenditure | 180 |
| Government expenditures on goods and services | 60 |
| Government transfer payments and subsidies | 20 |
| Total taxes paid | 90 |
| Exports to the rest of the world | 120 |
| Imports from the rest of the world | 140 |

1. Use Fact 15.1. Calculate the government budget balance.
2. Use Fact 15.1. Calculate the private sector budget balance.
3. Use Fact 15.1. Calculate the rest of the world's balance with this economy.
4. Use Fact 15.1. Which of the balances calculated in problems 1, 2, and 3 is a surplus and which is a deficit?

5. Use Fact 15.1. Is this economy a net lender to or a net borrower from the rest of the world?
6. Use Fact 15.1. If the interest rate at which this economy can borrow or lend is 10 percent a year, what is the equation for the government's intertemporal budget constraint in the current year?

**Fact 15.2** An economy has an interest rate of 10 percent a year and an inflation rate of 6 percent a year. The economy's GDP real GDP growth rate is 5 percent a year. Its current debt is $1 trillion and its current GDP is $10 trillion. The government has a basic deficit equal to 10 percent of GDP.

7. Use Fact 15.2. Calculate the current debt-GDP ratio.
8. Use Fact 15.2. Calculate the debt-GDP ratio at the end of one year.
9. Use Fact 15.2. Calculate the steady-state debt-GDP ratio.
10. Use Fact 15.2. Calculate the steady-state deficit.

## Answers

### Fill in the Blanks

1. debt-GDP ratio
2. external debt
3. federal, federal, provincial, local
4. budget constraint
5. borrowing, lending, intertemporal budget constraint
6. debt
7. money, government debt
8. basic deficit
9. hyperinflation
10. debt, taxes

### True or False

1T 5F 9F 13T 17T
2F 6F 10T 14F 18F
3F 7T 11F 15T 19T
4F 8T 12F 16T 20T

### Multiple Choice

1c 5a 9e 13c 17b
2d 6d 10e 14d 18c
3c 7c 11b 15a 19e
4b 8d 12b 16c 20d

### Short Answer Questions

1. The federal deficit is the deficit of the federal government. The total government deficit is the combined deficits of federal, provincial, and local governments.
2. A deficit is a flow, measured in dollars per unit of time. A debt is a stock, measured as dollars at a point in time. Deficits are the flows that add to the stock of debt.
3. Businesses' budget balance equals business saving minus business investment. Business saving is equal to business profits minus taxes minus dividend and interest payments to households. Business investment is the purchase of new plant, equipment, and buildings by firms, as well as the net change in inventories.
4. Whether external debt imposes a burden on future generations depends on the rate of

return and the rate of economic growth achieved with the borrowed resources.

5. A budget constraint defines the limits of expenditure—the maximum that can be spent given the resources available to finance that spending.
6. Most of the deficit that persisted during the 1980s and most of the 1990s arose from increases in expenditure, especially increases in transfer payments and subsidies and debt interest. Taxes increased as a percentage of GDP, but not by as much as the increase in expenditure.
7. An intertemporal budget constraint states the limits of expenditure at each point in time and the links between spending, borrowing, and lending.
8. (a) As a rule, people dislike expenditure to fluctuate. They prefer to smooth their expenditure over time. People smooth expenditure by borrowing when incomes are low and repaying the loans when incomes are high or by lending when incomes are high and borrowing when incomes are low.

   (b) Governments smooth their expenditure by borrowing more in recessions and less in booms.

   (c) Households smooth their expenditure (consumption) by saving less in recessions and more in booms.
9. (a) The inflation tax is the tax that people implicitly pay when rising prices reduce the real value of money and the government debt they hold.

   (b) No, this tax is not a legislated tax.
10. The government debt changes each year by an amount equal to the interest rate paid on the debt held by the public plus the basic deficit.
11. From the end of World War II through 1976, the debt of the Canadian federal government as a percentage of GDP steadily declined. By 1976, it was 30 percent of GDP. The federal government had a deficit from the mid-1970s until 1997 and its debt has steadily increased, exceeding 55 percent of GDP by the late 1980s and 76 percent by 1996. By 1998, the debt decreased to 72 percent of GDP.
12. The sum of the government budget balance, the private sector budget balance, and the rest of world balance is zero.
13. Government sector receipts, which include personal taxes, corporation taxes, and indirect taxes, increased slightly though the 1980s and 1990s but personal income taxes increased the fastest.

    Expenditure has fluctuated more than receipts. Most of the fluctuations have arisen from transfer payments and subsidies that fluctuated with the business cycle. Expenditures on goods and services have gradually decreased as a percentage of GDP, but transfer payments and debt interest have increased.
14. The real deficit is calculated by deflating current debt by the current price level and then subtracting the debt from the previous period deflated by the previous period's price level.
15. If the growth rate exceeds the real interest rate, real GDP grows at a faster rate than the outstanding debt interest. Eventually there is a stable relationship between debt and income.

## Problem Solving

1. \$10 billion
2. –\$30 billion
3. \$20 billion
4. Private sector has a deficit and the other two sectors have surpluses
5. Borrower
6. $(D_{t+1} - D_t) = 0.1D_t - 10$
7. 0.1
8. 0.19
9. 10
10. $1.1Y_t$

Chapter 16

# Why Macroeconomists Disagree About Policy

## Perspective and Focus

You have now completed your study of macroeconomic theory. You have studied the forces that determine the level of real GDP and its main expenditure components—consumer expenditure, investment, government expenditures, and net exports. You have also studied what determines labour market variables—employment, unemployment, and real wage rates. You've studied what determines financial market variables, such as the quantity of money supplied and demanded and the interest rate. You've also studied how this all comes together to determine real GDP and the price level, both in the short run and the long run. Finally, you've studied the way in which debts accumulate as a result of an ongoing deficit and the dynamic relationships between deficits and debts.

You are now ready to tackle some policy questions. These questions center on the role of government in the macroeconomy and the influence of changes in physical policy and monetary policy on the main macroeconomic variables.

This first policy chapter sets the broad scene by examining the range of opinion among macroeconomists about the potential effects of policy on the economy.

## Learning Objectives

*After studying this chapter, you will be able to:*

- Describe the conflicting policy advice given by macroeconomists and others
- Distinguish among targets, instruments, and indicators of macroeconomic policy
- Distinguish between rules and discretion
- Explain the content and consequences of monetarist policy advice
- Describe Japan's experience with monetarist policies
- Explain the content and consequences of activist policies
- Describe the consequences of pursuing activist policies in the 1960s
- Explain why monetarists and activists offer conflicting advice
- Explain the consensus policy of targeting nominal GDP

## Increasing Your Productivity

This chapter is not a heavy one in terms of analysis but your understanding and appreciation of it will be greatly enhanced if you are completely familiar with the *IS-LM* analysis developed in Chapter 7 for the closed economy and Chapter 8 for the open economy. If you are not thoroughly familiar with this material, go back to Chapters 7 and 8 and refresh your understanding of that material before embarking on the present chapter.

The second thing to keep in mind as you work through this chapter is that the analysis abstracts from ongoing inflation and economic growth. This abstraction does not mean that the analysis is irrelevant to an economy with inflation and economic growth. It means simply that in studying the central issues involved in economic *fluctuations*, a clearer picture and a sharper focus can be obtained by ignoring the ongoing inflation and growth trends. Thus the diagrammatic analysis of the consequences of each alternative stabilization policy studies movements in real GDP and the price level around their trends.

The final part of this chapter studies nominal GDP targeting and summarizes an emerging consensus about macroeconomic policy. Be sure that you understand the figure depicting the nominal GDP target, Figure 16.11. Such a target is a band and the goal is to place the price level and real GDP in a given year inside this band. In a sense nominal GDP targeting is a recognition that demand management policies can do no more than stabilize aggregate demand. They have no ability to stabilize aggregate supply. Controversy may exist but there is no disagreement on this proposition.

As you work through the material in this chapter, try to form your own critically and carefully arrived at position on the appropriateness of alternative stabilization policies. Repeatedly ask yourself the question, to what extent is my conclusion driven by my preferences about inflation, unemployment, and real growth and to what extent is it driven by my best assessment of the way the economy works?

## Self Test

### Fill in the Blanks

1. Statistical descriptions of the economy that could be used to study the effects of alternative policies before they were implemented are called ____________ ____________.
2. ____________ ____________ are the objectives that macroeconomic policy seeks to achieve.
3. The four main target variables are ________, ____________ ____________, ____________ ____________ and ____________.
4. The main daily macroeconomic indicators are ____________ ____________, ____________ ____________, and ____________ ____________.
5. Macroeconomic policy instruments fall into two groups: ___________ policy instruments and ___________ policy instruments.
6. A macroeconomic policy rule is a macroeconomic policy that operates according to a ___________ ___________.
7. A prescription of behaviour that is the same regardless of the state of the economy is a ____________ ____________.
8. Discretionary macroeconomic policy is a policy that reacts to the ________ state of the economy.
9. ____________ ____________ is a policy that reacts to the state of the economy.
10. ____________ ____________ ____________ is a policy that targets nominal GDP growth.

### True or False

1. Macroeconomic indicators are variables that provide information, on a frequent basis, about the current state and direction of the economy.
2. A macroeconomic policy rule is a macroeconomic policy that reacts to changing economic conditions.
3. A discretionary macroeconomic policy is a policy that does not react to the current state of the economy.
4. Following monetarist policy advice in the face of an aggregate supply shock leads to movements in real GDP and the price level in the same directions.
5. Nominal GDP targeting is based on the presumption that it is possible to make aggregate demand more stable than it would be in the absence of activist policy.
6. Nominal GDP equals real GDP multiplied by the price level.
7. Calculations with statistical models of the Canadian economy suggest that nominal GDP targeting could indeed be used to decrease the variability of real GDP and inflation, keeping the economy closer to its full-employment level and avoiding excesses of inflation and deflation.
8. Monetarists advocate feedback rules for the money supply and fiscal policy.
9. Target variables are variables that macroeconomic policy seeks to influence.
10. Monetary policy instruments are the monetary base, bank rate, and short-term interest rates.
11. Macroeconomists agree about policy objectives but not about the way the economy works.
12. Monetarists advocate feedback rules while activists advocate fixed rules.
13. Monetarist policy advice, if followed, results in no fluctuations arising from aggregate demand shocks.
14. Monetarist policies can avoid stagflation.

15. Activist policies can avoid demand shocks only if the policy maker has perfect foresight.
16. Activist policies can eliminate stagflation.
17. If policy makers to not have perfect foresight, activist policies lead to bigger price level fluctuations than those arising from monetarist policies.
18. Successful nominal GDP targeting stabilizes real GDP and the price level when demand shocks occur.
19. Random temporary shocks hit the economy from time to time. Monetarist advice is based on the fact that policy makers can forecast these shocks.
20. When a negative random shock to aggregate demand occurs, activist advice is to increase the money supply, increase government expenditures on goods and services, or cut taxes.

## Multiple Choice

1. A macroeconomic policy that does not react to changing economic conditions is known as
(a) a variable rule.
(b) an activist rule.
(c) a feedback policy rule.
(d) a discretionary rule.
(e) a fixed rule.

2. Variables the provide information about the current state of the economy
(a )include interest rates and exchange rates.
(b) include the money supply and unemployment.
(c) are called macroeconomic indicators.
(d) include stock prices and consumer prices.
(e) all of the above.

3. The Bank of Canada
(a) and the government are in total agreement about the fiscal and monetary policies that should be pursued.
(b) follows monetarist policy similar to that followed by the Bank of Japan in the 1980s.
(c) pursued "monetarism" as defined by macroeconomists during the late 1970s and early 1980s.
(d) is more concerned with potential inflation than with high employment.
(e) none of the above.

4. The consequences of following monetarist policy advice when the economy is hit by aggregate demand shocks are
(a) nominal GDP deviating from potential GDP and the price level deviating from its actual level.
(b) real GDP deviating from potential GDP and the price level deviating from its actual level.
(c) real GDP deviating from its potential GDP and the price level deviating from its expected level.
(d) nominal GDP deviating from potential GDP and the price level deviating from its expected level.
(e) real GDP deviating from potential GDP but the price level remaining constant.

5. A monetarist policy in the face of a negative aggregate supply shock results in
(a) inflation.
(b) disinflation.
(c) stagflation.
(d) hyperinflation.
(e) none of the above.

6. The macroeconomic policy targets are the objectives that macroeconomic policy seeks to achieve. The main target variables are
(a) unemployment.
(b) real GDP.
(c) the current account balance.
(d) inflation.
(e) all of the above.

7. Fiscal policy instruments are
(a) government expenditures goods and services.
(b) the monetary base.
(c) transfer payments.
(d) taxes.
(e) (a), (c), and (d).

8. A feedback policy is a policy that reacts to the current state of the economy. It is also known as

(a) an activist macroeconomic policy.
(b) a non-discretionary macroeconomic policy.
(c) a fixed policy.
(d) a variable policy.
(e) a discretionary macroeconomic policy.

9. If real GDP is (or is forecasted to be) below potential GDP, then an increase in aggregate demand by increasing the money supply, increasing government expenditures on goods and services or cutting taxes is known as
(a) fixed policy rule advice.
(b) activist policy advice.
(c) variable policy advice.
(d) conflicting policy advice.
(e) monetarist policy advice.

10. In recent years, opinion has converged on the nature of a desirable and possible macroeconomic stabilization policy. It is
(a) real GDP targeting.
(b) national income targeting.
(c) personal disposable income targeting.
(d) nominal GDP targeting.
(e) real national income targeting.

11. Stabilizing the economy is beyond our reach because
(a) there are too many policy disagreements.
(b) we do not have sufficient knowledge of how the economy works.
(c) politicians and central bankers are ignorant of the knowledge about how the economy works that is available to economists.
(d) we do not spend enough resources on economic research.
(e) monetary and fiscal policy are always operating in opposite directions to each other.

12. An economy is subject only to temporary aggregate demand shocks and policy affects aggregate demand with a one period time lag.
(a) Monetarist policy achieves greater stability of real GDP than activist policy.
(b) Activist policy achieves greater stability of real GDP than monetarist policy.
(c) Activist and monetarist policy have the same effect on real GDP.
(d) Not possible to say which of these two policies have the larger or smaller effect on real GDP.
(e) Long-run aggregate supply responds more with activist policies than with monetarist policies.

13. An economy is subject a permanent aggregate demand shock and policy affects aggregate demand with a one period time lag. Over the 2 time periods,
(a) the price level fluctuates more with monetarist policy than with activist policy.
(b) the price level fluctuates more with activist policy than with monetarist policy.
(c) the price level fluctuates the same regardless of the policy.
(d) it is not possible to say under which policy the price fluctuates more.
(e) the average inflation rate is higher with monetarist policy.

14. An economy experiences a negative, temporary shock to long-run aggregate supply.
(a) Monetarist policy achieves greater stability of real GDP than activist policy.
(b) Activist policy achieves greater stability of real GDP than monetarist policy.
(c) Activist and monetarist policy have the same effect on real GDP.
(d) Not possible to say which of these two policies have the larger or smaller effect on real GDP.
(e) Long-run aggregate supply responds more with activist policies than with monetarist policies.

15. An economy experiences a negative, permanent shock to long-run aggregate supply.
(a) The price level fluctuates more with monetarist policy than with activist policy.
(b) The price level fluctuates more with activist policy than with monetarist policy.
(c) The price level fluctuates the same regardless of the policy.
(d) It is not possible to say under which policy

the price level fluctuates more.
(e) The average inflation rate is higher with monetarist policy.

16. When monetarist policies were pursued in Japan during the 1980s,
(a) inflation accelerated.
(b) real GDP growth collapsed.
(c) inflation gradually moderated and real GDP growth remained steady.
(d) inflation moderated and real GDP growth accelerated.
(e) the policy had no effect on inflation.

17. Nominal GDP targeting prevents
(a) real GDP from falling when there is a negative aggregate supply shock.
(b) real GDP from falling when there is an aggregate demand shock.
(c) short-run aggregate supply from fluctuating when long-run aggregate supply is stable.
(d) long-run aggregate supply from fluctuating.
(e) both (b) and (c).

18. For a positive random shock to aggregate demand,
(a) activist advice is to hold the money supply constant.
(b) monetarist advice is to hold the money supply constant.
(c) activist advice is to decrease taxes.
(d) activist advice is increase government expenditures.
(e) all of the above.

19. A positive aggregate supply shock hits the economy and a policy lag exists. In the period of the shock, the economy experiences
(a) inflation if monetarist advice is followed but not if activist advice is followed.
(b) inflation but not an increase in unemployment.
(c) inflation and an increase in unemployment.
(d) stagflation if activist advice is followed but not if monetarist advice is followed.
(e) none of the above.

20. A temporary decrease in investment that is unexpected leads to
(a) an permanent decrease in the price level if a feedback policy if adopted.
(b) a temporary decrease in the price level if a fixed rule policy is adopted.
(c) a temporary decrease in unemployment if a fixed rule policy is adopted.
(d) a permanent increase in unemployment if a fixed rule policy is adopted.
(e) (b) and (c).

## Short Answer Questions

1. What is a macroeconomic indicator? Give some examples.
2. (a) What are macroeconomic policy instruments?

   (b) What are fiscal policy instruments?

   (c) What are monetary policy instruments?
3. (a) Explain the policy advice of the monetarist.

   (b) What is the main instrument of macroeconomic policy for the monetarist? Explain.
4. Describe Japanese-style monetarism as pursued by the Bank of Japan from 1978 to 1990.
5. Explain the policy advice of activists.
6. The essence of the dispute between activists and monetarists turns on the question of information and the use that may be made of new information. Explain these assertions.
7. Why is nominal GDP targeting most useful for coping with aggregate supply shocks?
8. What are econometric models?
9. What are the consequences of following an activist policy in the face of a negative aggregate supply shock?
10. What are the three steps involved in macroeconomic stabilization policy?
11. What is the theory of aggregate demand based on?
12. Describe the U.S. economy during the 1960s.

13. What are the four main target variables?

14. What is nominal GDP targeting?

15. What is the main argument against nominal GDP targeting?

## Problem Solving

### Practice Problems

1. You are given the following information about Hibiscus Island's long-run aggregate supply, short-run aggregate supply, and aggregate demand:

$$y = 750 \qquad (16.1)$$

$$y^s = 150P \qquad (16.2)$$

$$y^d = 150M/P + e. \qquad (16.3)$$

The expected value of $e$ is zero.

(a) Calculate the long-run level of real GDP.

(b) Calculate the rational expectation of the price level.

(c) Calculate equilibrium real GDP if the value of $e$ is 25.

(d) Calculate the equilibrium price level if the value of $e$ is 25.

### Solutions to Practice Problems

1. (a) Calculate the long-run level of real GDP.
In the long run, the economy is on its long-run aggregate supply curve. So, the long-run level of real GDP is 750.

(b) Calculate the rational expectation of the price level.
The rational expectation of the price level is equal to the price level at which the *LAS* curve intersects the *SAS* curve. Solving Equations (16.1) and (16.2) for $P$ gives an expected price level of 5.

(c) Calculate equilibrium real GDP if the value of $e$ is 25.
Before the equilibrium value of real GDP can be found, it is necessary to calculate the expected money supply. The expected aggregate demand curve intersects the long-run aggregate supply curve at the expected price level.
The expected price level is 5, long-run real GDP is 750 and the expected shock is 0. Substituting for $P$, $y$, and $e$ in Equation (16.3) gives a money supply of 25.
Therefore the equation to the aggregate demand curve before the shock hits is
$y^d = 3{,}750/P$.

Once the shock hits, the aggregate demand curve becomes

$$y^d = 3{,}750/P + 25. \qquad (16.4)$$

Equilibrium real GDP is determined by the intersection of the aggregate demand and short-run aggregate supply curves. Solving Equations (16.4) and (16.2) for $y$ gives equilibrium real GDP equal to 763.

(d) Calculate the equilibrium price level if the value of $e$ is 25.
At the equilibrium, real GDP is 763. Substituting for $y$ in either the aggregate demand or the short-run aggregate supply curves gives a price level of 5.08.

## Problems to Solve

**Fact 16.1** You are given the following information about Hibiscus Island's long-run aggregate supply, short-run aggregate supply, and aggregate demand:

$$y = 1{,}000$$

$$y^s = 100P$$

$$y^d = 100M/P + e.$$

The expected value of $e$ is zero.

1. Use Fact 16.1. Calculate long-run equilibrium real GDP.

2. Use Fact 16.1. Calculate the rational expectation of the price level.

3. Use Fact 16.1. Calculate equilibrium real GDP if the value of $e$ is 50.

4. Use Fact 16.1. Calculate the equilibrium price level if the value of $e$ is 50.

5. Use Fact 16.1. Calculate equilibrium real GDP if policy responds by decreasing the

money supply so as to offset the effect of $e$ on aggregate demand.

6. Use Fact 16.1. If monetary policy operates with a one period time lag, calculate equilibrium real GDP in the next period following the shock that increases $e$ to 50 if the money supply is decreased to offset the effect of $e$ on aggregate demand and if the shock to $e$ is temporary and in the next period is equal to 0.
7. Use Fact 16.1. Calculate the equilibrium price level in the situation described in the Problem 6.
8. Does real GDP fluctuate most in Problems 5 and 6 or in the case in which the money supply is held constant.
9. Does the price level fluctuate most in Problems 5 and 6 or in the case in which the money supply is held constant.
10. In Problems 5 and 6, which policy is activist and which is monetarist?

## Answers

### Fill in the Blanks

1. econometric models
2. Macroeconomic policy targets
3. unemployment, real GDP, current account balance, inflation
4. interest rates, stock prices, exchange rates
5. fiscal, monetary
6. fixed formula
7. fixed rule
8. current
9. Feedback policy
10. Nominal GDP targeting

### True or False

1T 5T 9T 13F 17T
2F 6T 10T 14F 18T
3F 7T 11F 15T 19F
4F 8F 12F 16F 20T

### Multiple Choice

1e 5c 9b 13b 17b
2e 6e 10d 14b 18b
3d 7e 11b 15b 19e
4c 8e 12c 16c 20b

### Short Answer Questions

1. Macroeconomic indicators are variables that provide information, on a frequent basis, about the current state and direction of the economy. The main daily indicators are interest rates, stock prices, and exchange rates. The main monthly indicators include the money supply, unemployment, consumer prices, industrial production, new housing starts, and retail sales.
2. (a) Macroeconomic policy instruments are variables manipulated by the federal government or the Bank of Canada to influence macroeconomic policy targets.

   (b) Fiscal policy instruments are government expenditures on goods and services, transfer payments, and taxes.

   (c) Monetary policy instruments are the monetary base, bank rate, and short-term interest rates.

3. (a) Monetarists offer the following policy advice. First, set government expenditures, transfer payments, and taxes at levels that achieve an efficient allocation of resources and a fair distribution of income and wealth. (Fairness, an ethical concept, has to be determined in the political and social arena and cannot be objectively determined by an economic analyst.) Second, let the foreign exchange rate be flexible and pay no attention to the current account balance. Third, make the money supply grow at a constant rate.

   (b) The main instrument of macroeconomic policy for the monetarist is the money supply. Monetarists advocate setting the growth rate of a monetary aggregate (either the monetary base or a monetary aggregate such as M1 or M2+) so that, on the average, the inflation rate will be zero. This money supply growth rate can be computed as the growth rate of real GDP multiplied by the income elasticity of the demand for money minus the long-term growth in the velocity of circulation of money. Once calculated, monetarists advocate, the chosen monetary aggregate should be made to grow at the predetermined rate with no deviation from it, regardless of the state of the economy, the state of the government's budget, or any other economic factor.

4. In the period 1978 to 1990, the Bank of Japan pursued a monetarist policy of targeting the growth rate of a monetary aggregate and keeping its actual growth rate close to the target. The particular monetary aggregate targeted was a broad one—M2 plus certificates of deposit (CDs).

5. Activists offer the following advice. If real GDP is (or is forecasted to be) below potential GDP, increase aggregate demand by increasing the money supply, increasing government expenditures on goods and services, or cutting taxes.

   If real GDP is (or is forecasted to be) above potential GDP, decrease aggregate demand by decreasing the money supply, decreasing government expenditures on goods and services, or increasing taxes.

6 The monetarist asserts that the Bank of Canada has no information advantage over private agents and that it can do nothing that private agents will not do for themselves. Any attempt by the Bank of Canada to fine-tune or stabilize the economy by making the money supply react to previous shocks everybody knows about will not keep real GDP any closer to potential GDP and will make the price level more variable.

   Activists assert that the Bank of Canada has an effective informational advantage. They agree that individuals form their expectations rationally, using all the information available to them. But they also assert that individuals get locked into contracts based on expectations of the price level that, after an aggregate demand shock, turn out to be wrong. The Bank of Canada can act after private agents have tied themselves into contractual arrangements based on a wrong price level expectation to compensate for and offset the effects of those random shocks.

7. Nominal GDP targeting is most useful for coping with aggregate supply shocks because it imposes discipline on the capacity of the economy to respond without an unending burst of inflation.

8. Econometric models are statistical descriptions of the economy that could be used to study the effects of alternative policies before they were implemented.

9. Initially, activist policy leads to a rise in the price level but no decrease in real GDP. If the shock is temporary, real GDP remains at its initial level, but the price level does not fall. If the shock is permanent, real GDP eventually decreases and the price level rises further.

10. The three steps involved in macroeconomic stabilization policy are formulating the objectives as the values of the policy target variables, undertaking research to discover stable policy-invariant relationships among the variables, and choosing the setting and the rules governing changes in the policy instruments

11. The theory of aggregate demand is based on theories of consumption, investment, the demand for money, and international trade and capital flows.

12. During the Kennedy years real GDP expanded, unemployment declined, and

inflation remained remarkably low. In the second half of the 1960s, the Johnson administration pursued policies similar to the Kennedy administration, but fiscal expansion was more vigorous. Real GDP grew, unemployment fell, and inflation began to accelerate. By the end of the 1960s, inflation was more than 5 percent a year and was still accelerating at the time of the aggregate supply shocks of the 1970s.

13. The four main target variables are unemployment, real GDP, the current account balance, and inflation.
14. Nominal GDP targeting is a policy that targets nominal GDP growth.
15. The main argument against nominal GDP targeting centers on our ability to forecast movements in nominal GDP far enough ahead to be able to implement policies that can decrease the variability of nominal GDP relative to what it would be in the absence of active intervention. If policy actions take several months or a year or more, then forecasts of a year or more ahead are required to be able to set policy instruments at the right levels to stabilize nominal GDP.

## Problem Solving

1. 1,000
2. 10
3. 1,025
4. 10.25
5. 1,000
6. 975
7. 9.75
8. Problem 6 and monetarist policy give the same fluctuations in real GDP.
9. Problem 6 gives the largest fluctuations in the price level.
10. Problems 5 and 6 are activist.

# Chapter 17

# Stabilizing the Canadian Economy

## Perspective and Focus

The previous chapter studies some general issues concerning stabilization policy. This chapter focuses on the specific problems of stabilizing the Canadian economy. It describes the Bank of Canada and the tools at its disposal. It then examines the alternative policies that can be pursued by the Bank of Canada so as to keep real GDP growth stable and inflation under control. And like previous chapters, it builds on the *IS-LM* framework.

## Learning Objectives

*After studying this chapter, you will be able to:*

- Describe the balance sheets of the Bank of Canada and chartered banks and define various monetary aggregates
- Describe the policy instruments available to the Bank of Canada
- Explain how open market operations influence the money supply and interest rates
- Explain the difference between money supply targeting and interest rate targeting
- Explain the lags in the operation of the Bank of Canada's monetary policy
- Describe the Bank of Canada's evolving policies between 1962 and 1998

## Increasing Your Productivity

This chapter, like the previous one, is not heavy on new analytical material. It applies and extends the *IS-LM* model of aggregate demand. It does so, however, with a new twist and being aware of the new twist will allow you to make progress more easily. The new twist is money supply targeting versus interest rate targeting.

If the central bank targets the interest rate, its action makes the supply of money perfectly elastic at its targeted interest rate. The effect of such an action is to make the *LM* curve irrelevant for the determination of equilibrium in the *IS-LM* framework. Instead, equilibrium is determined at the point of intersection of the *IS* curve and the target interest rate. Once you have understood this fact, the comparison of interest rate targeting and money supply targeting is very straightforward. In one case you are studying the predictions from the *IS-LM* model, and in the other case you are studying the predictions of a model in which only the *IS* curve and fixed interest rate are relevant. In effect, you are comparing the *IS-LM* model and the aggregate expenditure model of Chapter 5.

An implication of interest rate targeting is that the aggregate demand is vertical. To appreciate this outcome, just think about the effect on the money market of a change in the price level. Other things being equal, a change in the price level changes the real money supply and the interest rate. Since the Bank of Canada is pegging the interest at its target level, the money supply adjusts automatically to compensate for any change in the price level. As a result, the real money supply does not change. With no change in the real money supply, there is no change in the real GDP, so the *AD* curve is vertical. The *AD* curve shifts if there is a *change* in the target interest rate because the resulting change in the interest rate brings a change in aggregate expenditure.

## Self Test

### Fill in the Blanks

1. Bank reserves are the deposits held by __________ __________ at the Bank of Canada, together with currency held in the vaults and tills of __________.
2. Notes and coins held by households and firms is __________ __________ __________ __________.
3. The monetary base is the sum of __________ __________ and currency held by the public.
4. M1 is currency held by the public plus __________ __________ at chartered banks.
5. __________ is equal to __________ plus savings deposits and notice deposits at chartered banks plus deposits at trust and

mortgage companies, credit unions and caisse populaires, and other financial institutions.

6. An ____________ is the purchase or sale of government securities by the Bank of Canada in order to change the monetary base.
7. The ____________ the overnight lending rate, the smaller is the quantity of monetary base that chartered banks plan to hold.
8. Government deposit shifting is the shifting of government funds between the Bank of Canada and ____________ ____________.
9. The reserves that chartered banks regard as necessary to conduct their business are ____________ ____________.
10. Excess reserves equal ____________ ____________ minus ____________ ____________.
11. The money multiplier is the change in the ____________ per one-dollar change in ____________.
12. The time lag between an economic event and observing that event is an ____________ lag; the time lapse between observing the economy and being able to decide how much information the observation provides is an ____________ lag.
13. The ____________ effects of policy actions on indicators or targets are the impact effects. ____________ effects are the drawn-out effects that take place as households and firms respond to policy actions.
14. The development of new financial products such as credit cards, interest-bearing chequing accounts, and money market funds is ____________ ____________.
15. During the era of the Diefenbaker dollar, the world was operating on a ____________ ____________ ____________.

True or False

1. The governor of the Bank of Canada is appointed by the Bank's board of directors.
2. The bank rate is the interest rate paid by chartered banks when they borrow from each other.
3. The Bank of Canada can influence the money supply by changing the supply of monetary base through an open market operation.
4. Monetary base is the total deposits held by chartered banks at the Bank of Canada, together with currency held in the vaults and tills of chartered banks.
5. Effectiveness lags are the time lapses from the implementation of a policy action to its effects on the target variables.
6. Dynamic effects are the instantaneous effects of policy actions on indicators or targets.
7. The time lags in the operation of monetary policy are not only long but also variable.
8. The money multiplier is the change in the money supply per one-dollar change in the monetary base.
9. The act under which the Bank of Canada operates has not changed since the bank was created in 1935.
10. The Bank of Canada can increase the monetary base with an open market purchase of securities or by lowering the overnight lending rate.
11. Currency held by the public is part of M1 but not part of the monetary base.
12. An open market purchase of securities by the Bank of Canada decreases the monetary base.
13. The larger the percentage of the money supply held as currency, the smaller is the money multiplier.
14. By targeting interest rates rather than the money supply, the Bank of Canada can prevent instability in the demand for money from effecting aggregate demand.
15. By targeting the interest rate rather than the money supply, the Bank of Canada can prevent fluctuations resulting from changes in business expectations about future profits from influencing aggregate demand.
16. By targeting the money supply rather than interest rates, the Bank of Canada can narrow the range of fluctuations in aggregate demand arising from instability in the demand for money function.

17. By targeting interest rates rather than the money supply, the Bank of Canada makes aggregate demand more elastic.

18. Interest rate targeting causes inflation if the interest rate target is set too low.

19. If the Bank of Canada could make its decision more quickly, then there would be no major time lags in the operation of monetary policy.

20. Financial innovation shifted the demand for money function in the 1980s and 1990s.

## Multiple Choice

1. The Bank of Canada was created in
(a) 1925.
(b) 1935.
(c) 1945.
(d) 1899.
(e) 1933.

2. The monetary base consists of
(a) bank deposits at the Bank of Canada.
(b) the sum of bank reserves and currency held by the public.
(c) the money supply.
(d) government securities held by the Bank of Canada.
(e) gold held by the Bank of Canada.

3. The Bank of Canada's main instruments for influencing the money supply include
(a) printing money.
(b) reserve requirements.
(c) the purchase and sale of government securities.
(d) both (b) and (c).
(e) all of the above.

4. The interest rate at which the Bank of Canada is willing to lend funds and the rate that it pays the chartered banks on their deposits at the Bank of Canada is the
(a) discount rate.
(b) bank rate.
(c) transactions rate.
(d) reserve rate.
(e) current rate.

5. The Bank of Canada controls the
(a) bank rate by setting the overnight lending rate.
(b) overnight lending rate by setting the bank rate.
(c) overnight lending rate by setting the quantity of reserves that chartered banks must hold.
(d) bank rate by setting the quantity of reserves that chartered banks must hold.
(e) none of the above.

6. The lower the overnight lending rate,
(a) the greater is the quantity of monetary base that chartered banks plan to hold.
(b) the smaller is the quantity of monetary base that chartered banks plan to hold.
(c) the greater is the quantity of deposits that the government of Canada transfers to chartered banks.
(d) the smaller is the quantity of deposits that the government of Canada transfers to chartered banks.
(e) none of the above.

7. The assets of the Bank of Canada are mainly
(a) gold.
(b) bank reserves.
(c) government securities.
(d) both (a) and (c).
(d) all of the above.

8. An open market
(a) purchase of government securities by the Bank of Canada increases the monetary base.
(b) purchase of government securities by the Bank of Canada decreases the monetary base.
(c) sale of government securities by the Bank of Canada increases the monetary base.
(d) sale of government securities by the Bank of Canada has no effect on the monetary base
(e) none of the above

9. The quantity of monetary base demanded is equal to

(a) $\frac{(a+b)}{(1+a)}M.$

(b) $\frac{(a-b)}{(1+a)}M.$

(c) $\frac{(a-b)}{(1-a)}M.$

(d) $\frac{(a-b)}{(1+b)}M.$

(e) $\frac{(b-a)}{(1+a)}M.$

10. The monetary base includes
(a) demand deposits held by the public.
(b) demand deposits held by the government.
(c) currency held by the public.
(d) government securities.
(e) all the liabilities of the Bank of Canada.

11. Assets of chartered banks include
(a) bank reserves and demand deposits.
(b) currency held by the public and government securities.
(c) demand deposits and fixed-term deposits.
(d) bank reserves, loans, and investments.
(e) loans, investments, and currency held by the public.

12. Other things being equal, the money multiplier is larger,
(a) the larger the public's demand for currency as a proportion of total deposits.
(b) the larger the banks' demand for reserves as a proportion of total deposits.
(c) the smaller the public's demand for currency as a proportion of total deposits.
(d) the larger is the sum of the public's demand for currency and the banks' demand for reserves as a proportion of total deposits.
(e) the larger is an open market operation.

13. Targeting the interest rate rather than the money supply when there are shocks to the *IS* curve
(a) increases the fluctuations in the amount of money held.
(b) increases fluctuations in investment.
(c) decreases fluctuations in consumption.
(d) increases fluctuations in aggregate demand.
(e) both (a) and (d).

14. Shocks to the *IS* curve can be effectively reduced by
(a) interest rate targeting.
(b) money supply targeting.
(c) increasing the money supply whenever there is a positive shock to investment.
(d) cutting interest rates when spending increases.
(e) none of the above.

15. With money supply targeting, a financial innovation that decreases the demand for money,
(a) increases the interest rate and decreases real GDP.
(b) decreases the interest rate and increases real GDP.
(c) decreases the interest rate and decreases real GDP.
(d) increases the interest rate and increases real GDP.
(e) has an ambiguous effect on the interest rate and real GDP.

16. With interest rate targeting, a decrease in the target interest rate
(a) increases aggregate demand.
(b) results in a movement along the aggregate demand curve.
(c) increases aggregate supply.
(d) increases short-run aggregate supply but not long-run aggregate supply.
(e) increases investment but decreases consumption.

17. If the interest rate is targeted and the target interest rate is below its full-employment level
(a) the price level begins to rise, decreasing aggregate demand and decreasing real GDP to its full-employment level.
(b) the price level begins to increase but aggregate supply falls.
(c) real GDP and the price level both decrease.
(d) the price level increases without limit but real GDP returns to its long-run aggregate supply level.
(e) the price level begins to increase without limit and real GDP remains above its long-run level.

18. With interest rate targeting,
(a) an increase in the demand for money has a larger effect on real GDP and the price level than it does with money supply targeting.
(b) a decrease in the demand for money has a smaller effect on real GDP and the price level than it does with money supply targeting.
(c) an increase in investment demand has a smaller effect on real GDP and the price level than it does with money supply targeting.
(d) an increase in consumption demand has a smaller effect on real GDP and price level than it does with money supply targeting.
(e) a decrease in short-run aggregate supply has a larger effect on real GDP than it does with money supply targeting.

19. Since 1989, the Bank of Canada has
(a) developed monetary policy to accommodate inflation.
(b) pursued interest rate targeting and brought interest rates down.
(c) pursued published inflation targets.
(d) abandoned open market operations.
(e) adopted a "checklist" approach that pays attention to the exchange rate and monetary aggregates.

20. An open market sale of government securities to chartered banks
(a) increases their desired reserves.
(b) decreases their desired reserves.
(c) increases their actual reserves.
(d) decreases their actual reserves.
(e) has no effect on their actual reserves.

## Short Answer Questions

1. In what year was the Bank of Canada established? By what act is the Bank of Canada currently governed?
2. What is the overnight lending rate?
3. What are the two stages in the effectiveness lags. Explain each stage.
4. (a) What are the main instruments the Bank of Canada uses to influence the money supply?

   (b) Which instrument is used to influence the course of the economy?
5. Explain what the size of the money supply depends on.
6. Explain how an open market operation changes the money supply.
7. What is the money multiplier?
8. Under what type of targeting do fluctuations in the demand for money bring fluctuations in interest rates and aggregate demand?
9. What happens if the interest rate is set too low when the Bank of Canada is following a policy of interest rate targeting?
10. What are time lags in the operation of monetary policy?

## Problem Solving

### Practice Problems

1. You are given the following information about Green Island in 1999.

| Item | $ million |
|---|---|
| Currency held by public | 10 |
| Bank reserves | 5 |
| M1 | 110 |

(a) Calculate Green Island's monetary base in 1999.

(b) Calculate the amount of demand deposits

held at chartered banks in 1999.

(c) Calculate the money multiplier.

**Solutions to Practice Problems**

1. (a) Calculate Green Island's monetary base in 1999.

The monetary base is the sum of bank reserves and currency held by the public. Bank reserves are $5 million and currency held by the public is $10 million so the monetary base is $15 million.

(b) Calculate the amount of demand deposits held at chartered banks in 1999.

M1 is the currency held by the public plus demand deposits at chartered banks. So demand deposits equal M1 minus the currency held by the public.

M1 is $110 million and currency held by the public is $10 million. Demand deposits at chartered banks are $100 million.

(c) Calculate the money multiplier.

The money multiplier is (1 + *a*) divided by (*a* + *b*), where *a* is the proportion of total deposits that the public holds as currency and *b* is the proportion of total deposits that banks hold as reserves. On Green Island, *a* is 0.1 and *b* is 0.05. The money multiplier is 1.1/0.15, which is 7.33.

## Problems to Solve

1. On Coral Island, the public holds $5,000 of currency, banks hold $10,000 of reserves, and the public holds $20,000 in demand deposits at chartered banks.

(a) Calculate M1.

(b) Calculate the monetary base.

2. You are given the following information about Space World:

| Item | $ million |
|---|---|
| Demand deposits at chartered banks | 20 |
| Savings and notice deposits at chartered banks | 5 |
| Currency held by the public | 15 |
| Deposits at all other financial institutions | 5 |
| Gold reserves | 1 |
| Foreign currency deposits | 1 |

(a) Calculate M1.

(b) Calculate M2+.

**Fact 17.1**

| | Year | |
|---|---|---|
| Item | 1997 | 1998 |
| Currency held by public | 150 | 180 |
| Bank reserves | 50 | 60 |
| M1 | 1,150 | 1,380 |

3. Use Fact 17.1.

(a) Calculate the monetary base in 1997 and 1998.

(b) Calculate the change in the monetary base.

(c) Calculate the amount of demand deposits at chartered banks in 1997 and 1998.

(d) Calculate the money multiplier.

4. Use Fact 17.1. The central bank conducts an open market purchase of government securities in 1999 of 50. Calculate the 1999 values of

(a) M1.

(b) the amount of currency held by the public.

(c) the amount of demand deposits held at chartered banks.

(d) the amount of bank reserves.

**Fact 17.2** You are given the following information about an economy:

$c = 100 + 0.9(y - t)$

$i = 50 - 50r + e_1$

$g = 100$

$t = 100$

$M/P = 0.15y + 50 - 50r + e2$

$M = 500$

$P = 1.$

$e_1$ is a random shock to investment demand and $e_2$ is a random shock to the demand for money.

5. Use Fact 17.2. Calculate the multiplier effect on aggregate demand

(a) of a random shock to investment demand with interest rate targeting.

(b) of a random shock to investment demand with money supply targeting.

(c) a random shock to the demand for money with money supply targeting.

(d) a random shock to the demand for money with interest rate targeting.

Calculate the slope of the aggregate demand curve at the equilibrium point with

(e) money supply targeting

(f) interest rate targeting

## Answers

### Fill in the Blanks

1. chartered banks, chartered banks
2. currency held by the public
3. bank reserves
4. demand deposits
5. M2+, M1
6. open market operation
7. higher
8. chartered banks
9. desired reserves
10. actual reserves, desired reserves
11. money supply, monetary base
12. observation, interpretation
13. instantaneous, Dynamic
14. financial innovation
15. gold exchange standard

### True or False

1F 5T 9F 13T 17F
2F 6F 10T 14T 18T
3T 7T 11F 15F 19F
4F 8T 12F 16F 20T

### Multiple Choice

1b 5b 9a 13e 17e
2b 6a 10c 14b 18b
3c 7c 11d 15b 19c
4b 8b 12c 16a 20d

### Short Answer Questions

1. The Bank of Canada was established in 1935. It is currently governed by the provisions of the Bank of Canada Act of 1967.
2. The overnight lending rate is the interest rate paid by chartered banks when they borrow from each other or from other financial institutions.
3. The two stages of effectiveness lags are the impact effects and the dynamic effects. Impact effects are the instantaneous effects of policy actions on indicators or targets. Dynamic effects are the drawn-out effects that take place as households and firms respond to

policy actions.

4. (a) The main instruments the Bank of Canada uses to influence the money supply are open market operations, the overnight lending rate, and government deposit shifting.

   (b) Open market operations is the only instrument that is used to influence the course of the economy.

5. The size of the money supply depends partly on the actions of the Bank of Canada and partly on the response of the chartered banks and other financial institutions, as well as the general public.

6. An open market purchase by the Bank of Canada increases the monetary base. Banks now have excess reserves and they increase lending. As banks lend their excess reserves, creating additional loans and additional deposits, they also stimulate a demand for currency to be held by the public. This process of lending and money creation comes to an end when the total quantity of bank deposits has increased so that the extra demand for reserves by the banks and the extra demand for currency by the general public equals the additional monetary base created.

7. The money multiplier is the change in the money supply per one-dollar change in monetary base.

8. Targeting the money supply means that fluctuations in the demand for money bring fluctuations in interest rates and aggregate demand.

9. If the interest rate is set too low, real GDP is greater than potential GDP. The economy is above full employment and the wage rate increases. The rising wage rate shifts the *SAS* curve upward and the price level rises. If the interest rate is not adjusted, an inflation process with no natural limit begins. Only if interest rates are increased to shift the aggregate demand curve leftward can the inflation process be ended.

10. The time lags in the operation of monetary policy are observation lags, interpretation lags, decision lags, implementation lags, and effectiveness lags.

## Problem Solving

1. (a) \$25,000

   (b) \$15,000

2. (a) \$35 million

   (b) \$45 million

3. (a) Monetary base 1997 = 200; Monetary base 1998 = 240

   (b) +40

   (c) Demand deposits 1997 = 1,000; Demand deposits 1998 = 1,200

   (d) 5.75

4. (a) 1,667.5

   (b) 217.5

   (c) 1,450

   (d) 72.5

5. (a) 10

   (b) 4

   (c) –4

   (d) 0

   (e) –0.0005

   (f) ∞

**Chapter 18**

# Stabilizing the World Economy

## Perspective and Focus

This chapter broadens your vision away from the problems of the Canadian economy to the interactions among economies and the problems of the global economy. This chapter builds on and makes use of the *IS-LM* model of the open economy that you studied in Chapter 8.

## Learning Objectives

*After studying this chapter, you will be able to:*

- Describe the main trends in the global economy
- Describe the main features of the international monetary system
- Explain how exchange rates are determined
- Explain some of the major movements in foreign exchange rates
- Explain how the balance of payments is determined
- Explain the global business cycle and its international transmission

## Increasing Your Productivity

One point in the analysis of this chapter that often causes students problems is the definition of the exchange rate. In this chapter, the exchange rate is defined as units of foreign currency per unit of domestic currency. The chapter uses yen and dollars, and the exchange rate is measured as yen per dollar. If the exchange rate goes down from 140 yen per dollar to 120 yen per dollar, the yen strengthens and the dollar weakens. A dollar costs a smaller number of yen and you get fewer yen for your dollar.

It is possible to define the exchange rate the other way around as dollars per yen. When the exchange rate is expressed as dollars per yen and its value declines, the dollar strengthens. When the exchange rate is expressed as dollars per yen and its value rises, the dollar weakens.

Another potential stumbling block in this chapter is the concept *dollar-denominated assets*. Financial assets can be denominated in any currency. The currency of denomination defines the units in which the asset will be repaid or redeemed. A Canadian dollar asset is one that is worth a certain number of Canadian dollars. How much that asset will ultimately be worth in terms of Canadian dollars or Japanese yen depends on the exchange rate between the currencies. The currency of denomination defines the nature of the legal obligation being undertaken.

The third potential stumbling block in this chapter is the distinction between stocks and flows. Dollars that flow across the foreign exchange market in either direction do not determine the price or value of the currency in terms of another currency. The demand for currency and the supply of currency are stock concepts. They are the demand for and supply of a stock of assets. Stocks are influenced by flows and flows result from changes in desired stocks. But it is the demand for dollar-denominated assets by domestic and foreign holders and the supply of dollar-denominated assets that determine the equilibrium price of a dollar in the foreign exchange market.

With these concepts clear, you will have no difficulty with the analysis in this chapter.

## Self Test

### Fill in the Blanks

1. A monetary system in which most major countries fix the value of their currency in terms of gold and permit gold to freely enter and leave the country is the ______________ ______________.
2. A set of arrangements and institutions for governing the financial relations among countries is the ______________ ______________.
3. Devaluation is a ____________ in the value of a ____________ exchange rate.
4. ____________ is an increase in the value of a fixed exchange rate.
5. The quantity of dollar assets demanded is the quantity of ______________ ______________ denominated in Canadian dollars that people plan to hold at a given point in time. The quantity of dollar assets

supplied is the quantity of ____________ ____________ denominated in Canadian dollars available to be held at a point in time.

## True or False

1. An international monetary system is a set of arrangements and institutions for governing the financial relations among countries.
2. Other things remaining constant, the lower the interest rate on dollar assets, the greater is the demand for dollar assets; the lower is the interest rate on yen assets, the lower is the demand for demand for dollar assets; the lower is the future exchange rate, the greater is the demand for dollar assets.
3. For a nation to make a credible revaluation of its currency, it must have a large enough stock of foreign exchange reserves to convince people that it can maintain the new higher value for its currency.
4. Under a managed float, speeding up or slowing down the growth rate of the money supply sets up the same dynamic overshooting adjustments as is done under flexible exchange rates.
5. A severe monetary contraction in Singapore and Indonesia during 1997 and 1998 prevented a large depreciation of the Singapore dollar and the Indonesian rupiah.
6. Since a higher Canadian real exchange rate increases Canadian imports and decreases Canadian exports, Canadian net exports rise, resulting in a larger current account surplus or a smaller current account deficit.
7. A speedup of the growth rate of the Canadian money supply leads to a depreciation of the currency that overshoots its long-run value and a gradual decrease in the inflation rate.
8. The International Monetary Fund provides assistance to countries with long-term balance of payment problems and the World Bank provides short-term financing to developing countries with intermittent shortages of foreign exchange.
9. A tightening of monetary policy increases interest rates, increases the exchange rate, and increases the current account deficit.
10. A decrease in the value of a fixed exchange rate is known a revaluation.
11. The Japanese yen depreciated more than the U.S. dollar, British pound, and Canadian dollar during the 1980s.
12. The international monetary system is based on fixed exchange rates.
13. Other things being equal, an increase in interest rates in Canada causes an increase in the demand for dollar-denominated financial assets.
14. With a fixed exchange rate, the supply of dollar assets is perfectly elastic.
15. The quantity of dollar assets demanded is a flow.
16. The lower the exchange rate, the higher is the expected rate of return on dollar assets and the greater is the quantity of dollar assets that people plan to hold.
17. Under a fixed exchange rate, the domestic economy experiences a greater decrease in real GDP as a result of a world recession than under a flexible exchange rate.
18. A decrease in interest rates in the rest of the world increases real GDP in the domestic economy under flexible exchange rates but decreases real GDP in the domestic economy under fixed exchange rates.
19. A country can completely insulate itself from foreign supply shocks by having a flexible exchange rate.
20. The 1970s was a decade in which there is a clear international business cycle.

## Multiple Choice

1. The global macroeconomy consists of some

(a) four billion people residing in 300 countries.

(b) six billion people living in 150 countries.

(c) thirty billion people residing in 500 countries.

(d) fifty billion people living in 100 countries.

(e) one billion people residing in 50 countries.

2. The most important aspect of an international monetary system is its rules governing the determination of exchange rates. These include

(a) fixed exchange rates.

(b) flexible exchange rates.

(c) managed-floating exchange rates.

(d) both (a) and (b).

(e) all the above.

3. Which of the following exchange rates does the monetary authority pay attention to in the foreign exchange market in an attempt to smooth out fluctuations in the exchange rate?

(a) Fixed exchange rate.

(b) Flexible exchange rate.

(c) Managed-floating exchange rate.

(d) Pegged exchange rate.

(e) both (a) and (b).

4. With a flexible exchange rate, the Bank of Canada

(a) supplies more dollar assets when the exchange rate rises.

(b) takes no action to change the supply of dollar assets.

(c) supplies more dollar assets when the exchange rate falls.

(d) demands more dollar assets when the exchange rate falls.

(e) none of the above.

5. Which of the following measures the value of a national currency in terms of the foreign goods and services that it will buy?

(a) Nominal Exchange Rate (NER).

(b) Implicit Price Deflator (IPD).

(c) Consumer Price Index (CPI).

(d) Real Exchange Rate (RER).

(e) none of the above.

6. Which of the following is the most important short-run influence on the real exchange rate?

(a) Flexible exchange rate.

(b) Nominal exchange rate.

(c) Fixed exchange rate.

(d) Floating exchange rate.

(e) Pegged exchange rate.

7. The *IS* curve under

(a) flexible exchange rates is steeper than under fixed exchange rates.

(b) flexible exchange rates is less steep than under fixed exchange rates.

(c) fixed exchange rates is less steep than under flexible exchange rates.

(d) fixed exchange rates is as steep as under flexible exchange rates.

(e) none of the above.

8. A world recession hits. In a domestic economy with a flexible exchange rate, the *IS* curve

(a) shifts leftward and the *LM* curve shifts leftward.

(b) shifts leftward and the *LM* curve shifts rightward.

(c) shifts rightward and the *LM* curve shifts leftward.

(d) does not shift and the *LM* curve shifts leftward.

(e) shifts leftward and the *LM* curve does not shift.

9. The international monetary system of the 1990s is a

(a) fixed exchange system.

(b) flexible exchange system.

(c) managed-floating system.

(d) pegged exchange system.

(e) gold standard system.

10. The supply curve of dollar-denominated assets under fixed exchange rates is

(a) vertical at the chosen value for the exchange rate.

(b) horizontal at the chosen value for the exchange rate.

(c) upward sloping at the chosen value for the exchange rate.

(d) downward sloping at the chosen value for the exchange rate.

(e) none of the above.

11. Which of the following statements is true?
(a) There is no international transmission of disturbances under fixed exchange rates.
(b) International transmission of disturbances is stronger under fixed exchange rates than under flexible exchange rates.
(c) There is no international transmission of disturbances under flexible exchange rates.
(d) International transmission of disturbances is stronger under flexible exchange rates than under fixed exchange rates.
(e) none of the above.

12. Each of the following results in an increase in the demand for dollar-denominated assets *except*
(a) an increase in the interest rate on dollar-denominated assets.
(b) a decrease in the interest rate on yen-denominated assets.
(c) an expectation that the dollar will strengthen against the yen.
(d) an expectation that the interest rate on yen-denominated assets will increase.
(e) an increase in the volume of transactions undertaken using dollars

13. The slope of the supply of dollar-denominated assets curve depends on the exchange rate regime and
(a) is more elastic with a fixed exchange rate than a managed-floating exchange rate.
(b) is more elastic with a flexible exchange rate than a managed-floating exchange rate.
(c) is more elastic with a managed-floating exchange rate than a fixed exchange rate.
(d) can sometimes be more elastic with a managed-floating exchange rate than with a fixed exchange rate.
(e) varies from day to day depending on the actions on the central bank.

14. Compared with a fixed exchange rate, a managed-floating exchange rate regime results in
(a) smaller fluctuations in the exchange rate.
(b) smaller fluctuations in the quantity of dollar-denominated assets.
(c) larger fluctuations in the exchange rate.
(d) larger fluctuations in the supply of dollar-denominated assets.
(e) both (b) and (c).

15. Compared with a flexible exchange rate regime, under a managed-floating exchange rate regime
(a) the exchange rate fluctuates by more.
(b) the exchange rate fluctuates by less.
(c) it is not possible to say whether the exchange rate fluctuates by more or less.
(d) there are larger fluctuations in the quantity of dollar-denominated assets.
(e) both (b) and (d).

16. If the supply of dollar-denominated assets decreases, then with a flexible exchange rate system, the currency
(a) appreciates but initially by less than it eventually appreciates.
(b) does not change until the balance of payments adjusts.
(c) depreciates but initially by more than it eventually depreciates.
(d) appreciates but initially by more than it eventually appreciates.
(e) could appreciate or depreciate depending on expectations.

17. Under flexible exchange rates, a decrease in real GDP in the rest of the world
(a) does not decrease domestic income because the exchange rate adjusts.
(b) decreases the domestic interest rate initially but capital flows adjust to keep real GDP constant.
(c) decreases the domestic interest rate with no change in domestic real GDP.
(d) decreases the domestic interest rate and decreases domestic real GDP.
(e) decreases the domestic interest rate but as the exchange rate adjusts, the interest rate returns to its original level.

18. A decrease in world interest rates
(a) decreases real GDP under flexible exchange rates and increases real GDP under fixed

exchange rates.

(b) decreases domestic real GDP under fixed exchanges and increases domestic real GDP under flexible exchange rates.

(c) increases domestic real GDP under flexible exchange rates and increases it under fixed exchange rates.

(d) has no effect on domestic real GDP regardless of the exchange rate regime.

(e) decreases domestic real GDP under flexible exchange rates and decreases it under fixed exchange rates.

19. The international business cycle

(a) was more synchronized under the fixed exchange rate period of the 1960s than in later decades.

(b) was more synchronized in the 1970s when exchange rates were flexible.

(c) was more synchronized in the early 1980s when exchange rates were flexible.

(d) converged to a single cycle by 1990.

(e) demonstrates the power of flexible exchange rates to isolate economies from the problems of others.

20. With a fixed exchange rate, the supply curve of Canadian dollar assets is

(a) perfectly elastic.

(b) perfectly inelastic.

(c) upward sloping.

(d) downward sloping.

(e) constantly shifting to keep the exchange rate at its fixed level.

## Short Answer Questions

1. Distinguish between devaluation and revaluation of a currency.

2. What are Canadian dollar-denominated assets? Give some examples.

3. Name three factors that influence the relative return on dollar assets.

4. Explain the role of the monetary authority with a

(a) fixed exchange rate.

(b) flexible exchange rate.

(c) managed-floating exchange rate.

5. (a) What is meant by the quantity of dollar assets supplied?

(b) What is meant by the supply of dollar assets?

6. How does the monetary authority influence the balance of payments by its intervention?

7 .Why is it possible that the world economy will be less stable under flexible exchange rates than under fixed exchange rates?

8. What was the Bretton Woods system?

9. What have been the main trends in world exports between 1968 and 1998?

10. How does a change in aggregate demand in one country transmit to other countries?

## Problem Solving

### Practice Problems

1. Jodi has $1,000. By holding dollar assets, she can get a return of 8 percent a year. At the same time, the interest rate on yen assets is 3 percent a year. The exchange rate is 160 yen per dollar today and is expected to be 150 yen per dollar one year from today.

(a) What is Jodi's rate of return if she holds her $1,000 in dollar assets for one year?

(b) What is her expected rate of return on yen assets if she holds her $1,000 in yen assets for one year?

### Solutions to Practice Problems

1. (a) What is Jodi's rate of return if she holds her $1,000 in dollar assets for one year?
If she holds her $1,000 in dollar assets her rate of return will be 8 percent a year.

(b) What is her expected rate of return on yen assets if she holds her $1,000 in yen assets for one year?
If she holds her $1,000 in yen assets for the year, she must initially convert her dollars at the spot exchange rate. Doing this gives her 160,000 yen. At the end of the year she will have 160,000(1 + 0.03), or 164,800 yen. But she will then have to convert the yen back into

dollars. She expects that when she does this she will have 164,800/150, or 1,098.67 dollars. Her expected rate of return is (1,098.67 – 1,000)/1,000, which is 9.87 percent a year.

## Problems to Solve

1. Fran has $100. By holding dollar assets, she can get a return of 10 percent a year. At the same time, the interest rate on yen assets is 5 percent a year. The exchange rate is 130 yen per dollar today and is expected to be 120 yen per dollar one year from today.

   (a)What is Fran's rate of return if she holds $100 in dollar assets for one year?

   (b)What is Fran's expected rate of return on yen assets one year from now if she holds $100 in yen assets for one year from today?

2. When the number of yen per dollar decreases, what effect does it have on the

   (a) dollar?

   (b) yen?

3. Random fluctuations in the demand for dollar assets lead to random fluctuations in the exchange rate and/or in the quantity of dollar assets in existence. How do fluctuations in the exchange rate and the quantity of dollar assets in existence compare under a

   (a) fixed exchange rate regime?

   (b) flexible exchange rate regime?

   (c) managed-floating exchange rate regime?

4. How does the exchange rate influence the balance of payments?

5. How does the balance of payments influence the exchange rate?

**Fact 18.1** You are given the following information:

| | |
|---|---|
| Interest rate in Japan | 3 percent a year |
| Interest rate in Canada | 10 percent a year |
| Today's exchange rate | 150 yen per dollar |

6. Use Fact 18.1. Calculate

   (a) the expected exchange rate one year in the future.

   (b) the expected rate of return for a Canadian investing in Japan when the yen are converted to dollars.

7. Use Fact 18.1. Calculate

   (a) the expected rate of return for a Japanese investing in Canada when the dollars are converted into Japanese yen

   (b) the expected rate of appreciation or depreciation of the dollar against the yen.

8. If Canada tries to establish a fixed exchange rate at a rate higher than what the market believes can be sustained, what will happen to the exchange rate and to Canadian foreign exchange reserves?

9. Explain why an increase in the supply of dollar-denominated assets leads to a depreciation of the currency under flexible exchange rates and why, in the process, the exchange rate undershoots its long-run equilibrium value.

10. Explain how an increase in world real GDP is transmitted to the domestic economy

    (a) under fixed exchange rates.

    (b) under flexible exchange rates.

## Answers

### Fill in the Blanks

1. international gold standard
2. international monetary system
3. decrease, fixed
4. Revaluation
5. net financial assets, net financial assets

### True or False

1T 5F 9T 13T 17T
2F 6F 10F 14T 18F
3T 7F 11F 15F 19F
4T 8F 12F 16T 20T

### Multiple Choice

1b 5d 9c 13a 17e
2e 6b 10b 14e 18a
3c 7b 11b 15e 19b
4b 8e 12d 16d 20a

### Short Answer Questions

1. A devaluation of a currency is a decrease in the fixed exchange rate and a revaluation of a currency is an increase in the fixed exchange rate.
2. Canadian dollar-denominated assets are promises to pay so many Canadian dollars under given circumstance on a given date. Examples are Bank of Canada notes, the monetary base, M1, M2+, and Canadian government debt held by the public.
3. Three factors that influence the relative return on dollar assets are the dollar interest rate, the foreign interest rate, and the future exchange rate.
4. (a) Under a fixed exchange rate, the monetary authority pegs the foreign currency price of the domestic currency and stands ready to buy or sell foreign assets in exchange for domestic assets.

   (b) Under a flexible exchange rate, the monetary authority pays no attention to the foreign exchange value of its currency. There is a given quantity of dollar assets in existence and this quantity is independent of the exchange rate.

   (c) Under a managed-floating exchange rate, the monetary authority pays attention to the foreign exchange market and attempts to smooth out fluctuations in the exchange rate. To do this, it increases the quantity of dollar assets supplied when the dollar appreciates and decreases the quantity supplied when the dollar depreciates.
5. (a) The quantity of Canadian dollar assets supplied is the quantity of net financial assets denominated in Canadian dollars available to be held at a point in time.

   (b) The supply of Canadian dollar assets is the relationship between the quantity of dollar assets supplied and the exchange rate.
6. The official settlements account of the balance of payments records the transactions by the monetary authority in the foreign exchange market. By its intervention, the monetary authority influences the balance of payments. A decision to use foreign reserves to buy dollar assets worsens the balance of payments. A decision to use dollar assets to buy foreign reserves improves the balance of payments.
7. Under flexible exchange rates, the exchange rate can overshoot changes in the price level, resulting in changes in the real exchange rate. Such changes in the real exchange rate bring fluctuations in net exports. These fluctuations, in turn, disturb real economic activity. This source of macroeconomic disturbance is absent in a fixed exchange rate world.
8. The Bretton Woods system was an international monetary system based on the U.S. dollar being linked to gold and the values of all other currencies being fixed in terms of the U.S. dollar. This system operated until the early 1970s.
9. World exports expanded rapidly during the 1970s but fell sharply through the mid-1980s before rising again. Exports from the developing countries contributed most to the decline in world exports in the 1980s. Since 1968, world exports have expanded more than five-fold.
10. A change in aggregate demand in one country transmits to other countries through net exports.

## Problem Solving

1. (a) 10 percent

   (b) 13.75 percent

2. (a) The dollar depreciates.

   (b) The yen appreciates.

3. (a) With a fixed exchange rate, the exchange rate remains constant but fluctuations in the quantity of dollar assets in existence are greatest.

   (b) With a flexible exchange rate, the quantity of dollar assets in existence is fixed and fluctuations in the exchange rate are greatest.

   (c) With a managed-floating exchange rate, the fluctuations in the exchange rate are smaller than under a flexible exchange rate and the fluctuations in the quantity of dollar assets are smaller than in the case of a fixed exchange rate.

4. The exchange rate influences the balance of payments through its effects on international relative prices—real exchange rates.

5. The balance of payments influences the exchange rate through expectations and intervention.

6. (a) 140.45

   (b) 10 percent

7. (a) 3 percent

   (b) depreciation of approximately 7 percent

8. To answer this question draw a diagram similar to that in Figure 18.8(b) in the textbook. The unsustainable revaluation sets up an expectation of the future devaluation. The demand for dollar-denominated assets decreases and foreign exchange reserves have to be used to maintain the exchange rate. The reserves keep falling until they reach a point below which they can fall no further. At this point the new higher unsustainable exchange rate is abandoned and the currency depreciates, probably to a level lower than that from which it started.

9. To answer this question use Figure 18.9 and Figure 18.10 in the textbook. The detailed answer is contained in the extended caption to these two figures.

10. (a) An increase in world real GDP shifts the *IS* curve to the right and the domestic interest rate rises. The exchange rate is fixed so it does not change. The domestic interest rate now exceeds the world interest rate, so funds flow into the domestic economy. The domestic money supply increases and the *LM* curve shifts to the right. In the process, the interest rate gradually falls but real GDP continues to increase. The process comes to an end when the domestic interest rate equals the world interest rate.

    (b) Under flexible exchange rates, an increase in world real GDP shifts the *IS* curve rightward increasing the interest rate and real GDP. There is no change in the money supply.

## Chapter 19

# Consumption and Saving

## Perspective and Focus

The chapters that appear in this part of the book, take a deeper look at the determination of the components of aggregate expenditure and aggregate demand. This chapter looks at consumption and saving. It digs more deeply behind the consumption function that you studied in Chapter 5. You may be studying this chapter in sequence or you may be studying it immediately after you've studied Chapter 5. It works well either way, so you should not be alarmed whichever of these orders you've been asked to study the chapter in.

## Learning Objectives

*After studying this chapter, you will be able to:*

- Describe the main facts about consumption, saving, and income, both over time and across income groups
- Describe a household's intertemporal and lifetime budget constraints
- Explain how consumption and saving decisions are made
- Define permanent income and explain the permanent income hypothesis
- Explain the life-cycle hypothesis
- Explain the behaviour of consumption and saving in Canada and other countries in the 1980s and 1990s
- Explain the effects of taxes on consumption and saving
- Explain the effects of money and credit on consumption and saving

## Increasing Your Productivity

This chapter contains an analysis of the household's choice of the timing of its consumption. The basic analysis is an application of the microeconomic theory of indifference curves and the determination of substitution and wealth effects. (The wealth effect is the intertemporal analog of the income effect in a choice made at a given point in time). If you are studying microeconomics at the same time as macroeconomics, then now is a good opportunity to cross-fertilize the two parts of the discipline.

The core of the chapter is contained in section 19.3. The permanent income hypothesis in section 19.4 and the life-cycle hypothesis in section 19.5 are extensions of this basic model. There is no point in moving forward to these parts until you are thoroughly familiar with the basic model in section 19.3.

This chapter is a good one for illustrating the method of scientific analysis in economics. It shows you how economists develop models to interpret data and how theories result from this process.

## Self Test

### Fill in the Blanks

1. The limits to a household's consumption over its lifetime is the ________ ________ ________.
2. A household's endowment is the ________ ________ that a household will receive over its lifetime.
3. ________ ________ is the amount of a sum of money that, if invested in the present, at the current interest rate, would accumulate to the future sum over a given number of year.
4. Human capital is the ________ of current and future ________ ________.
5. The marginal rate of intertemporal substitution is the amount of ________ consumption the household is willing to give up to have one additional unit of ________ consumption.
6. The proposition that consumer expenditure is proportional to permanent income is the ________ ________ ________.
7. The average income the household expects to receive over the rest of its life is called ________ ________.
8. Transitory income is the difference between the current period's ________ income and the previous period's ________ income.

9. The life-cycle hypothesis is the proposition that households smooth their ______________ over their lifetimes.

10. The maximum amount of current consumption that can be financed by borrowing against future labour income is known as a ______________.

## True or False

1. Cross-section data record the values of variables over time—from one quarter or year to the next.

2. The long-run consumption function is the average relationship between real personal consumer expenditure and real personal disposable income over a long period of time.

3. In the household's intertemporal budget constraint, total income is its labour income, $YL_t$, and its income from assets, $rA_{t-1}$.

4. Human capital is another name for the present value of current and future labour income.

5. The effect of interest rate changes on consumption choices has two components. They are an income effect and a saving effect.

6. The percentage of personal disposable income saved in Canada decreased from almost 18 percent in 1982 to 9 percent in 1997.

7. A permanent tax change influences permanent disposable income and has a large effect on consumer expenditure.

8. Temporary changes in the money supply change the nominal interest rate and the expected inflation rate.

9. Transitory income, the difference between the current period's actual income and the previous period's permanent income, has a small and perhaps zero effect on consumer expenditure.

10. According to the permanent income hypothesis, households smooth their consumption over their lifetimes, accumulating assets while they are working and consuming out of assets in their retirement years.

11. The short-run marginal propensity to consume is higher than the long-run marginal propensity to consume.

12. In cross-section data, the marginal propensity to consume decreases as disposable income increases.

13. Wealth is equal to the present value of current and future labour income.

14. An increase in the interest rate decreases the amount of consumption that can be undertaken.

15. Permanent income is always greater than current income.

16. The marginal propensity to consume out of transitory income is smaller than to consume out of permanent income.

17. According to the life cycle hypothesis, the propensity to consume out of labour income increases with age.

18. According to the life cycle hypothesis, the marginal propensity to consume out of assets increases with age.

19. The country with the highest saving rate as a percentage of GDP is Japan.

20. The saving rate as a percentage of GDP in Canada is lower than that in the United States and lower than the world average.

## Multiple Choice

1. Which of the following constraints represents the intertemporal budget constraint?

(a) $C_t + A_t \leq YL_t - (1 + r)A_{t-1}$.

(b) $C_t + A_t \leq YL_t + (1 + r)A_{t-1}$.

(c) $C_t - A_t \leq YL_t + (1 + r)A_{t-1}$.

(d) $C_t - A_t \leq YL_t - (1 - r)A_{t-1}$.

(e) $C_t + A_t \leq YL_t + (1 - r)A_{t-1}$.

2. In the household's intertemporal budget constraint, ($YL_t$) is the household's labour income and ($rA_{t-1}$) is the household's

(a) returns from durable goods.

(b) returns from equities.

(c) income from assets.

(d) interest from capital.

(e) economic profits.

3. The household's saving is equal to
(a) $A_{t-1} + A_t$.
(b) $A_{t-1} - A_t$.
(c) $A_{t+1} + A_t$.
(d) $A_t - A_{t-1}$.
(e) $A_t - A_{t+1}$.

4. A household's wealth is equal to
(a) $YL_1 + YL_2/(1 - r)$.
(b) $YL_1 - YL_2/(1 - r)$.
(c) $YL_1 + YL_2/(1 + r)$.
(d) $YL_2 - YL_1/(1 + r)$.
(e) $YL_2 + YL_1/(1 - r)$.

5. The slope of the household's indifference curve equals the household's
(a) marginal rate of technical substitution.
(b) marginal rate of utility substitution.
(c) average rate of technical substitution.
(d) average rate of utility substitution.
(e) marginal rate of intertemporal substitution.

6. The two components of the effect of interest rate changes on consumption choices are
(a) a substitution effect and an income effect.
(b) a substitution effect and a wealth effect.
(c) an income effect and a wealth effect.
(d) an income effect and a saving effect.
(e) a substitution effect and a saving effect.

7. Suppose the government budget starts out balanced and the government cuts taxes. It borrows to cover the deficit. At some time in the future the debt plus the interest on it has to be repaid. Rational households recognize this fact and realize that the tax cut has not changed their permanent income or shifted their lifetime budget constraint. This is known as the
(a) Ricardo-Barro hypothesis.
(b) Ricardo-Malthus hypothesis.
(c) Ricardo-Sargent hypothesis.
(d) Ricardo-Lucas hypothesis.
(e) Keynes-Barro hypothesis.

8. The intertemporal theories of consumption and saving recognize only one constraint on the household's consumption choice, which is its
(a) one pay period budget constraint.
(b) lifetime budget constraint.
(c) one year budget constraint.
(d) liquidity budget constraint.
(e) investment budget constraint.

9. The maximum amount that a household can borrow to finance current consumption out of future labour income is an additional constraint on consumption, known as
(a) credit constraint.
(b) liquidity constraint.
(c) capital constraint.
(d) saving constraint.
(e) none of the above.

10. All of the following are true about the Canadian consumption function *except*
(a) the long-run marginal propensity to consume is greater than the short-run marginal propensity to consume.
(b) the short run consumption function shifts upward over time.
(c) the marginal propensity to consume diminishes in the cross-section data as income increases.
(d) consumption expenditure is highly unpredictable and volatile.
(e) at a disposable income of a little less than \$10,000 a year, consumer expenditure equals disposable income.

11. Other things being equal, the higher the interest rate,
(a) the greater the level of wealth.
(b) the lower the level of wealth.
(c) the greater is labour income in the current period.
(d) the less the household can consume in the current period.
(e) the more consumption will fluctuate over time.

12. Permanent income is
(a) the part of a household's income that it will always be able to rely on.
(b) income from a job that is secure.
(c) interest from bonds that is guaranteed.
(d) household average income.
(e) the average income that the household expects to receive over the rest of its life.

13. According to the permanent income hypothesis,
(a) the higher a household's measured income the higher is its level of consumption.
(b) the higher is the household's permanent income the higher is its consumption.
(c) the higher a household's transitory income the higher its consumption.
(d) the higher a household's transitory income the lower its consumption.
(e) the long-run marginal propensity to consume is the same as the short-run marginal propensity to consume.

14. According to the life-cycle hypothesis,
(a) households consume more when their incomes higher.
(b) households smooth their income over their working lives.
(c) the marginal propensity to consume out of disposable labour income increases as the household gets older.
(d) the marginal propensity to consume out of assets increases as the household gets older.
(e) those who are retired save most.

15. Choose the best statement.
(a) Liquidity-constrained households consume more than other households.
(b) Liquidity-constrained households consume less than other households.
(c) A liquidity-constrained household might consume more or less than an unconstrained household.
(d) Liquidity constraints make the consumption function highly unpredictable.
(e) Liquidity constraints are more important than disposable income in determining consumption expenditure.

16. According to the Ricardo-Barro hypothesis,
(a) consumption depends on disposable income not aggregate income.
(b) consumption depends on aggregate income not disposable income.
(c) consumption depends on net-of-tax wealth.
(d) consumption depends on pre-tax wealth.
(e) consumption does not depend on taxes at all.

17. Inflation
(a) increases interest rates and decreases current consumption.
(b) increases interest rates and increases current consumption.
(c) increases interest rates and has no effect on current consumption.
(d) increases interest rates and has an ambiguous effect on current consumption.
(e) has no effect on interest rates.

18. Other things being equal, a one-dollar increase in the government deficit is predicted to
(a) increase household consumption by more than one dollar.
(b) decrease household saving by one dollar.
(c) decrease household consumption by less than one dollar.
(d) increase household consumption one dollar.
(e) increase household saving by one dollar.

19. The maximum amount that a household can borrow to finance current consumption out of future labour income is an additional constraint on consumption, known as
(a) intertemporal budget constraint.
(b) human capital constraint.
(c) liquidity constraint.
(d) permanent income constraint.
(e) transitory income constraint.

20. A temporary tax change that is going to be reversed in the future has
(a) no effect on permanent income and no effect on consumer expenditure.

(b) no effect on permanent income and decreases consumer expenditure.

(c) decreases permanent income and has no effect on consumer expenditure.

(d) decreases permanent income and decreases consumer expenditure.

(e) none of the above.

## Short Answer Questions

1. Briefly explain the distinction between time-series data and cross-sectional data.
2. What does aggregate consumer expenditure depend on?
3. Wealth has previously been defined as the difference between total assets and total liabilities. What is another way of defining wealth?
4. What two variables influence the lifetime budget constraint?
5. What is meant by a liquidity constraint?
6. With the presence of a liquidity constraint there are two important influences on consumer expenditure other than the interest rate and the household's endowment. What are these two important influences on consumer expenditure?
7. What does the term *present value* mean?
8. What happens to household saving when the government increases its deficit by one dollar?.
9. What is the distinction between the long-run and the short-run consumption function?
10. Explain and distinguish the intertemporal budget constraint and the lifetime budget constraint.
11. Explain how an increase in the interest rate changes the lifetime budget constraint.
12. What is the permanent income hypothesis?
13. What is permanent income?
14. What is the life cycle hypothesis?
15. What happens to the marginal propensities to consume out of assets and out of labour income as the age of the household increases?

## Problem Solving

### Practice Problems

1. Suppose that the Dundee Family's life runs from age 20 to age 80 and that its retirement age is 65. During the working years, its income is $50,000 each year and the interest rate is zero. The Dundee Family prefers constant consumption of $35,000 each year over its entire lifetime. It has $100,000 of assets at age 20.

   (a) Calculate the Dundee Family human capital.

   (b) Calculate the Dundee Family's assets at age 65.

   (c) Calculate the Dundee Family's saving when it is 30 years.

   (d) Calculate the Dundee Family's marginal propensity to consume out of labour income when the Dundee Family is 40 years.

### Solutions to Practice Problems

1. (a) Calculate the Dundee Family human capital.

   The Dundee Family's human capital is the sum of its lifetime labour income, which is $2,250,000.

   (b) Calculate the Dundee Family's assets at age 65.

   The Dundee Family's assets at age 65 are given by the following formula:

   $A_t = A_0 + (YL - C)(t - 20)$

   where $A_0$ represents assets at age 20, $YL$ is labour income each year, $C$ is annual consumption, and $t$ is current age.

   Substituting into the formula gives

   $A_t = \$100,000 + \$15,000 \times (65 - 20)$,

   which equals $775,000.

   (c) Calculate the Dundee Family's saving when it is 30 years.

   The Dundee Family's income is $50,000 a year and its annual consumption is $35,000, so its saving is $50,000 minus $35,000, which equals $15,000.

   (d) Calculate the Dundee Family's marginal propensity to consume out of labour income when the Dundee Family is 40 years.

The marginal propensity to consume out of labour income, when t = 40 is given by the formula

$b = (R - t)/(L - t)$,

where $R$ is the age at retirement (65), $L$ is the age at death (80), and t is the current age. Substituting into the formula, gives $b$ equal to 0.625.

## Problems to Solve

**Fact 19.1** The Lee Family receives a labour income of $50,000 in year 1 and $55,000 in year 2. It can borrow and lend at an interest rate of 10 percent a year.

1. Use Fact 19.1. According to the lifetime budget constraint,

   (a) if the household consumes zero income in year 1, how much can be consumed in year 2?

   (b) if the household borrows all available funds against its labour income in year 2, how much could be consumed in year 1?

   (c) how much would the household have to repay in (b)?

2. Use Fact 19.1. The Lee Family's labour income increases by 10 percent in year 1 and year 2. According to the lifetime budget constraint,

   (a) by how much does labour income increase in year 1 and year 2?

   (b) what is maximum consumption in year 2?

   (c) what is maximum consumption in year 1?

**Fact 19.2** You are given the following information about an economy:

A marginal propensity to consume out of permanent income is 0.8. The speed of adjustment of permanent income to actual income is 0.4.

3. Use Fact 19.2. Calculate the marginal propensity to consume in the short run.

4. Use Fact 19.2. Calculate the marginal propensity to consume in the long run.

5. Use Fact 19.2. Calculate the effects of a $100 million windfall—increase in income—on consumption in the period in which the windfall occurs.

6. Use Fact 19.2. Calculate the effect of the windfall in Problem 5 on consumption in the long run.

**Fact 19.3** A household consists of two 50 year-old people. They have assets valued at $1 million and they plan to retire at age 60. They expect to live to 80 years.

7. Use Fact 19.3. Calculate the household's lifetime consumption constraint.

8. Use Fact 19.3. Calculate the household's marginal propensity to consume out of assets.

9. Use Fact 19.3. Calculate the household's marginal propensity to consume out of labour income.

10. Use Fact 19.3.

    (a) What is the household's marginal propensity to consume out of assets in the year in which it retires?

    (b) What is the household's marginal propensity to consume out of labour income at the beginning of its last year at work?

## Answers

### Fill in the Blanks

1. lifetime budget constraint
2. labour income
3. Present value
4. present value, labour income
5. future, current
6. permanent income hypothesis
7. permanent income
8. actual, permanent
9. consumption
10. liquidity constraint

### True or False

1F 5F 9T 13T 17F
2T 6F 10F 14F 18T
3T 7T 11F 15F 19F
4T 8F 12T 16T 20F

### Multiple Choice

1b 5e 9b 13b 17d
2c 6b 10d 14d 18e
3d 7a 11b 15c 19c
4c 8b 12e 16c 20a

### Short Answer Questions

1. Time-series data records the values of variables over time—from one quarter or year to the next.

   Cross-section data records the values of an economic variable for different groups in a population at a point in time.
2. Aggregate consumer expenditure depends on permanent income (or lifetime average income), the interest rate, current disposable income, and available credit.
3. Another way of defining wealth is that it is the maximum amount that can be consumed in the current period if nothing is consumed in later periods.
4. The lifetime budget constraint is influenced by the interest rate and labour income.
5. Liquidity constraint is the maximum amount of current consumption that can be financed by borrowing against future labour income.
6. The other two important influences on consumer expenditure other than the interest rate and the household's endowment are disposable income and available credit.
7. Present value is the amount of a sum of money that, if invested in the present, at the current interest rate, would accumulate to the future sum over a given number of years.
8. If the government increases its deficit by one dollar, that action creates a liability for households to pay interest on that dollar in perpetuity. The value of the liability created is equivalent to the dollar the government has spent. Other things being equal, a one-dollar increase in the government deficit is predicted to increase household saving by one dollar.
9. The long-run consumption function is the average relationship between real personal consumer expenditure and real personal disposable income over a long period of time. The short-run consumption function is the relationship between real personal consumer expenditure and real personal disposable income over shorter periods.
10. The intertemporal budget constraint states how current consumption and next period's assets are related to current assets and current income. The lifetime budget constraint describes the connection between lifetime consumption and wealth.
11. An increase in the interest rate rotates the lifetime budget line on the endowment point. The lifetime budget line becomes steeper.
12. The permanent income hypothesis is the proposition that consumer expenditure is proportional to permanent income.
13. Permanent income is the average income the household expects to receive over the rest of its life.
14. The life-cycle hypothesis is the proposition that households smooth their consumption over their lifetimes.
15. The older the household, the larger is the marginal propensity to consume out of assets and the smaller is the marginal propensity to consume out of labour income.

## Problem Solving

1. (a) $110,000
   (b) $100,000
   (c) $55,000
2. (a) $5,000 and $5,500 respectively
   (b) $121,000
   (c) $110,000
3. 0.32
4. 0.8
5. $32 million increase
6. There is no change in consumption in the long run.
7. $C(80 - t) = \$1\text{million} + (60 - t)YL$
8. 1/30
9. 1/3
10. (a) 1/20
    (b) 1/21

## Chapter 20

# Investment

## Perspective and Focus

Like Chapter 19, this chapter also digs more deeply into one of the components behind aggregate expenditure—investment. You first encountered investment in Chapter 6 and here we study it more deeply. Chapter 20 may be studied in sequence or immediately following Chapter 6. Either way, the chapter contains everything that you need to make good progress with the material. You do not need to be concerned if you have not studied Chapters 7 to 19 before beginning this chapter.

The core of the chapter is sections 20.2 and 20.4.

## Learning Objectives

*After studying this chapter, you will be able to:*

- Describe the volatility of investment in Canada and other countries
- Explain the accelerator theory of investment
- Describe the accelerator in Canada and the United States
- Explain how the rental rate of capital is determined
- Explain how monetary policy affects investment
- Explain how taxes affect investment
- Explain why there are alternating waves of optimism and pessimism
- Explain how fluctuations in investment bring fluctuations in real GDP and interest rates

## Increasing Your Productivity

Focus most of your attention in this chapter initially on section 20.2 (capital, investment, and the accelerator theory) and section 20.4 (investment and the rental rate of capital).

The accelerator theory is an analysis of the connection between the desired capital stock and the current capital stock and the influence that the gap between the desired and actual capital stocks has on investment. It is not a theory of the desired capital stock. The desired capital stock depends on the rental rate of capital, which in turn depends on the interest rate.

It is also worth spending some time studying investment in Canada to see how the accelerator and interest rate mechanisms work. The key point of this chapter is that the investment demand curve fluctuates a great deal.

## Self Test

### Fill in the Blanks

1. Residential fixed investment is the expenditure by ________ and ________ on new houses and ________ ________.
2. ________ ________ ________ is the expenditure by firms on new plant, buildings, and equipment.
3. The accelerator mechanism is the mechanism linking the ________ of net investment to the change in ________.
4. The accelerator mechanism in the U.S. economy is ________ than in Canada.
5. A capital-intensive technique is a technique that uses a ________ amount of capital and a ________ amount of labour.
6. A labour-intensive technique is a technique that uses a large amount of ________ and a small amount of ________.
7. The rental rate of capital is the cost of using a piece of ________, expressed in terms of dollars per hour.
8. An alternative name to rental rate of capital is ________ ________ ________ ________.
9. Tobin's $q$ is the ratio of the ________ ________ of a firm to the price of the firm's capital assets.
10. A situation in which no reallocation of assets will increase the return on a portfolio for a given amount of risk is ________ ________.

## True or False

1. Investment is the least volatile component of aggregate demand.
2. The three components of investment are changes in inventories, residential fixed investment, and nonresidential fixed investment.
3. In order to see the connection between the stock of capital and the flow of investment, investment may be divided into net investment and replacement investment.
4. In the national income and product accounts, replacement investment is called capital consumption allowance.
5. A technique that uses a large amount of capital and a small amount of labour is called a labour-intensive technique.
6. Capital is a flow. It is measured as the rate of purchase of new plant, buildings, and equipment over a particular period of time.
7. Other things being equal, the higher the real interest rate, the higher is the level of gross investment.
8. A permanent change in the money supply growth rate that brings a permanent change in the inflation rate leaves the real interest rate unaffected and, in the long run, has no effect on the desired capital stock or investment.
9. Monetary policy can have an important effect on the desired capital stock and investment by influencing the after-tax rental rate.
10. Despite the fact that tax changes appear to affect investment, they are not regarded as a reliable tool for stabilizing fluctuations in investment and aggregate demand.
11. Fluctuations in investment in Canada are very similar to fluctuations in global investment.
12. Net investment fluctuates more than replacement investment
13. The accelerator mechanism links the level of net investment to the change in real GDP.
14. The higher is the inflation rate, other things being equal, the higher is the real rental rate of capital.
15. The higher the depreciation rate the higher is the rental rate of capital
16. The variables that affect the real rental rate are the real interest rate and the depreciation rate.
17. If the marginal product of capital exceeds the rental rate firms have too much capital
18. Investment only increases when the real interest rate declines
19. An increase in the corporate income tax rate increases the rental rate of capital
20. An investment tax credit decreases the rental rate of capital.

## Multiple Choice

1. Which of the following represents the second largest component of gross private domestic investment?

(a) Nonresidential fixed investment.
(b) Residential fixed investment.
(c) Changes in inventories
(d) Replacement investment.
(e) Fixed investment.

2. The mechanism linking the level of net investment to the change in output is known as

(a) internal funds mechanism.
(b) accelerator mechanism.
(c) classical mechanism.
(d) Tobin's $q$.
(e) Tobin's $r$.

3. An alternative name for the rental rate of capital is

(a) rental cost of capital.
(b) purchase price of capital.
(c) marginal product of capital.
(d) user cost of capital.
(e) wear and tear cost of capital.

4. Which of the following represents Tobin's $q$?

(a) $q = MPK/P_k$.

(b) $q = SMV/P_k$.

(c) $q = MPK/SMV$.

(d) $q = P_k/SMV$.

(e) $q = R/MPK$.

5. The accelerator mechanism must be modified in order to take account of the dependency of the desired capital-sales ratio on

(a) income.

(b) rental income.

(c) labour income.

(d) real interest rate.

(e) economic profits.

6. Monetary policy can influence investment through

(a) the interest rate effect.

(b) the exchange rate effect.

(c) the real balance effect.

(d) the income effect.

(e) (a), (b), and (c).

7. Three main sources of tax effects on the after-tax rental rate are

(a) corporate income taxes, social security taxes, and investment tax credits.

(b) depreciation deductions, investment tax credits, and personal income taxes.

(c) corporate income taxes, depreciation deductions, and investment tax credits.

(d) personal income taxes, corporate income taxes, and social security taxes.

(e) depreciation deductions, corporate income taxes, and personal income taxes.

8. If one ignores changes in the price of capital, the rental rate is equal to

(a) $P_k(\delta - r)$.

(b) $P/k(\delta + r)$.

(c) $P_k(\delta + r)$.

(d) $P_k(\delta/r)$.

(e) $P_k(\delta \times r)$.

9. Net investment

(a) equals the change in the capital stock plus depreciation.

(b) minus gross investment equals replacement investment

(c) is the replacement of worn out capital.

(d) is equal to the change in the capital stock.

(e) is the capital consumption allowance.

10. The accelerator mechanism means that

(a) when real GDP is high investment is high.

(b) when real GDP is rising investment is rising.

(c) when real GDP is rising investment is high.

(d) when investment is rising real GDP is high.

(e) the change in investment is correlated with the level of real GDP.

11. The rental rate of capital is

(a) only relevant if a firm actually rents its capital equipment.

(b) a theoretical price of no practical importance.

(c) expressed an a percentage of the price of capital.

(d) is equal to the price of a capital asset multiplied by the interest rate.

(e) is the cost of using a piece of capital equipment regardless of whether the capital is actually rented.

12. The rental rate of capital is higher,

(a) the higher is the price of capital.

(b) the higher is the rate of depreciation.

(c) the higher is the rate of inflation.

(d) the higher is the real interest rate.

(e) all of the above except (c).

13. If the marginal product of capital exceeds the real interest rate firms can lower their costs by

(a) increasing their capital stock.

(b) decreasing their capital stock.

(c) renting more capital.

(d) renting less capital.

(e) none of the above.

14. If the marginal product of capital exceeds the real rental rate firms can lower their costs by

(a) buying or renting more capital equipment.

(b) buying or renting less capital equipment.

(c) buying some capital and renting it out.

(d) decreasing the amount of capital they own.
(e) financing their capital investment by selling bonds.

15. If a firm has a marginal product of capital divided by its stock market value that exceeds the interest rate on bonds, then
(a) it pays to buy shares in that firm.
(b) it pays to sell shares in that firm.
(c) it pays to take a bank loan and buy bonds.
(d) it pays to buy stock in the firm only if the economy is expanding.
(e) it pays to sell stock in the firm if the economy is contracting.

## Short Answer Questions

1. (a)What are the three components of gross private domestic investment?

   (b)Rank these components from largest to smallest.

2. What is meant by the accelerator mechanism?
3. How is investment influenced by monetary policy?
4. What are the three main sources of tax effects on the after-tax rental rate?
5. (a)What is meant by the rental rate of capital?

   (b)What is meant by the user cost of capital?

6. What are *animal spirits*?
7. (a)How do modern macro theorists explain sunspots?

   (b)How do sunspot effects operate in reality?

8. Describe the fluctuations in net investment and replacement investment in Canada.
9. How is Tobin's $q$ calculated?
10. Describe the Canadian accelerator.

## Problem Solving

### Practice Problems

1. La Bella Pizza is considering buying a new pizza oven for $3,000. If it buys the oven it has to borrow from the bank and the interest rate on the loan is 8 percent a year. Zippy Rentals is willing to rent La Bella Pizza an oven for $500 a year. The price of pizza ovens is expected to increase by 5 percent a year, and they depreciate at 15 percent a year.

   Calculate the highest price that La Bella Pizza is willing to pay for a pizza oven.

### Solutions to Practice Problems

1. Calculate the highest price that La Bella Pizza is willing to pay for a pizza oven.
The highest price that La Bella Pizza is willing to pay for the oven is the price that makes the implicit rental rate equal to $500.

$$\text{Rental rate} = P_k\left(\delta + r_m - \frac{\Delta P_k^e}{P_k}\right)$$

$$500 = P_k(0.15 + 0.08 - 0.05)$$

So, $P_k = \$2,777.78$.

## Problems to Solve

**Fact 20.1** An earthmover costs $100,000 and the depreciation rate is 20 percent a year. The interest rate is 5 percent a year and there is no inflation.

1. Use Fact 20.1. What is the expected rate of appreciation of earthmover prices?
2. Use Fact 20.1. What is the real interest rate?
3. Use Fact 20.1. What is the rental rate of the earthmover?
4. Use Fact 20.1. What is the real rental rate of the earthmover?
5. Use Fact 20.1. Suppose this earthmover can be rented for $30,000 per year. Does it pay to buy or to rent?
6. Use Fact 20.1. Whichever it pays to do in Problem 5, does the firm do it?

**Fact 20.2** XYZ Inc. owns 10 earthmovers of the type described in Fact 20.1. They are all brand new. Also the firm has made wise investment decisions and this quantity of earthmovers exactly minimizes its cost. The stock market value of the firm is $900,000.

7. Use Fact 20.2. What is the value of the firms Tobin's *q*?

8. Use Fact 20.2. Will people buy or sell shares in this firm?

**Fact 20.3** Refer to Fact 20.2. The government introduces a 25 percent corporate income tax rate.

9. Use Fact 20.3. How does this income tax rate affect the firms rental rate?

10. Does the firm now buy more earthmovers or sell some?

**Fact 20.4** Refer to Fact 20.2. The government introduces an investment tax credit permitting firms to deduct 10 percent of the purchase price of new capital against their income when computing their income tax liability.

11. Use Fact 20.4. How does this investment tax affect the rental rate of capital?

12. Use Fact 20.4. Does the firm now acquire more capital or less?

13. You are thinking of buying a big screen Magnavox television set for $2,000. The price of such televisions is expected to decrease by 20 percent a year. If you did purchase this television set you would have to borrow the money from the bank at 10 percent interest per year. The television depreciates at 10 percent per year. A friend owns exactly the same television set and you can rent it from him for $20 per month.

    (a)What is the implicit rental rate if you purchase the television set?

    (b)Is it cheaper to rent the television from your colleague for one year or purchase it from the store?

14. You are trying to decide whether to buy a condominium or rent one. The price of the condominium is $100,000 and the mortgage interest is 10 percent a year. Condominium prices are expected to increase by 5 percent a year and depreciate by 2 percent a year.

    (a) What is the maximum rent you would pay for such a condominium?

    (b) What is the implicit rental rate?

15. ABC Rentals has capital that cost $1,000,000. Its marginal product of a capital is $90,000, and the interest rate on bonds is 10 percent. Calculate

    (a) the stock market value of the firm.

    (b) Tobin's *q*.

    (c) the rental rate of capital.

## Answers

### Fill in the Blanks

1. households, firms, apartment buildings
2. Nonresidential fixed investment
3. level, output
4. stronger
5. large, small
6. labour, capital
7. capital equipment
8. user cost of capital
9. stock market value
10. portfolio equilibrium

### True or False

1F 5F 9F 13T 17F
2T 6F 10T 14F 18F
3T 7F 11T 15T 19T
4T 8T 12T 16F 20T

### Multiple Choice

1b 4b 7c 10c 13e
2b 5d 8c 11e 14a
3d 6e 9d 12e 15a

### Short Answer Questions

1. (a) The three components of gross private domestic investment are changes in inventories, residential fixed investment, and nonresidential fixed investment.

   (b) The largest component of gross private domestic investment is nonresidential fixed investment; the second largest component is residential fixed investment; and changes in inventory are the smallest component.

2. The accelerator mechanism is the mechanism linking the level of net investment to the change in output. The mechanism arises from the fact that firms desire to maintain a particular relationship between the level of their sales and the level of their capital stock. Because the change in the capital stock is net investment, a change in sales leads to a temporary increase in net investment.

3. Monetary policy can influence investment through the interest rate effect, the exchange rate effect, and the real balance effect.

4. The three main sources of tax effects on the after-tax rental rate are corporate income taxes, depreciation deductions, and investment tax credits.

5. (a) The rental rate of capital is the cost of using a piece of capital equipment, expressed in terms of dollars per hour.

   (b) The user cost of capital is an alternative name for the rental rate of capital since most capital equipment is not rented, it is bought and used by its owners.

6. Keynes's *animal spirits* describe the forces at work generating swings in mood and changes in expectations. The name conjures up the idea of instinctive reactions to collective swings of moods rather than rational responses to changes in the objective environment.

7. (a) Modern theorists have used the term "sunspot" to denote any variable that in fact has no effect but that people believe has an effect on the economy.

   (b) So far, it is not known whether sunspot effects operate in reality. Sunspot effects are the subject of a great deal of current research.

8. Net investment fluctuates a great deal. Replacement investment has a steady growth with virtually no fluctuations.

9. Tobin's $q$ is calculated by dividing the stock market value of the firm by the price of capital, or equivalently by dividing the marginal product of the firm's capital by the rental rate of the firm's capital.

10. There is a strong relationship between net fixed investment and the change in real GDP. When real GDP increased in 1981, so did net nonresidential fixed investment and inventory investment. When real GDP crashed in 1982, net nonresidential fixed investment crashed with it. But when the recovery began in 1983, inventory investment increased but net nonresidential fixed investment did not recover until four years later. With a time lag, net nonresidential fixed investment did follow the path of the change in real GDP. The recession of the early 1990s is also reflected in both components of net investment.

## Problem Solving

1. 0
2. 0.05
3. $25,000 per year
4. $25,000 per year
5. Buy
6. Cannot tell because the firm needs to know the marginal product of capital
7. 0.9
8. Buy
9. With a 25 percent tax rate, the rental rate increases by 25 percent
10. Sell
11. The rental rate decreases by 10 percent
12. It pays to buy more capital (but not very much because the allowance applies only to new investment not to existing capital stock)
13. (a) $800

    (b) It is cheaper to rent
14. (a) $7,000

    (b) $7,000
15. (a) $900,000

    (b) 0.9

    (c) $100,000

## Chapter 21

# Money and Asset Holding

## Perspective and Focus

This chapter also probes more deeply behind the determinants of aggregate demand. This chapter focuses on the microeconomic foundations of the demand for money that lies behind the *LM* curve.

## Learning Objectives

*After studying this chapter, you will be able to:*

- Describe the trends in the velocity of circulation of various monetary aggregates
- Explain the opportunity cost of holding money
- Explain the inventory theory of the demand for money
- Explain the precautionary theory of the demand for money
- Explain the speculative theory of the demand for money
- Explain the modern quantity theory of the demand for money
- Explain how financial innovation has changed the demand for money in Canada
- Explain the effect of the demand for money on aggregate economic fluctuations

## Increasing Your Productivity

The key to understanding what is going on in this chapter is the concept of opportunity cost. You first encountered this concept in your very first lecture in economic principles. The concept pays handsome dividends in this chapter. It is the concept applied to holding money. The concept of the opportunity cost of holding money is summarized in Table 21.1 and once you have understood the concept of the opportunity cost of holding money and what constitutes that opportunity cost for different monetary aggregates you will have no difficulty with the rest of the chapter. You will race through the material on financial innovation and the influence of financial innovation on the velocity of circulation of the various monetary aggregates.

A potential stumbling block for students not familiar with calculus is the material on the inventory theory of the demand for money. The diagrammatic analysis of this theory, summarized in Figures 21.2 and 21.3 are adequate. It would though be a good idea to try and understand the square root formula for this explains why the demand for money has economies of scale.

## Self Test

### Fill in the Blanks

1. ________ is the narrowest definition of money.
2. ________ consists of M1 plus personal savings deposits and non-personal notice deposits at chartered banks.
3. ________ is the broadest definition of money.
4. ________ consists of M2 plus non-personal fixed-term deposits at chartered banks and foreign currency deposits of residents booked in Canada.
5. The average number of times one dollar of money finances transactions in a given time period is the ________ ________ ________.
6. Income velocity of circulation is ________ divided by the ________ ________ ________.
7. The ________ theory of the demand for money is based on the idea that people minimize the cost of managing their inventories of money.
8. The ________ theory of the demand for money is based on the idea that money is held, in part, as a kind of general insurance against an uncertain future.
9. The ________ theory of the demand for money is based on the idea that people hold the mixture of money and other assets that gives the best available combination of risk and return.
10. Eurodollars are bank deposits held in ________ denominated in a variety of currencies. The expansion of Eurodollars has ________ the velocity of circulation of M1 and M2+.

## True or False

1. M2 consists of M1 plus personal savings deposits and non-personal notice deposits at chartered banks.

2. The velocity of circulation of money is the average number of times one dollar of money finances transactions in a given time period.

3. The inventory theory does not appear to be a good theory insofar as it does not account for the variations in the amount of money held as income and interest rates vary, but it does account for the absolute level of money holding.

4. The modern quantity theory of the demand for money, in effect, combines the elements of the inventory, precautionary, and speculative theories systematically into a unified theory of asset allocation.

5. The income velocity of circulation of money is GDP multiplied by the quantity of money.

6. The precautionary theory of the demand for money is based on the idea that money is held, in part, as a kind of general insurance against an uncertain future.

7. Money market mutual funds are financial institutions that issue shares redeemable at variable prices against which cheques can be written.

8. The quantity of money demanded fluctuates when the interest rate changes, but changes in the interest rate caused by some other factor do not change the demand for money.

9. M3 consists of M2 plus non-personal fixed-term deposits of residents booked at chartered banks.

10. The opportunity cost of holding fixed-term deposits is the interest rate on bonds and stocks plus the interest rate on long-term deposits.

11. The velocity of circulation of M1 trended upward from 1970 to 1990 and trended downward since 1990.

12. The opportunity cost of holding money is the goods that are foregone by not making a purchase.

13. The opportunity cost of holding currency is zero.

14. The opportunity cost of holding a savings deposit is the interest rate on higher yielding assets.

15. Money holding is subject to economies of scale. An increase in the scale of expenditure does not, in general, lead to a proportional increase in the amount of money held.

16. When the $2 bill was replaced by a $2 coin, the demand for M1 increased.

17. The amount of money held is so volatile that it is not possible to predict how interest rate changes will influence the quantity of money held.

18. The average cash holding by a household varies directly with the number of trips to the bank.

19. There is no reason to believe that the demand for money held depends on wealth. It only depends on income.

20. Fluctuations in the velocity of circulation are simply a reflection of movements up and down the demand for money curve.

## Multiple Choice

1. M1 includes

(a) currency in circulation.

(b) savings deposits at chartered banks.

(c) demand deposits at chartered banks.

(d) non-personal notice deposits at chartered banks.

(e) both (a) and (c).

2. The theory that is based on the idea that people minimize the cost of managing their inventories of money is called the

(a) speculative theory of the demand for money.

(b) precautionary theory of the demand for money.

(c) transactions theory of the demand for money.

(d) time theory of the demand for money.

(e) inventory theory of the demand for money.

3. The total cost of managing a household's cash inventory is equal to
(a) $bn + rY/n$.
(b) $bn + rY/2n$.
(c) $bn - rY/2n$.
(d) $bn \times rY/2n$.
(e) $bn + 2n/rY$.

4. The modern quantity theory of the demand for money systematically combines elements of the
(a )inventory theory.
(b) precautionary theory.
(c) speculative theory.
(d) both (b) and (c).
(e) all the above.

5. The modern quantity theory of the demand for money states that households allocate their given stock of wealth across
(a) money.
(b) bonds.
(c) real capital.
(d) human capital.
(e) all of the above.

6. Bank deposits denominated in a variety of currencies, including Canadian dollars, held in Europe are known as
(a) Eurodollars.
(b) British dollars.
(c) European dollars.
(d) German dollars.
(e) none of the above.

7. Cash management accounts
(a) include daily interest chequing accounts.
(b) are available only to large personal customers of chartered banks.
(c) include sweep accounts.
(d) includes non-personal savings accounts.
(e) include money market mutual funds as well as (a) and (d).

8. Fluctuations in the velocity of circulation induced by changes in the interest rates do not cause fluctuations in aggregate economy activity. These fluctuations in velocity are a consequence of a
(a) change in the demand for money.
(b) movement along the demand for money curve.
(c) counterclockwise movement in the demand for money curve.
(d) clockwise movement in the demand for money curve.
(e) either (c) or (d).

9. Financial innovation that decreases the demand for money and
(a) shifts the *LM* curve to the right.
(b) shifts the *LM* curve to the left.
(c) decreases interest rates.
(d) increases real GDP.
(e) all the above except (b).

10. Fluctuations in aggregate economic activity can result from fluctuations in the velocity of circulation resulting from
(a) changes in interest rates.
(b) changes in the supply of money.
(c) financial innovation.
(d) (a) and (b) only.
(e) (b) and (c) only.

11. M2+ has
(a) cycles and a downward trend.
(b) cycles and an upward trend.
(c) no cycles and a downward trend.
(d) no cycles and an upward trend.
(e) none of the above.

12. The opportunity cost of holding currency is equal to
(a) zero.
(b) the inflation rate.
(c) the interest rate on bonds.
(d) the interest rate on demand deposits.
(e) the interest rate on credit cards.

13. The opportunity cost of holding a fixed-term deposit is
(a) the interest rate on savings deposits.
(b) the interest rate on bonds.

(c) the inflation rate.

(d) the interest rate on fixed-term deposits.

(e) the interest rate on bonds minus the interest rate on fixed-term deposits.

14. According to the inventory theory of the demand for money

(a) the higher the interest rate, the smaller is the number of trips to the bank.

(b) the higher the level of income, the smaller is the number of trips to the bank.

(c) the larger the number of trips to the bank, the larger is the amount of money held on the average.

(d) as income increases, the amount of money held on the average increases and by the same percentage as the increase in the interest rate.

(e) as the interest rises, the amount of money held on the average falls and by a smaller percentage than the increase in the interest rate.

15. According to the modern quantity theory of money, the demand for money depends on

(a) the real interest rate and wealth.

(b) the nominal interest rate and wealth.

(c) human capital.

(d) the rate of return on currency.

(e) the rate of return on capital plus the rate of return on currency.

16. The expansion of credit cards have had the following effect on the demand for money.

(a) The demand for M1 has increased but M2 has decreased.

(b) The demand for M1 has decreased and the demand for M2 has increased.

(c) The demand for all types of money has decreased.

(d) The effect on the demand for money is ambiguous.

(e) There has been no effect on the demand for money.

17. The velocity of circulation increases when

(a) interest rates rise.

(b) interest rates fall.

(c) financial innovation leads to a decrease in the demand for money.

(d) financial innovation leads to an increase in the demand for money.

(e) both (a) and (c).

18. During the late 1970s and early 1980s, the introduction of daily interest chequing accounts

(a) decreased the velocity of circulation of M1 and increased the velocity of circulation of M2+.

(b) increased the velocity of circulation of M1 and decreased the velocity of circulation of M2+.

(c) increased the velocity of circulation of M1 and M2+.

(d) decreased the velocity of circulation of M1 and M2+.

(e) did not change the velocity of circulation of M1 or M2+.

19. A financial innovation that decreases the demand for money

(a) shifts the *LM* curve to the left, lowers the interest rate, and increases real GDP.

(b) shifts the *LM* curve to the right, increases the interest rate, and increases real GDP.

(c) has no effect on the *LM* curve.

(d) shifts the *LM* curve to the left, increases the interest rate, and decreases real GDP.

(e) shifts the *LM* curve to the right, decreases the interest rate, and increases real GDP.

20. An inventory that is the first-line defence against random fluctuation is a

(a) buffer stock.

(b) buffer flow.

(c) speculative stock.

(d) speculative investment.

(e) precautionary investment.

## Short Answer Questions

1. On what idea is the speculative theory of the demand for money based?

2. What did Milton Friedman suggest in his formulation of the modern quantity theory of money?

3. What does the proposition that the quantity of money demanded depends on permanent income imply?
4. (a) What are Eurodollars?

   (b) Why are Eurodollars attractive to banks?

   (c) How were Eurodollars invented?
5. What are cash management accounts?
6. Define the narrowest definition of money in Canada.
7. State the two reasons for the importance of the square root formula.
8. Briefly summarize the trends in the velocity of circulation of the various monetary aggregates.
9. What is meant by financial innovation.
10. What is the opportunity cost of holding money?

## Problem Solving

### Practice Problems

1. Sammy earns $1,800 a month and he spends $400 on rent and other monthly expenses as soon as he is paid. He keeps the rest in cash and in an interest-earning chequing account and spends it at an even pace over the month. It costs Sammy $1.75 each time he goes to the bank. His bank pays 1 percent interest each month.

   (a) How many times does Sammy go to the bank each month?

   (b) How much does Sammy withdraw each time he goes to the bank?

   (c) What is Sammy's average currency holding?

   (d) What is Sammy's average holding of chequing deposits?

   (e) What is Sammy's average money holding?

   (f) What does it cost Sammy to manage his inventory of cash?

   (g) How much of Sammy's cost of managing his cash inventory is the opportunity cost of holding cash and how much is the cost of transactions?

### Solutions to Practice Problems

1. (a) How many times does Sammy go to the bank each month?

   Sammy earns $1,800 a month and immediately pays $400 on rent and other monthly expenses. This leaves $1,400 in his interest-earning chequing account.

   Sammy makes $n$ trips to the bank where

$$n = \sqrt{\frac{rY}{2b}}.$$

   The interest rate, $r$, is 0.01 a month, his monthly cash expenditure, $Y$, is $1,400, and the cost of a trip to the bank, $b$, is $1.75. Substituting in the above equation gives

$$n = \sqrt{\frac{0.01 \times \$1{,}400}{2 \times \$1.75}} = 2.$$

   Sammy makes 2 trips to the bank each month.

   (b) How much does Sammy withdraw each time he goes to the bank?

   Sammy's total withdrawals during the month are $1,400, and he makes 2 trips to the bank each month. So, on each trip to the bank he withdraws

$$\$1{,}400 \div 2 = \$700.$$

   (c) What is Sammy's average currency holding?

   Average currency holding is given by the equation

$$AC = \frac{Y}{2n}.$$

   Monthly cash expenditure, $Y$, is $1,400 and the number of trips to the bank, $n$, is 2, so average currently holding is

$$\frac{\$1{,}400}{2 \times 2} = \$350.$$

   (d) What is Sammy's average holding of chequing deposits?

Sammy's average holding of chequing deposits is equal to his average cash expenditure minus his average currency holding. That is,

$$\frac{\$1{,}400}{2} - \$350 = \$350.$$

(e) What is Sammy's average money holding?
Sammy's average money holding is his average holding of cash plus chequing deposits which equals his average monthly cash expenditure. Sammy's average money holding is $700.

(f) What does it cost Sammy to manage his inventory of cash?
Sammy's total cost of managing his cash holding is

$$TC = bn + \frac{rY}{2n}$$

$$TC = (\$1.75 \times 2) + \frac{(0.01 \times \$1{,}400)}{2 \times 2} = \$7.00.$$

(g) How much of Sammy's cost of managing his cash inventory is the opportunity cost of holding cash and how much is the cost of transactions?
Sammy's opportunity cost of holding cash, $rY/2n$, equals $3.50, and his transactions costs, $bn$, equals $3.50.

## Problems to Solve

1. Wei Ming receives a cash income of $2,000 per month and spends it uniformly throughout the month.

   (a) What is Wei Ming's average cash holding?

   (b) What is Wei Ming's average cash holding when she uses half of the income to buy bonds?

2. The Sukkar Family gets paid once a month and immediately writes cheques to pay all the bills. It then has $1,600 left to deposit into its interest-bearing bank account which pays an interest rate of 1 percent a month. Furthermore, the Sukkar Family spends its cash in equal amounts over the month.

   The Sukkar Family makes two trips to the bank each month to withdraw cash. Calculate the Sukkar Family's average cash holding.

3. The Sukkar Family in problem 2 decides to increase the number of trips to the bank to four each month. Calculate the Sukkar Family's average cash holding.

4. Professor Ho earns $4,000 per month each month of the year. As soon as she receives her income each month she pays the rent of $1,400 and puts $200 into a retirement account. The remainder of the income is spent evenly throughout the month.

   (a) What is Professor Ho's demand for money?

   (b) What is Professor Ho's average holding of money?

5. Sally earns $3,900 a month and she spends $600 on rent and other monthly expenses as soon as she is paid. She keeps the rest in cash and in an interest-earning chequing account and spends it at an even pace over the month. It costs Sally $2.75 each time she goes to the bank. Her bank pays 1.5 percent interest each month.

   (a) How many times does Sally go to the bank each month?

   (b) How much does Sally withdraw each time he goes to the bank?

   (c) What is Sally's average currency holding?

   (d) What is Sally's average money holding?

   (e) What does it cost Sally to manage her inventory of cash?

   (f) How much of Sally's cost of managing her cash inventory is the opportunity cost of holding cash and how much is the cost of transactions?

## Answers

### Fill in the Blanks

1. M1
2. M2
3. M2+
4. M3
5. velocity of circulation
6. GDP, quantity of money
7. inventory
8. precautionary
9. speculative
10. Europe, increased

### True or False

1T 5F 9F 13F 17F
2T 6T 10F 14F 18F
3F 7F 11T 15T 19F
4T 8T 12F 16T 20F

### Multiple Choice

1e 5e 9e 13e 17e
2e 6a 10e 14e 18b
3b 7c 11a 15b 19e
4e 8b 12d 16c 20a

### Short Answer Questions

1. The speculative theory of the demand for money is based on the idea that people hold the mixture of money and other assets that gives the best available combination of risk and return.
2. Milton Friedman suggested that wealth could be measured as permanent income. The key proposition in the modern quantity theory of money is that the quantity of money demanded depends inversely on the nominal rate and positively on permanent income.
3. It immediately implies that there will be time lags in the relationship between the quantity of money demanded and current income. Because permanent income responds gradually to changes in current actual income, the quantity of money demanded will respond only gradually to changes in current income. Thus there will be a time lag between a change in income and the change in the quantity of money demanded.
4. (a) Eurodollars are bank deposits (originally denominated in U.S. dollars but now available in all the major currencies) held in Europe.

   (b) They are attractive to banks because there are no required reserves on these deposits so banks can lend the entire amount deposited, thereby increasing their profits.

   (c) They were invented when the Soviet Union wanted to hold the proceeds of its international trade in U.S. dollars but did not want to put the money in the United States.
5. Cash management accounts are a financial innovation available to corporations and other large customers of banks. One such account is the sweep account—at the end of the business day, the bank sweeps the balances from chequable deposits and places them in overnight investments. Cash management accounts have the effect of decreasing the demand for money and increasing the velocity of circulation of all types of money.
6. M1, the narrowest definition of money, consists of currency (Bank of Canada notes and coins) in circulation and demand deposit balances at chartered banks.
7. First, it makes a very precise prediction about the demand for cash. It predicts that as the amount of expenditure undertaken using cash increases, the amount of cash held increases, but only by the square root of the increase in expenditure. If spending increases fourfold, cash holdings increase only twofold. It also predicts that the higher the interest rate on the next convenient asset, the smaller is the amount of currency held. Again, the responsiveness is very precise. A 1 percent increase in interest rates bring a one-half percent decrease in the amount of currency held.

   Second, the formula easily generalizes to deal with other components of money.
8. The velocity of circulation of M1 cycled around a rising trend until 1990 when it began a downward movement. M2+ has cycled around a falling trend.
9. Financial innovation is the development of new financial products, items such as credit cards and types of bank deposits and other

securities.

10. The opportunity cost of holding money is the interest forgone on an alternative asset minus the interest rate on the type of money in question.

Problem Solving

1. (a) $1,000
   (b) $500
2. $400
3. $200
4. (a) $1,200
   (b) $1,200
5. (a) 3
   (b) $1,100
   (c) $550
   (d) $1,650
   (e) $16.50
   (f) $8.25, $8.25 respectively

## Notation Used in *Modern Macroeconomics*

### Chapter 2: Circular Flow of Income and Expenditure

- *C* Consumer expenditure
- *E* Expenditure
- *EX* Exports
- *G* Government expenditures
- *IM* Imports
- *I* Investment
- *S* Saving
- *T* Taxes

### Chapter 3: Classical Model

- *k* Propensity to hold money
- *MD* Quantity of money demanded
- *MP* Marginal product of labour
- *P* Price level
- *r* Real interest rate
- *R* Nominal interest rate
- *W* Money wage rate
- *y* Real GDP
- $\pi$ Inflation

### Chapter 4: *AD-AS* Model

- *c* Consumer expenditure
- *ex* Exports
- *g* Government expenditures
- *i* Investment
- *im* Imports
- *M/P* Real money supply
- *P** Foreign price level
- *r* Interest rate
- *s* Saving
- *S* Spot exchange rate

| | |
|---|---|
| $T$ | Taxes |
| $y$ | Real GDP |
| $y^*$ | Foreign income |

## Chapter 5: Aggregate Expenditure Model

| | |
|---|---|
| $a$ | Autonomous consumer expenditure |
| $b$ | Marginal propensity to consume |
| $c$ | Consumer expenditure |
| $ex$ | Exports |
| $g$ | Government expenditures |
| $im$ | Imports |
| $k$ | Multiplier |
| $m$ | Marginal propensity to import |
| $y$ | Real GDP |
| $s$ | Saving |
| $t$ | Taxes |

## Chapter 6: Closed Economy *IS–LM* Model

| | |
|---|---|
| $a$ | Autonomous consumer expenditure |
| $b$ | Marginal propensity to consume |
| $c$ | Consumer expenditure |
| $g$ | Government expenditures |
| $h$ | Sensitivity of investment to the interest rate |
| $i$ | Investment |
| $i_0$ | Investment at a zero interest rate |
| $k$ | Multiplier |
| $k$ | Sensitivity of quantity of real money demanded to real income |
| $\ell$ | Sensitivity of quantity of real money demanded to the interest rate |
| $M$ | Quantity of money |
| $M^d$ | Quantity of money demanded |
| $m_0$ | Quantity of real money demanded at zero real income and zero interest rate |
| $P$ | Price level |
| $r$ | Interest rate |
| $s$ | Saving |

| | |
|---|---|
| $t$ | Taxes |
| $y$ | Real GDP |

## Chapter 8: Open Economy *IS–LM* Model

| | |
|---|---|
| $a$ | Autonomous consumer expenditure |
| $b$ | Marginal propensity to consume |
| $c$ | Consumer expenditure |
| $ER$ | Exchange rate |
| $ex$ | Exports |
| $ex_1$ | Sensitivity of exports to foreign real income |
| $ex_2$ | Sensitivity of exports to the real exchange rate |
| $g$ | Government expenditures |
| $h$ | Sensitivity of investment to the interest rate |
| $im$ | Imports |
| $im_1$ | Sensitivity of imports to foreign real income |
| $im_2$ | Sensitivity of imports to the real exchange rate |
| $i$ | Investment |
| $i_0$ | Investment at a zero interest rate |
| $k$ | Multiplier |
| $k$ | Sensitivity of quantity of real money demanded to real income |
| $\ell$ | Sensitivity of quantity of real money demanded to the interest rate |
| $M$ | Quantity of money |
| $M^d$ | Quantity of money demanded |
| $m_0$ | Quantity of real money demanded at zero real income and zero interest rate |
| $nx$ | Net exports |
| $P$ | Price level |
| $P_f$ | Foreign price level |
| $r$ | Interest rate |
| $r_f$ | Foreign interest rate |
| $s$ | Saving |
| $t$ | Taxes |
| $y$ | Real GDP |

## Chapter 9: Neoclassical Growth Model

| | |
|---|---|
| $k$ | Capital stock |
| $b$ | Consumption rate (average and marginal propensities to consume) |
| $n$ | Population |
| $y$ | Real GDP |

## Chapter 9: *Ak* Growth Model

| | |
|---|---|
| $A$ | Capital productivity |
| $b$ | Consumption rate (average and marginal propensities to consume) |
| $k$ | Capital stock |
| $n$ | Population |
| $y$ | Real GDP |

## Chapter 10: Real Business Cycle Model

| | |
|---|---|
| $\theta$ | Capital's share of real GDP |
| $k$ | Capital stock |
| $1-\theta$ | Labour's share of real GDP |
| $n$ | Population |
| $y$ | Real GDP |
| $s/n$ | Saving per person |
| $Z$ | Technology coefficient |

## Chapter 13: Quantity Theory of Money

| | |
|---|---|
| $M$ | Money supply |
| $P$ | Price level |
| $V$ | Velocity of circulation |
| $Y$ | Real GDP |
| $\mu$ | Growth rate of money supply |
| $\Delta v$ | Velocity growth rate |
| $\pi$ | Inflation rate |
| $\rho$ | Real GDP growth rate |

## Chapter 12: Labour Market Flows

| | |
|---|---|
| $E$ | People employed |
| $f$ | Job find rate |
| $\ell$ | Job loss rate |
| $L$ | Labour force |
| $U$ | People unemployed |

## Chapter 13: Purchasing Power Parity

| | |
|---|---|
| $P$ | Domestic price level |
| $P_f$ | Foreign price level |
| $E$ | Exchange rate |
| $\Delta\varepsilon$ | Rate of appreciation of domestic currency |
| $\pi$ | Domestic inflation rate |
| $\pi_f$ | Foreign inflation rate |

## Chapter 15: Deficits and Debts

| | |
|---|---|
| $A$ | Assets |
| $B$ | Debt held by the public |
| $D$ | Debt |
| $d$ | Debt-GDP ratio |
| $E$ | Expenditure |
| $g$ | GDP growth rate |
| $G$ | Government debt |
| $M$ | Money created by the Bank of Canada |
| $P$ | Price level |
| $r$ | Interest rate |
| $T$ | Net taxes |
| $Y$ | GDP |
| $z$ | Basic deficit as a proportion of GDP |
| $\pi$ | Inflation rate |

## Chapter 17: Monetary Base and Money Supply

$a$ Public's demand for currency as a proportion of deposits

$b$ Banks' demand for reserves as a proportion of deposits

$BR$ Bank reserves

$CP$ Currency held by the public

$D$ Bank deposits

$M$ Monetary supply

$MB$ Monetary base

## Chapter 18: Exchange Rate and Balance of Payments

$E$ Exchange rate

$ER$ Nominal exchange rate

$P$ Price of domestic goods and services

$P_f$ Price of foreign goods and services

$r^d$ Interest rate on dollar assets

$r^y$ Interest rate on yen assets

$RER$ Real exchange rate

## Chapter 19: Consumption Function

$a$ Marginal propensity to consume out of assets

$A$ Assets

$b$ Marginal propensity to consume out of labour income

$C$ Consumer expenditure

$h$ Speed of adjustment of permanent income

$k$ Marginal propensity to consume out of permanent income

$L$ Age at death

$P$ Price level

$r$ Interest rate

$R$ Age at retirement

$S$ Saving

$t$ Current age

$Y$ Household income

$YL$ Labour income

$Y^P$ Permanent income

$\pi$ Inflation rate

## Chapter 20: Accelerator Theory

$I$ Gross investment

$I^N$ Net investment

$I^R$ Replacement investment

$K$ Capital stock

$K^*$ Desired stock capital

$P$ Price level

$P_k$ Price of capital

$r$ Real interest rate

$r_m$ Nominal interest rate

$RR$ Real rental rate

$Y$ Actual sales

$Y^e$ Expected permanent sales

$z$ Tax credit rate

$\delta$ Depreciation rate

$\pi^e$ Expected inflation rate

$u$ Corporate income tax rate

## Chapter 20: Tobin's *q*

$MPK$ Marginal product of firm's capital

$P_k$ Price of the firm's capital

$q$ Tobin's $q$

$r$ Interest rate

$R$ Rental rate of firm's capital

$SMV$ Stock market value of the firm

$\nu$ Desired capital-sales ratio

## Chapter 21: Inventory Demand for Money

| | |
|---|---|
| $b$ | Cost of one trip to the bank |
| $r$ | Interest rate on chequable deposits |
| $Y$ | Monthly cash expenditure |
| $n$ | Number of trips to the bank |